D1383975

The Right to be Educated

STUDIES TO COMMEMORATE THE TWENTIETH ANNIVERSARY
OF THE ADOPTION BY THE UNITED NATIONS OF THE UNIVER-
SAL DECLARATION OF HUMAN RIGHTS, DECEMBER 10, 1948

The Right to be Educated

STUDIES TO COMMEMORATE THE TWENTIETH ANNIVERSARY
OF THE ADOPTION BY THE UNITED NATIONS OF THE UNIVER-
SAL DECLARATION OF HUMAN RIGHTS, DECEMBER 10, 1948

*Sponsored by the International
Federation of Catholic Universities*

EDITED BY ROBERT F. DRINAN

Foreword by Arthur J. Goldberg

CORPUS BOOKS

Washington and Cleveland

CORPUS PUBLICATIONS

EDITORIAL OFFICE
1330 Massachusetts Ave., N.W
Washington, D.C. 20005

SALES & DISTRIBUTION
2231 West 110th Street
Cleveland, Ohio 44102

Copyright © 1968 by Robert F. Drinan

All rights reserved. No part of this book may be reproduced in any form without permission from the publisher, except for brief passages included in a review appearing in a magazine or newspaper.

"Catholic Americans and the Future of the Public School"   Copyright © Doubleday & Company, Inc.

Library of Congress Catalog Card Number: 68-9033
FIRST PRINTING 1968
Printed in the United States of America

Foreword

I am grateful for the invitation of my good friend Father Hesburgh, President of the International Federation of Catholic Universities, to contribute a Foreword to this important book, and I appreciate the spirit of ecumenism which prompted his request.

In the present era, perhaps more than any preceding era, the ideas by which men live cease to be particular to this or that national or religious group, and tend to become universal in scope. The United Nations has contributed to this tendency —especially in one of the most influential documents that ever emerged from it, the Universal Declaration of Human Rights, whose twentieth anniversary is the occasion of International Human Rights Year.

For those of us whose religious and national traditions have long since acknowledged the rights which all men derive from their divine origin, the basic ideas in the Universal Declaration are by no means new. But the effort to promote the enjoyment of such rights among all peoples is indeed new, and it is a momentous development in human history.

Among these rights, the right to be educated, and thus to develop one's innate capacities, is clearly essential. Its fulfillment for the majority of the world's people is still very incomplete or totally lacking; and in no country is it com-

65501

pletely fulfilled. This book, bringing together the knowledge and insight of leading Catholic authorities on this important subject, will be of interest to all—Catholic and non-Catholic alike—who desire to help bring the great liberating influence of education to more of the peoples of the world.

THE HONORABLE ARTHUR J. GOLDBERG
Former United States Representative
to the United Nations

Preface

In June 1966 I was pleased to receive, in my capacity as President of the International Federation of Catholic Universities, a letter from His Eminence Cardinal Cicognani, Secretary of State to His Holiness, in which a request was made in the name of His Holiness that the International Federation of Catholic Universities arrange an appropriate event to commemorate the International Human Rights Year in 1968. Cardinal Cicognani's letter was gratefully received by the officers of the International Federation of Catholic Universities and promptly acted upon. A committee made up of scholars from Catholic universities in the United States and Canada, under the chairmanship of Father Robert F. Drinan, S. J., Dean of the Boston College Law School, was established by the Federation in order to implement the directives of Cardinal Cicognani's letter.

Although Cardinal Cicognani's letter mentioned "the many possibilities" by which the "contribution of Christianity to the affirmation of the dignity of the human person" could be "highlighted during the various programs planned for 1968," His Eminence's letter suggested as "opportune" the publication of "a volume of essays and studies, compiled by learned and experienced teachers of law and sociology from the many Catholic universities of the world." The committee appointed by the Administrative Council of the International Federation of Catholic Universities concurred in the judgment that a volume of essays would be an "opportune" way to signalize the International Year of Human Rights. Indeed this committee was of the view—a view thoroughly vindicated by this volume—that a volume of essays would be an ideal way to demonstrate the truth enunciated by Cardinal Cicognani when he stated that the "declaration, defence, and the vindication of human rights constitute an important part of the activity and teaching of the Church throughout the centuries."

The committee which planned this collection of essays properly judged that it would not be wise to try to cover all or even several of the thirty articles contained in the Universal Declaration of Human Rights. Because of the particular preciousness of the human right to an education to the planners of this volume and because of the special devotion of the International Federation of Catholic Universities to everything that affects the right to knowledge, it was decided to explore and analyze the enormous implications of one of the crucial and central guarantees contained in Articles 26 and 27 of the Universal Declaration of Human Rights—the right of everyone to an education and the right of everyone "to participate in the cultural life of the community, to enjoy the arts and to share in scientific advancement and its benefits."

The theme of the human right to an education selected for analysis in this volume is particularly appropriate not only for the International Federation of Catholic Universities, but also for the Catholic scholars in America. It is appropriate for Catholic scholars to explore in depth the right to know in order to understand more profoundly the consequences of the vast commitment which American Catholics have made to Catholic schools. A searching analysis of the right to know is, moreover, appropriate for Catholic educators because of the ambivalent attitude which some Catholics have always had towards the public school in the whole history of America. Because of the paradox evident in the phenomenon that Catholics support their own schools with enormous generosity while sometimes they have neutral or negative attitudes towards the public school, it is fitting that Catholic educators explore the profound implications and apparent contradictions in the contemporary position of American Catholics with respect to the human right to be educated.

The position of the Church with regard to the right to an education was clarified and re-emphasized in several of the documents that emerged from Vatican II. The "Declaration on Christian Education," for example, enunciated the Church's position in these words: "Since every man of whatever race, condition, and age is endowed with the dignity of a person, he has an inalienable right to an education. . . ."

At least three overwhelming convictions come to the reader from an examination of the essays in this volume. These convictions are 1) the profundity and richness of Catholic thought on the subject of human rights, 2) the impressive involvement of Catholic scholars and Catholic organizations in the search for ways to implement human rights, and 3) the urgent necessity for Catholics to become more involved in the struggle on behalf of human rights and in particular for the attainment of the right to an education. Each of these convictions merits a brief comment.

The metaphysical and theological depths of Catholic thought with respect to the bases of human rights are revealed in the paper by Professor Carlos A. Sacheri of Laval University. Those bases are further explored as they relate to the philosophical foundations of the right to an education in the essay by Professor Germain G. Grisez of Georgetown University. The methods by which the Church's profound commitments to human rights can be translated into the political order are delineated in the statement of Professor Quentin L. Quade of Marquette University.

These three position papers focus on the truth that the Church's role is to form and fashion a theory for human rights rather than a table of the specific rights of men in a particular era. These three statements—reinforced by all of the essays in this document—illustrate the treasures which Christian tradition has to offer to a world torn apart by the presence of rich nations and poor nations, a world where illiteracy still keeps hundreds of millions of persons in the darkness and blindness of their own ignorance.

The second conclusion which arises from this volume is the encouraging participation of Catholics, singly and collectively, in the formation of a worldwide understanding of the meaning and urgency of human rights. The essay by Miss Catherine Schaefer, director of the Office for United Nations Affairs of the United States Catholic Conference, gives abundant evidence of the involvement of Catholic spokesmen and Catholic organizations in the crucially important work of the United Nations. The paper of Professor Cornelius F. Murphy of Duquesne University Law School reveals the mind of a philosopher and a lawyer at work on the vast implications and impact on American and international society of the Universal Declaration of Human Rights. Similarly the essay by Father Neil McCluskey, S.J., professor of education at Notre Dame University, indicates the extent of the involvement of American Catholics in the fulfillment of the right to an education. The ecumenical problems and dilemmas confronting Catholics in their efforts to enhance the right to an education are developed in the chapter by Father John Sheerin, C.S.P., editor of the *Catholic World*.

The efforts and limitations of Catholic colleges and universities in their work in the international field are highlighted by Professor William V. O'Brien of Georgetown University, the president of the Catholic Association for International Peace. Finally, the reflections on human rights in Africa by Mr. Thomas P. Melady, Pax Romana representative to the United Nations, manifest the intensity of the Church's concern for the right to an education in the emerging nations of Africa.

The third and most painful conclusion which one must draw from this important series of essays is the distressing truth that the Church, despite all its efforts, still cannot be said to be sufficiently concerned with the fulfillment of the sacred and precious right which everyone has to know, the right to have an education, and the right to share in the cultural life of society.

The papers in this volume could not in the nature of things

touch on all aspects of the right to an education. But from my own experience as one of the six Commissioners of the United States Commission on Civil Rights, I feel obliged to emphasize that, based on personal observation, the denial of the right to an education continues on a shockingly widespread scale in the culturally deprived and racially imbalanced schools of America. It is to be hoped that Catholics will deepen their concern over this basic injustice and that they will direct their profound philosophical and theological convictions about the human and inalienable right to be educated to the countless American schools where children are deprived of one of their most precious rights—the right to know.

On behalf of the International Federation of Catholic Universities I express the abiding loyalty of this organization to the Holy See and the sense of gratification and gratitude which the International Federation has experienced because of the gracious invitation to prepare this volume which has been extended to the Federation by Cardinal Cicognani. To the editor Rev. Robert F. Drinan, S.J., Dean of the Boston College Law School, and to all the authors I express my own gratitude and that of the officials and members of the International Federation of Catholic Universities. They have indeed exceeded our highest hopes.

May this volume give witness during the International Year of Human Rights to the profound conviction contained in Catholicism of the sacredness of all secular truths and the commitment which hopefully all Catholics will share in an ever deepening way that the right to be educated is one of the imprescriptible privileges which a wise Creator has placed in free men.

THEODORE HESBURGH, C.S.C.

N. 4584/66   Dear Father Hesburgh,

As you well know, the General Assembly of the United Nations has decided to commemorate solemnly the 20th Anniversary of the Universal Declaration on Human Rights; to this end, it has designated 1968 as the "International Year of Human Rights", and has proposed to convoke an international conference on this subject.

The declaration, the defence and the vindication of human rights constitute an important part of the activity and teaching of the Church throughout the centuries. The contribution of Christianity to the affirmation of the dignity of the human person deserves to be high-lighted during the various programs planned for 1968.

At the gracious direction of the Holy Father, consideration is being given to the possibility of emphasizing the doctrine and the activity of the Church in this field. Among the many possibilities, it seems opportune to publish a volume of essays and studies, compiled by learned and experienced teachers of Law and Sociology from the many Catholic Universities of the world. Such an undertaking could be initiated by the International Federation of Catholic Universities of which you are the distinguished President.

I request you, in the name of His Holiness, to give consideration to this proposal. When you next visit Rome, possibly before the Atomic Energy meetings, we could discuss this matter more at length; in the meantime, however, I would appreciate hearing your views on this subject as well as any suggestions or projects you might have.

With sentiments of esteem and cordial regard,

I am

Sincerely yours in Christ,

A. G. CARD. CICOGNANI

Very Rev. Fr. Theodor Hesburgh, CSC
President, International Federation
of Catholic Universities
Notre Dame, Indiana—USA

Contents

QUENTIN L. QUADE

1: Human Rights—The Church Speaking to Politics

In the language and literature of politics there are few concepts at once as important and as confused as the idea of human rights.

The testimony to its importance is convincing. Countless men have died in the name of human rights. Entire societies have been formed with some vision of human rights as the central social creed, while other societies have been thoroughly disrupted by internal elements pursuing such rights. And today the politics of many nations and much of the politics among nations is carried on in verbal categories of human rights.

But if the significance of the notion of human rights is evident, the fact of disagreement about its meaning is no less clear. There are radically diverse judgments about the *origins* of human rights: do they in some sense inhere in men, or are all rights simply the accidental derivatives of peculiar historical circumstances? When men claim this or that condition as a *right*, is this claim really anything more than interest masked in ideology? Even among men who share a common belief about the source of rights, there are great differences concerning the validity of specific rights and even greater differences regarding the priorities among particular agreed-upon rights. And, perhaps most crucially for our own time, men disagree fundamentally about whether there is a viable notion of *personal* rights or only rights of classes or masses.

To do a critical sorting-out of these conflicting judgments is obviously a task worth doing, but it cannot be the task of this essay. Rather, it will be necessary to provide a definition of the specific meaning here attached to the term "human rights," and then to ask how, if at all, Christian teaching relates to this key concept.

DEFINITION OF HUMAN RIGHTS

Perhaps for political understanding, this would be a useful usage: human rights may be understood as human needs or values whose moment has come in history for at least *some* people. The claimed right, in this sense, is a formalized request or demand that society recognize the legitimacy of some felt need or, perhaps, that society not only recognize but actually fulfill the need.

One response to such a definition may be that it is so broad as to blur the most important questions concerning human rights, such as those noted above. Indeed, this is true and designedly so. Any definition of this concept must be over-arching or pay the penalty of ignoring much current discussion of human rights.

Underpinning this broad definition of human rights are several judgments about the appearance in history of the needs which the claimed rights represent. First, it seems clear that similar human values may be proclaimed as human rights from and because of quite different ethical perspectives. Thus, for example, the "right to be educated"—the concern of this volume—may, with equal logic, be rooted in a personalist humanism or in a mass humanitarianism-logic of technology ethic. In such a case, the motives or starting points may be radically different, but the actual human conditions sought may bear striking resemblances. As will be seen below, such unintended congruences are of immense importance for the Christian when he turns to the question of what concretely to do about human rights.

A second assertion is that the human needs or values which are elevated to the status of "rights" (*somebody's* claimed rights) change from time to time, as do the priorities and intensities among them, according to historical circumstances. The "Rights of Englishmen," for instance, expanded in time and took on new meanings over centuries. *Magna Carta,* though absolutely crucial to the growth of constitutionalism and the relatively happy politics deriving from it, was extremely limited and highly negative, concerned as it was with restraint upon arbitrary central authority. Though that conception of rights remains essential to the spirit of British and, indeed, Western politics, the intervening years have found the notion of rights being applied more and more to such things as social and economic justice which the restrained government is expected to promote. In these terms of change, we may note that the right to be educated is a classic and characteristic example of the modern notion of rights.

RELATIVITY OF HUMAN RIGHTS

All of which is to say simply that there is a certain relativity implicit in the notion of human rights, even as regards their sum and substance. Yet this relativity does not negate essential qualitative differences among the human-values-claimed-as-rights. Though politically all rights may be seen as historical and circumstantial, some impress the observer as answering more fundamental human needs than others. The right to free speech and the right to jury trial are alike in that both emerge from historical development, but jury trial is only a method or device for attaining a superior value and may be substituted for without great damage; while freedom of speech strikes so close to what man is and must be that the mind boggles at trying to conceive of a substitute.

Thus we observe that not all "rights" are of equal value. More important, at some moments in time it is the paramount task of politics to determine precisely what, for a particular society, the priorities among various claimed rights should be. But this in turn suggests a further sense in which all rights are both relative and identical. That is, they all seek their realization in and are basically dependent upon the framework of political guarantees that exist within a given society. In the political community there will be multiple values, and many will be asserted as rights. Even abstractly there will be conflicts among these assertions, and concretely men will disagree about their importance or their reality. If, then, we are to discern the role of Christianity and the Christian in the achievement of human rights, we need to examine more deeply the political context within which the actual struggle for rights goes on. What are the dominant characteristics of this context, and what role for Christians is suggested by them?

ROLE OF THE CHURCHES
IN ADVANCING HUMAN RIGHTS

Even a cursory examination of the characteristics of international and national politics, and of politics in general, strongly suggests that the role of the organized Churches in advancing human rights can only be a limited one. But if limited, this role may nevertheless be crucial; and if the limited role is to be fulfilled, it is imperative that the confines of the possible be identified.

Pope John's *Pacem In Terris* and the Vatican Council's *Constitution on the Church in the Modern World* are addressed to all men—to the world. That is as it should be, but it is also in a sense illusory. For perhaps the first thing that would impress an objective observer—a Martian, let us say—about the earth is that there is hardly a world at all. Instead, this observer would note that there are many "worlds," though exactly how many would depend on the defining tool the observer employed. If he had recently read Jean Bodin, he might characterize the earth as being populated by 130-plus worlds, to correspond with the exact number of political sovereignties presently abounding. And though modern political science would instruct him about the limitations on the notion of sovereignty—"no nation can do whatever it likes, all nations are influenced by others"—he would observe nonetheless that such limitations are primarily in the order of relative power, not of intention or national thrust.

He would note, in short, that while individual nations are constantly concerned with their "national self-interest" or common good, and while some have been able to define and achieve this condition tolerably well, there is little in the way of a universal common good defined, achieved, or even sought after. There is, indeed, perhaps no more of this than what we hope is a common desire not to see the earth destroyed. A Christian, who seemingly is called to transcend national boundaries at least to the extent of recognizing all men as brothers, or any other person who universalizes his human obligations, may well look upon this political fragmentation as destructive of deeper ethical needs of man and may seek to promote more and more positive common interests or goods among all men. He may search the history of the nation-state phenomenon and conclude that the most important reasons and justifications for its existence are eroding and that the nation-state system is now basically self-sustaining and self-justifying. He may see the desirability and remotely the possibility of moving from nation-states to a larger, even all-inclusive community of mankind that would parallel his view of his own relationship to all his brothers. But even such a *telos* must be conditioned by the fact that for the present essentially anarchic states seek uncommon common goods narrowly defined and that these same states must be primary agents for whatever degree of world interest is actually to be promoted.

To complicate matters finally, it is necessary to observe that political multiplicity often represents much more than simply accidental boundaries imposed upon a larger culture which is essentially homogeneous—as may be said, for example, of Europe. Even if our Martian rejected sovereignty as his organizing concept, he could hardly ignore that portion of political diversity which actually represents profound cultural differences. And even less could he overlook the clash of conflicting ideologies which, whether "truly held" or only draped over national interests, tend to fan the fires of inter-nation discord.

Thus, even if Christianity spoke to the world with one voice on human rights and the political good, it would have to be aware that there were *many* listeners, each exercising its human prerogative to hear what it wants to hear. And if this does not adequately portray the difficulties of "speaking to the nations," then an equally brief examination of the nations themselves might.

In surveying the arena of international politics, one may legitimately speak of nations as parts of a system. But when one steps into the nation itself a quite different perspective is required. If nation-state sovereignty means subdued anarchy at the international level, it means something quite different *within* a given nation. Very simply it means that the nation in question is a free agent, free, that is, in the sense of being self-directing and self-defining. Within the limits of its power, it can do practically what it pleases. Looked at differently, it recognizes no authority, moral or otherwise, as its superior.

The actual confines of this freedom appear fairly promptly when a nation's foreign policy is analyzed. Even the super-powers operate within fairly strict limits of their own potential and the counter-potential of other states. Thus, the United States could practically limit the Soviet Union by containment, but could not practically go beyond containment to "rollback," even if this were abstractly desirable. And what is true of major powers is doubly true of lesser powers. Further, one may recognize with Hans Morgenthau and the school of political realism that many technically "doable" things would actually be counter-productive in terms of national interest, and that this notion of national interest is also a kind of limitation on national initiatives or freedom. Even granting these points, however, it remains true that even in its foreign policy a nation has wide latitude to define its own role and, indeed, even to specify for itself what its national interest is. One may say from a national interest perspective that, for example, the United States *should* do such and such; but one can hardly say it *must*, and even less say that it *will*.

FREEDOM OF NATION-STATES

But the full meaning of the modern nation-states' freedom is not seen until one looks at its potential within its own confines. Those who possess authority and exercise power in the state, whether they be a Nazi Party or a democratic majority confront only the limitations of their own imaginations and self-restraints and the physical capacity available to them. The differences between a Hitler and a majority are vast and demonstrable, and there is no suggestion here that on balance they are much the same. On the contrary, a democratic process in the very character of its operation *tends* toward humaneness by contrast with authoritarian and totalitarian systems. Yet the fact remains that no extra-political guarantees exist in any state system. One shudders when thinking of Hitler's "final solution" to the Jewish problem and Stalin's order to "liquidate the Kulaks as a class," and is not much relieved when his thoughts turn to South Africa's apartheid or even the often absent-minded but quite truly harmful racial policies of the United States' last hundred years. Thus the point is not, as some seem today to suggest, that one system is as bad as another, but rather that any state has some potential for human destructiveness; and this potential is illustrative of the basic freedom of the modern nation-state operating within its own confines.

This sense of limitlessness is augmented by several of the present century's most characteristic features. As secularism and ethical pluralism become more and more dominant, the sphere of the politically possible broadens. That is to say, the goals which government may pursue are less and less foreordained—instead, the goals themselvès, and not just the techniques, increasingly become legitimate objects of political discussion, debate, and action. This is not put forth as a warning or an ominous sign, but simply as an assertion about facts. When the political society admits no authority beyond itself, then the political process becomes not just a value-implementer, but a value-giver as well. If the process is a representative one, it will be tied to its community in formalizing social values, of course. But strictly speaking, nothing limits the community or the majorities that form within it.

To this general condition of value-openness, one needs to add the ingredient of modern technological capability. Hitler's "final solution" was, among other things, technically feasible, as would be a "solution" of the Negro problem in the United States by transplantation or liquidation. Science made possible the practical elimination of polio, and that same science now makes possible the elimination of unwanted or predictably defective fetuses. Hopefully, nothing will be done just because it can be done, but the fact remains that *whether* to do any or all of these things is for the modern, free society (if not for individuals) always an open question. While some of these questions may be answered more easily than others, none is answered *a priori* or by a superior, outside institution.

And finally in this context, one should note certain repercussions which flow from the condition of representative democracy. A dominant fact of such systems is the difficulty of assessing moral responsibility within them. In the age of kings, society found it difficult if not impossible to make the monarch politically responsible, but there could be little question about moral responsibility for state actions in such a situation. In the age of democracy, men have devised many ways, some more effective than others, of promoting the political responsibility of governors to governed; but one effect has been to blur and diffuse the ultimate moral responsibility for political acts. The democratic representative has an obligation not unlike the king's to seek the common good, but he must seek it and simultaneously conform himself to what he takes to be the limits of public opinion. Those limits may be flexible, and he by teaching and leading will in fact help to set them. But while he can lead, he cannot for long say "the public be damned," even if, as the case may be, "the public is a beast."

These are some of the most prominent characteristics of contemporary politics, and any church aspiring to speak to politics ought to recognize them. If it does, these special characteristics will be seen as both limits on the church's role in politics and as directives regarding how that role might fruitfully be fulfilled. Shortly, several suggestions about this role will be drawn from the preceding points; but first it is essential to probe more deeply into politics itself, irrespective of current characteristics, so as better to understand religion's relationship to it.

STATE, CHURCH, AND THE COMMON GOOD

One central characteristic of politics invites and even necessitates a religious-political inter-action: both the state and the church have as their concern the good for men. Making ultimate and definitive policy for its society is the task of the state; and such policy has to do with human value, defining that value when social members are unable to do it voluntarily. Politics concerns the *quality* of human life precisely when alternative and conflicting views of that quality are at issue.

In one sense, then, politics involves the determining of value priorities within and for society. But it is more than just a hierarchical ordering of values or principles. It seeks additionally to *harmonize* multiple values which are regularly conflicting. Without succumbing to a simple relativism in which all values are taken to be of equal importance (or unimpor-

tance), politics nonetheless strives to refrain from any single-
value theory in which the *preferred* position is taken also to be
the *exclusive* position.

This may be asserted, for example, as the core of democratic political activity. Priorities do have to be set; specific decisions do have to be made, and on these specific decisions
there will inevitably be "winners" and "losers." But neither the
win nor the loss tends to be complete or final. And this is so,
not because democratic citizens fail to take their principles seriously, but rather because they have elevated another principle
to a position of primacy: in respect of human equality and
dignity, democratic politics tries to distinguish between "true"
and "truly held" principles. And a kind of legitimacy is granted
to the latter irrespective of the "truth" expressed by the position, just because the citizen is seen as significant by the very
fact of what he is. Thus the state must, in ultimate issues, be
the arbiter of the humanly true and humanly good, but it must
not be the Fountain of Truth. Particularly this is so in this age
of technical potential for absolutism.

All of which is to say that politics—though incorporating
principles and values in policy and always searching for
them—is not just the identification of values abstractly; nor is
it, values in hand, simply an exegetical, deductive process of
drawing policy from principle. It includes these things, but it is
simultaneously an ordering and integrating of many values and
a testing of them in the concrete situation. And it is important
to note that the political process attends to issue, not singly
and in isolation, but attends to many related issues at once.
Looked at in this manner, the political act of judging what to
do here, now, is seen to have about it a certain uniqueness.
And related to this uniqueness, it has about it also a certain
autonomy. But though necessarily autonomous, the sensitive
political order is also open to value teaching from many
sources. Precisely because the political order does not claim
truth, it awaits specification about the good for society in particular circumstances.

OPPORTUNITIES FOR THE CHURCH

To look at some of the most prominent conditions of contemporary politics, as we have done, is in fact to identify the circumstances within which the churches must work in trying to promote human rights. Human rights may be *identified* abstractly, but they do not *exist* abstractly. They exist, where they exist at all, within political confines; and these same confines suggest what the proper role of the churches may be. If this seems a harshly limited basis for defining the churches' role, it is not because this writer seeks to limit; but rather because the limitations are genuinely there, and the churches are unlikely to do effectively even their limited task unless they concentrate their energies into these channels. Drawing upon this view of international and national politics, what may we say are the opportunities for the Church?

The modern nation-state and the preponderantly secular society over which it presides do not feel obliged to seek out the Church as teacher, let alone definer of their actions. As was noted above, this nation-state is "free," in the sense that it has few foreordained directions it feels bound to follow. But precisely because it is free in this sense and thus quite perpetually engaged in defining and re-defining its directions, it is *open* to teaching—open to counsel as to what its objectives ought to be. This, it would seem, provides the primary opportunity which the Churches have to make an impact upon the political order and the decisions about human life that order consistently makes. In particular, this suggests two primary and related avenues of religious involvement in political matters. In both cases, the role of religion is that of a potential specifier of some of the values or principles taken into the political act situation. Precisely because of that uniqueness and autonomy in the political act which was suggested previously, the role of religion is never to do the act itself, but rather to influence that act.

First, and very generally, the Church relates to politics as one of the primary shapers of the social ethos. This refers to the "givens" and general patterns within society, the premises which tend to give a society its distinctiveness. These values in turn are likely to be given concrete form in the policies of that country. It may be that the explicit religious roots of such values have been forgotten or so interwoven with historical development as to be practically indistinguishable. But if one asks, for example, why the United States is as it is, where her characteristics come from, it seems impossible to offer an explanation without heavily accenting the religious component. In this very fundamental sense, religion has helped (in Paul Ramsey's terms) provide *directions* but not *directives* to political society.

But the second avenue of religious influence is far more crucial for the purposes of current and future politics. It has two elements: the capacity of the Church to mold the individual's value structure and the capacity of the individual to help determine the policies of his nation. Is there, can there be, a distinctive Christian ethic? The answer, it would seem, must be a carefully qualified affirmative. There is no claim here that a Christian perspective is necessarily unique. Love of fellow men as a norm of action, for example, may be arrived at through other religious or philosophical processes. And to the Christian, this can hardly be either surprising or deflating—Christ's prescriptions presumably apply to all and presumably represent a universal *potential* within all men. His prescriptions are not *unnatural* prescriptions. But it remains true that those who are Christian may *consciously* conform their ethical beliefs to clear Christian teaching. One may, for example, conclude to an essential equality among all men on various grounds. A Christian may conclude to it on *Christian* grounds, on the basis of Christ's testimony; and he may undertake certain actions on the ground of his belief.

And thus the second element: in societies where politics is in flux or representative (a form of sustained but controlled flux), it is individuals and collections of individuals inspired by *something* who actually act politically, who determine policy and shape attitudes. This is the second avenue by which religion may influence the political order: through the actions of the believer as citizen or magistrate. A citizen of the United States may, for instance, on religious grounds desire a more generous foreign aid program, conceiving it as a vehicle for helping his fellow men. He may have other motives which support the religious motive, e.g., he may conceive of foreign aid as a stimulus to world stability—and again we note there is nothing strange nor wrong with such motivational congruence. In seeking increased foreign aid, this citizen-believer will not try to force his will on his fellow citizens because, both as a Christian and as a democrat, he respects their integrity, but he will still act out his own convictions by trying to convince his fellows of the desirability of his policy proposal. In so doing, he would, presumably, appeal to a variety of motives which exist among the citizens of his country.

If he does these things, he is not simply bringing the Gospel to his society in some evangelical sense. Rather, he is injecting what he takes to be some of the Gospel's *implications* into the politics of his nation or his world. He is, from one point of view, only another political actor pleading his special case at the bar of political opinion. But from another perspective, he may supremely and identifiably be a *Christian*. His motive (love), his method (convince rather than coerce), and his immediate objective (aid to the needy) may all reflect his interpretation of Christian commitment—all of this despite the fact that they may also reflect distinct but complementary impulses and that others may do similar things for consciously different reasons.

In these ways, the Church or religion may relate to politics, and relate crucially. But religion does not become politics, nor should it, if both are to maintain their integrity. With this foundation, it is possible to examine the content and the meaningfulness of the Church's teaching on human rights.

CHURCH AS TEACHER TO POLITICS

How does the institutional Church conceive its role as teacher
to politics? What is the Church's teaching on human rights?
What is the root or origin of rights in this view, and how are
they to be fulfilled? Within this context, what is the role of the
Christian, particularly the laymen, taken to be? And how does
this theoretical structure square with the "political realities"
outlined above? An examination of several of the documents of
Vatican Council II provides at least an initial response, and a
quite hopeful one at that, to these questions. Of particular importance in this regard are the *Constitution on the Church in
the Modern World,* the *Decree on the Apostolate of the Laity,*
and the *Declaration on Religious Freedom.*

"The role and competence of the Church being what it is,
she must in no way be confused with the political community,
nor bound to any political system" (*Church in the Modern
World,* #76). Though this may seem an obvious truth, it is a
crucial one in the modern setting where the relationship of
religion to politics is a subject of fiery debate. Here and elsewhere Vatican II showed a significant awareness of the
Church's limited but significant role in the political order. The
role is not that of political actor, but that of normative teacher
to politics. "The Church guards the heritage of God's Word
and draws from it religious and moral principles, without always having at hand the solution to particular problems. She
desires thereby to add the light of revealed truth to mankind's
store of experience, so that the path which humanity has taken
in recent times will not be a dark one" (*Ibid.,* #33).

And Vatican II bases this Church modesty on the reality of
the moral political act: it tends to be a complex situation, with
multiple and competing values and interpretations, and thus
ultimately requires judgment *in the situation.*

Often enough the Christian view of things will itself suggest
some specific solution in certain circumstances [an ethically

simple situation?]. Yet it happens rather frequently, and legitimately so, that with equal sincerity some of the faithful will disagree with others on a given matter. Even against the intentions of their proponents, however, solutions proposed on one side or another may be easily confused by many people with the Gospel message. Hence it is necessary for people to remember that no one is allowed in the aforementioned situations to appropriate the Church's authority for his opinion (*Ibid.*, #43).

As we observed above, the actual political meaning of human rights—e.g., their priorities and how precisely to implement them within societies—is a matter on which men with "equal sincerity" disagree, and sometimes violently. According to Vatican II's self-definition, the Church in such situations is not a likely source for problem-solving. But this does not detract from the role the Church does play in even so sensitive an area as human rights: the role of teacher of principle. The most fundamental contribution of the Church to the promotion of human rights is *not* in providing a catalogue of such rights, a sort of Bill of Rights according to Jesus Christ. Rather it is that the Church proposes, in effect, a *basis* for a theoretical structure of human rights and for practical steps to their achievement. The basis is simply a view of man which sees him (personally) as *dignified* and *valuable*. In this there is no uniqueness, of course. But the *reason* for the dignity and value is at least distinctive: the Church views man as personally valuable because created by God in his own image and attended to by God through the intervention of Christ.

For by his [man's] interior qualities he outstrips the whole sum of mere things. He finds re-enforcement in this profound insight whenever he enters into his own heart. God, who probes the heart, awaits him there. . . . Thus, when man recognizes in himself a spiritual and immortal soul; he is not being mocked by a deceptive fantasy springing from mere physical or social influences. On the contrary he is getting to the depths of the very truth of the matter (*Ibid.*, #14).

From this assertion about man, it is a rather short step to a doctrine of human rights conceived as providing the conditions for this valuable man to fulfill himself. "Only in freedom can man direct himself toward goodness. . . ." "For its part, authentic freedom is an exceptional sign of the divine image within man. For God has willed that man be left 'in the hand of his own counsel'. . . . Hence man's dignity demands that he act according to a knowing and free choice" (*Ibid.*, #17).

It is not astounding that the Church as Church does not bring forth a new or unique Bill of Rights. The work of Christ is not taken to be that of Destroyer and Grand Innovator. Rather, he is seen as the Restorer or Reconstructor or Re-Integrator of the human being. "To the sons of Adam he restores the divine likeness which had been disfigured from the first sin onward. Since human nature as he assumed it was not annulled, by that very fact it has been raised up to a divine dignity in our respect too" (*Ibid.*, #22). What man is and what man needs are matters to be *discovered* in the study of man and the model man, Christ himself.

> If by the autonomy of earthly affairs we mean that created things and societies themselves enjoy their own laws and values which must be gradually *deciphered*, put to use, and regulated by men, then it is entirely right to demand that autonomy. . . . For by the very circumstance of their having been created, all things are endowed with their own stability, truth, goodness, proper laws, and order (*Ibid.*, #36, emphasis added).

THE CHURCH NOT A POLICY-MAKER

Thus it is centrally not cravenness which causes the Church to refrain from trying to be a policy-maker (though there may have been craven acts). Rather, it is a recognition of the implicit autonomy present in much of human enterprise. And

> . . . far from thinking that works produced by man's own talent and energy are in opposition to God's power, and that the rational creature exists as a kind of rival to the Creator,

> Christians are convinced that the triumphs of the human race are a sign of God's greatness and the flowering of his own mysterious design. . . . Hence it is clear that men are not deterred by the Christian message from building up the world, . . . They are, rather, more stringently bound to do these very things (*Ibid.*, #34).

The command of Christ to love is a charge to do—loving is doing. Christ is thus an inspiration to discern what needs to be done for men and to intervene in social affairs in such a way as to achieve it.

When the Council did elaborate lists of human rights, it did so as a teacher of principle, not as a policy-maker.

> Therefore, there must be made available to all men everything necessary for leading a life truly human, such as food, clothing, and shelter; the right to choose a state of life freely and to found a family, the right to education, to employment, to a good reputation, to respect, to appropriate information, to activity in accord with the upright norm of one's own conscience, to protection of privacy and to rightful freedom in matters religious too (*Ibid.*, #26).

It sought to instill in minds and consciences the values represented by these proclaimed rights, but it did not attempt to do the political act of determining precisely how any or all of the rights should be acted upon here and now. In this sense, it remained true to its self-definition of function.

But it also recognized the incompleteness of preachment alone, and laid the groundwork for a *full* theory of human rights—a theory of means as well as ends. The action dimension is presented squarely as the obligation of the individual Christians in the world, as differentiated from the institutional Church. To perceive the needs of man in general terms and to seek the specific avenues of fulfillment are distinguishable tasks, though both seemingly are essential parts of an integral Christian posture.

THE CHRISTIAN AS CITIZEN

But as soon as one says that part of a *Christian* theory of human rights is a concern or obligation to define the precise good for all men and to seek ways to bring it about, one realizes that he has left the realm of abstract, normative principle and has entered the realm of multiple values-in-conflict, the realm of politics, social action, and contingency where the problem is not just to perceive *a* good, but to perceive and distinguish many, to search for priorities and intensities among them, and to organize action to achieve them. To the extent that the Church has been effective as a teacher to nations, as one of the influences in shaping the social ethos, Christianity will already be present in this realm. But it may be more immediately and decisively present in quite a different way—through the active intervention of the Christian as citizen.

> This Council exhorts Christians, as citizens of two cities, to strive to discharge their earthly duties conscientiously and in response to the Gospel spirit. They are mistaken who, knowing that we have here no abiding city but seek one which is to come, think that they may therefore shirk their earthly responsibilities. For they are forgetting that by the faith itself they are more than ever obliged to measure up to these duties, each according to his own proper vocation (*Ibid.*, #43).

In the promotion of human rights, the things to be done, the vocations, are many and diverse, ranging perhaps from socio-psychological probings to ascertain contemporary needs to mustering electoral support for their fulfillment, to *ad hoc* voluntary associations confronting immediate problems. Because of their numbers, their positions, their vocations, and their prime political importance, laymen have the central responsibility for this action dimension. "The apostolate of the social milieu, that is, the effort to infuse a Christian spirit into the mentality, customs, laws, and structures of the community in which a person lives, is so much the duty and responsiblity of the laity that it can never be properly performed by others" (*Decree on the Apostolate of the Laity,* #13).

As noted above, this Christ-motivated citizen cannot pretend to be the Church or to speak with its authority. Nor in this order of contingency is he permitted the luxury of abstract certitude. But he is nonetheless the primary vehicle for a Christian presence in the affairs of this world.

> They exercise a genuine apostolate by their activity on behalf of bringing the Gospel and holiness to men, and on behalf of penetrating and perfecting the temporal sphere of things through the spirit of the Gospel. In this way, their temporal activity can openly bear witness to Christ and promote the salvation of men. Since it is proper to the layman's state in life for him to spend his days in the midst of the world and of secular transactions, he is called by God to burn with the spirit of Christ and to exercise his apostolate in the world as a kind of leaven (*Ibid.,* #2).

Human rights, if they are to be secured, will be secured within political structures. Politics, because it involves the identification of and action on human values, is open to value orientations from any source. This openness is opportunity for the Church and for the Christian. Ultimately politics asks what is man, what is the good for him, and how will the good be attained. The Church and its members are invited to respond to these political questions, which are their questions also from a religious perspective. The response, if it is to be effective, must encompass both rational normative principles and fruitful designs for implementation.

THE CHRISTIAN RIGHT TO BE EDUCATED

Within this broad theoretical structure, what is there Christianly to be said about the human right to be educated? On the level of principle, one may first say with Vatican II what one could always have said: "Since every man of whatever race, condition, and age is endowed with the dignity of a person, he has an inalienable right to an education corresponding to his proper destiny and suited to his native talents, his sex, his cultural background, and his ancestral heritage" (*Declaration on Christian Education,* #1). One can say, in other words, that man has always had a need (right) to be educated in the sense of perfecting his intellectual capacity, his man-ness. But there is also a modern condition which buttresses, perhaps even transforms that right in that it adds great urgency to its claim. I refer to the simple fact that many men *are* educated and the related fact that levels of education are quickly becoming prime criteria in determining the individual's basic status in life. Those who have not received or will not receive a certain level of educational opportunity are thus seriously disadvantaged relative to their fellow men. From this vantagepoint the right to be educated is both modern and pressing.

There is yet another reality which makes easy the abstract identification of education as right and good. The characteristic problems of modern times clearly call for mustering all the intellectual resources present in men.

> In order for individual men to discharge with greater exactness the obligations of their conscience toward themselves and the various groups to which they belong, they must be carefully educated to a higher degree of culture through the use of the immense resources available today to the human race. Above all the education of youth from every social background has to be undertaken, so that there can be produced not only men and women of refined talents, but those great-souled persons who are so desperately required by our times (*Church in the Modern World,* #31).

For these several reasons, the desire to promote educational opportunities for all men seems a rather clear component of contemporary Christian responsibilities.

But even if this much is granted, there is little in the principle or value which expressly says what needs to be done here and now. What is the action dimension of this Christian responsibility? Some of the more specialized essays following in this volume represent various "workings-out" of the general principle through the application of diverse specialties—and represent, therefore, the second level of a full theory of Christian relation to human needs. It will suffice here briefly to note several of the more important conditions that will have to be confronted if the right to be educated is to be secured. First, in talking about the right to be educated *vis-à-vis* the developing countries, this seems to be a fact: the prerequisite for actually delivering the right seems to be a strong (organizationally and financially) governmental sector. This is another sense in which the right to be educated is characteristically modern, in that it does depend upon government action. This in turn suggests to the Christian (or anyone with congruent interests) some of the lines of action he might take in promoting education universally.

Second, an apparently pregnant area of endeavor for the Christian seeking to foster educational opportunity would be to identify and clarify the many different motives in the modern world which are favorable to the spread of education. To put it negatively, the Christian must not fall prey to the "despair of contradictory concepts." The goal of universalized education may stem from quite diverse ultimate motives, and the Christian in the arena of action presumably should strive to harness as many of these impulses as possible. Today, for example, we see as a spur to educational efforts in the world what can be called the "logic of technology-mass humanitarianism" rationale. While this exists most clearly in communist countries such as the U.S.S.R. and China, it has some presence in emerging countries with no Marxist-Leninist creed. Countries which seek industrialization and technological advance quickly discover the need for an at least minimally educated citizenry. Here again, such impulses should be coop-

erated with by Christians who want the goal even if the
starting points are radically distinct.

To discover and exploit such means for achieving the objective, to convince the others needed to support the endeavor;
in short, to discern the human good and devise the implements
for attaining it—this is fully "to burn with the spirit of Christ."

CARLOS A. SACHERI

2: *Governments and the Right to be Educated*

THE GOAL OF THE STATE: THE COMMON GOOD

Let us begin by asking ourselves what is the good which every state must principally attain.

Every human being naturally tends towards living in common, since only the political society can give him the vast number of the diverse goods he would not be able to attain by his individual activity. On commenting on this, Saint Thomas adds that we tend towards a social life as towards an absolutely indispensable means of achieving our perfection.[1]

The problem arises when it is realized that the individual welfare of every member of the community and the community as a whole differ from each other both in nature and in purely quantitative terms.[2] Indeed, each man is a citizen by reason of the fact that, just as the welfare and the individual working of a part cannot be identified with the welfare and working of the whole, so the welfare of each individual differs essentially and specifically from the welfare of society, called the common good.

Let us observe in passing that the notion of the common good or welfare is poorly understood, even though everyone believes that he perfectly understands it; this only serves to increase the general confusion. It is sufficient to peruse the principal texts that expound or develop the Church's social doctrine to realize the carelessness with which these texts have been explained.

What is the difference between the good called individual, private, or singular, and the good we term common? It is a question of a difference in *nature*, for there are goods which are individual by their very nature, while others are common in themselves. Expressed in different terms, some goods cannot be owned or participated in except by one single person, others may be held and participated in by an unlimited number of persons. For instance, a morsel of food is in itself individual, since only one person can eat it; as soon as another eats it, the other automatically is deprived of it.

Mathematical science, on the other hand, is in itself common, and can be possessed and shared by all. Not only does the knowledge which an individual may attain from this discipline not exclude others from an equal possession of it, but the more a mathematician masters his science, the more will he give others access to the same knowledge.

These examples help us to understand why we should talk of a formal distinction between individual and common goods. Material goods, by their very nature, are individual, that is, they may be possessed only by individuals. We shall see the importance of this distinction when we come to speak of the "good" of education. It may be useful to remember the reflection made by Saint Augustine in *De Civitate Dei* to the effect that material goods are permanent occasions of discord between men, while spiritual goods tend to unite men.

The common good, however, is an analogous term and, as such, includes various meanings, which it is necessary to distinguish. The princial distinction occurs between the common temporal good (the goal of political society) and the common supernatural good, which is God as the ultimate end of the entire created universe.[3] Even in the temporal field, however, there are diverse common goods: the good or welfare of the family, of the company, of a profession, of the international community, and so on. Such specifications are perfectly legitimate, although they all presuppose and concern the common good of political society. It is precisely the common good of political society which will serve as a basis for determining the role of the state.

In what does this good of political society consist? Pius XI has defined it is *Divini Illius Magistri* as "the peace and security enjoyed by individuals in the exercise of their rights, and at the same time, the greatest spiritual and material welfare possible in this life, by means of the union and the coordination of the efforts of all." Indeed, just as the family is the institution which has as its end the conservation of human life (in the order of procreation), so also the political society, or the state, has as its particular end the total welfare of man (in the order of perfection). It follows that the goods that constitute the common good cannot be other than those goods which conduce to human happiness or fulfillment. Expressed in other terms, all goods proper to human beings form part of the common good; that is, the common good includes the three categories of goods described by Plato: external goods, corporeal goods, spiritual goods.

However, while the first two goods form only part of the common good, as means or instruments necessary for attaining spiritual goods, the latter are the only ones which are truly "common" by nature. Among the principal elements of the truly common good are science, justice, order, security; if these are attained, peace results, which is, as it were, the result and synthesis of these elements. Peaceful coexistence within order —in the words of Saint Augustine, *pax tranquillitas ordinis*—is the sign par excellence of the effective achievement of well-being in a given society. Thus we see the essentially dynamic character of political welfare. It is not so much something possessed and shared as it is moral well-being; to the attainment of this all contribute; all participate in it and enjoy it in common. The achievement of this requires the coordination of all the efforts and activities of the social body, renewed day by day.

Once these basic distinctions are established, we may approach another particularly delicate point: what is the relationship between the individual and the common good? It is especially necessary to avoid the error of considering these goods as if one excluded the other. This has been the error of all modern political thought since the end of the Middle Ages, when nominalism began the process of corrupting the entire metaphysical doctrine of the good.

Both types of good not only do not exclude each other but necessitate the presence of each other, so much so that without particular goods the common good is unattainable and, reciprocally, the failure to attain the common good makes impossible the obtaining of the particular good. The first point is clear if we consider that material goods necessary for the satisfaction of the most immediate needs of man's life are the condition (and not the cause, as Marxists affirm,) for any progress in knowledge, any just treatment of our neighbors, etc. Thus a minimum of material goods is necessary in order to dedicate oneself to the speculative life.[4] On the other hand, if men were to live according to the law of the jungle, subjugated to the whim of the most powerful, without the least security, without the least guarantee of just treatment, how could each individual obain the elements most indispensable for his subsistence? Human life would become totally unbearable.

That both types of good complement each other so intimately arises from the fact that the total good (or total welfare) of man, or happiness (*bonum humanum perfectum*), is made up *simultaneously* of types of good of an individual nature and types of good of a common nature. Both food and clothing as well as knowledge and moral virtue are indispensable to the human being. The fact that they are indispensable does not imply that they have the same importance or value; for this reason, each good should be obtained according to the necessities of the individual and, just as there is a hierarchy existing among the various human operations, so also the hier-

archy of the different types of good must be respected according to whether they serve lower or higher necessities.

Both forms of good, private and common, combine within
what may be termed *individual or personal good,* that is, the
good of all human beings.[5] The importance of this conclusion
makes itself evident with the realization that the radical and
common error both of modern liberalism and socialism in their
respective social doctrines has consisted in opposing, as mutu-
ally exclusive terms, individual and common good. Once this
false dialectical relationship is adopted, the consequences are
inevitably deduced by both the one and the other. The liberals
have tried to preserve the rights of the individual and to do
this have set up as a supreme norm in the social order the free
play of the "healthy egotism" of each person. They ignore the
directive function of the state because of their belief that individual interest identifies and unites itself spontaneously and
automatically with the general interest. This is because they
have adopted as a basic assumption Rousseau's belief in the
natural goodness of man.

Inversely, socialist totalitarianism defines the human being
as a member of the collectivity, a kind of anonymous cog in
the social machinery, to whom even the most essential human
rights are denied because of the belief that nothing in the
individual can differ from or oppose the objectives fixed by the
state. With this, the person as such disappears before the arbitrary nature of the state raised to the status of an absolute end.
In this point of view, *the common good is destroyed in its
"community"* in order to transform it into the *private good of
the state,* i.e. of those persons who exercise public power, using
it according to their appetites for power, glory, or riches.

Thus it may be seen that both from the liberal point of
view and that of Marxist socialism, the antagonism between
individual good and common good leads fatally to a false identification of the part with the whole, whether it be by reducing
the whole to its parts, or denying the parts all autonomy within

the social order. In this way all the fundamental problems which make for the ordering of the political society are indefinitely bound in an endless series of dialectical contradictions (individual, society, authority-liberty, etc.) which create as many insoluble conflicts.

The preceding thoughts allow us to approach the relationship between the state or political authority and the common good. We shall find the solution when we answer the question about the raison d'être of the state. Aristotle stated the common principle on this subject, namely, that in every reality composed of multiple parts there must exist an element capable of maintaining cohesion between these parts.[6] The existence of this principle of the unity of the whole imposes a relationship between each one of the parts and the unifying and ordering element of the whole. This observation is verified at all the levels of the material universe, but it has a practical application which is still more profound in human societies and, in particular, in the political society. In these, unlike in natural organisms, each part is in itself independent of the whole since each citizen is a being in himself, while the members of an organism do not exist on their own if separated from the group. Thus human societies form *an accidental whole, or an ordered whole*, whose unity is based solely on a common end to which all the members strive. And this common goal is none other than the common good analysed above.

However, it remains to determine the reason why an authority assuring the unity of the whole must exist. In every human society, and more exactly in every political society, this reason is precisely the specific distinction between the individual good and the common good. Because the common good differs essentially from the individual good, at the heart of each political community there must exist someone who has as his special mission, not his personal interest but the good of the total social body.

The truth of this assertion will be shown if we consider an

unlikely case. Let us suppose that in the republic of Utopia all the citizens are so virtuous that they collaborate spontaneously in every useful and noble task; as soon as they realize that there is something which needs doing, they rush to carry it out. It cannot escape the notice of such citizens that the organization and the maintenance of certain common services require a suitable financing, and that this depends on the contribution of each citizen. The problem arises not as to whether each member pays his contribution, but as to how much, when and where each one must pay. It is not only a question of moral *uprightness* but of *knowledge*. To know exactly the common necessities and the means to be used to satisfy them, simple individual foresight is not enough, and more perfect habits are required: special knowledge, wide experience, great social sensitivity, etc., which are not the usual equipment of the average citizen, nor even of the virtuous citizen (*rara avis*) in our example. While every person normally possesses the necessary preparation, the skill and experience to obtain his individual well-being, to exercise his professional activities, to form a home, to educate his children, etc., no one could sensibly affirm that every person is capable of facing the problems that involve the common good and of adequately solving them.

From this follows the need of every political society to hand over to one person or a group of persons the exercise of public power. It is the very nature of the common good which imposes as an absolute necessity the existence of a social authority capable of carrying this out. For this reason it is obvious that the reason for the existence of political power is none other than the efficient achievement of the common good of the political society. To achieve this two things are needed in the political leader: *clear judgment* to know what to do in each circumstance and *moral uprightness* to bring this about.

THE GENERAL FUNCTION OF THE STATE

Once we have outlined the notion of common good, the cornerstone of a just social doctrine, we may understand more easily the specific functions which the political authority, or state, must assume in relation to this common good.

The first point to be examined closely is the following: in what measure can the state by itself bring about the common good? The question, far from being gratuitous, obliges us to deepen our analysis. Indeed, it could easily be objected, with reference to the preceding reflections, that the state can bring about at most only some elements of the common good, but not all. Thus, for example, the moral perfection of citizens is essential to the good of the community and yet the state cannot by means of legal compulsion force the citizens to be virtuous.

Within the constituent elements of the political society, the authorities occupy a special place which has not always been clearly explained. Every society presupposes four essential elements: 1) the actions of the multitude (the material cause); 2) the common good (the final cause); 3) the order or cooperation expressed in the law (the formal cause); 4) the efficient cause, which in this case is double: the authority, as a principal cause, and the multitude or social body, as a subordinate cause.[7] This last distinction between the causality of the authority and that of the citizens is seldom presented correctly, despite the fact that it is the only distinction that allows us to preserve both the responsibility and the initiative of the citizens and the due preeminence of the public power.

In fact, if only the social body is assimilated in the efficient cause, the political authority will lose its reason for existence, since all the citizens will spontaneously achieve coordination purely by the contribution of individual efforts; this is none other than the liberal doctrine, which, starting out from the natural goodness of man, denies the state any participation in social activities if it does not limit itself to being the "prefect" who calls the most unruly pupils to order. If, on the other hand, we reduce the social body to a mere material cause, we fall directly into the totalitarian thesis according to which the individual person is defined as a mere "citizen," that is, a mere cog in the state machinery which provides all rights and is the source of all human values, both natural and spiritual. The individual is thus deprived of all personal autonomy and responsibility, as in the case of a shapeless and parasitic being, capable only of receiving gifts without creating or achieving anything in return.

We thus see the delicate balance in which the different elements of the political society are reciprocally held. Both the authority and the social body stand as an efficient cause, but not on the *same level or with equal suitability.* The body of citizens is the immediate cause of the social operations which they carry out, but the play of personal initiative would not be sufficient to permit the achievement of the common good, which as we have just seen, is different from the individual good. Political power, on the other hand, when it imposes on individual actions the coordination and hierarchy expressed in the laws, arranges all things by subordinating them to the attainment of the common good. For this reason it deserves the name of principal efficient cause, since without its action the social body could not reach its goal.

In the light of these distinctions, let us try to clarify the objection already formulated as to the impossibility of the state effectively attaining that perfection of common existence which is the virtuous life. A text of Pius XII, frequently quoted, will allow us to meet the objection. In his message of Jan. 5, 1942, Pius XII defines the common political good in the following terms: "All political and economic activity of the state should be geared to the permanent attainment of the common good, that is to say, *the totality of the external conditions necessary to the citizens for the development of their qualities on the religious, intellectual, moral, and material plains.*" Such a definition appears incongruous in relation to what has been explained in this study in defining the common good. Why is it necessary to term it "totality of the external conditions" when the definition given by Pius XI in *Divini Illius Magistri* speaks of the different goods which form the social good and not of conditions? On the other hand, it is obvious that *good* and *condition* cannot be identified, since the external conditions stand as means for the achievement and possession of goods.

In spite of the apparent incongruity, both notions may easily be reconciled if one observes that the definition given by Pius XII describes not the common good *in itself*, but this good considered from the point of view of the state, i.e., that it is a question of defining the essential function of the state with respect to the political good. This being so, we may resolve the difficulty. Indeed, the common good has already been defined as happy coexistence in possession of the essential human goods (virtue, culture, order, peace, etc.). It is also true that the state cannot force the citizens to be virtuous in themselves, since this could imply a substitution for personal action, and moral virtue emerges only from the virtuous interior disposition of each man. We may deduce from this that the specific mission of the state does not consist in causing knowledge or virtue but in creating the external conditions which make possible the practice of virtue, the progress of knowledge, etc., for each citizen.

This group of external conditions to which Pius XII alludes is not confined to the material elements necessary to the *bene esse* of society, such, for example, as a network of institutions of learning which make possible the diffusion of knowledge, but consists mainly in an institutional framework guaranteeing liberty and the exercise of human rights, at the same time ordering all activities according to the demand of social justice.

Thus one may point out the insufficiency of some modern exponents (Antoine, Schwalm, and M. Clément, among others) who limit the activity of the state to "the protection of fundamental personal rights and to the facilitating of the fulfilment of corresponding obligations."[8] Without doubt, the authority should rest on these two bases by assuming three main functions: 1) stating and detailing rights, through legislative activity, by fixing the area of what is lawful and unlawful, rights and obligations, by which everybody knows "what to expect" in his relations with justice; 2) securing of the exercise of right by efficiently protecting all people, and especially the weakest, and 3) resolving of the conflicts of right by means of an adequate judiciary organization given over to competent courts.

But this mission is not the limit of the political authority and does not even constitute its principal function. If the state or political authority is the director of the common good, its essential mission is that of creating and keeping a just public order of human coexistence.

It has been explained that individuals in the just use of their reason and liberty may attain by themselves their particular good and, in consequence, may exercise their corresponding personal rights without needing the contribution of the public power. For this reason,

> the power of the state begins properly speaking and attains, as it were, its own place and sphere in the realm of what is public, what is common, that is when there is a question of regulating private acts, not when these are seen in terms of one with another, but when they concern relations with the community, or affect and may have a repercussion on the community or on social life. The field of action proper to the state is thus the public sphere, that is, that which surpasses the limit of purely private relationships.[9]

The expression of this public order of coexistence is human law, or positive law, which, founded upon the actual order, must make concrete and determine through particular norms the universal moral principles which the circumstances and characteristics of each political society bear very much in mind (history, customs, social structure, accepted values, ways of being, etc.). The goal of positive law is no other than the benefit of man himself, that is, his happiness, achieved in and through the common good. Since human happiness consists in the virtuous life, the state must do everything possible to favor the practice of virtue and prevent the diffusion of immorality by means of an efficient public regulation of customs. Because its sphere of action is limited to the external actions of the citizens, it cannot regulate the course of personal conscience (*ordo intentionis*); thus authority may demand from each member the punctual payment of his taxes, but not that such a payment be accompanied by a broad smile of satisfaction. Saint Thomas explains clearly the necessity for positive law, after describing the virtuous citizen, when he states:

> But for those others—this kind does exist—who are of a wicked nature, who tend toward vice, for whom all persuasion and good counsel are of no effect, coercion and the threat of punishment become quite necessary in order that they may cease in the practice of evil. In this way, weakening in their insistence on doing evil, they do not disturb the peace of others with whom they live, and they in turn may finally, spontaneously, and freely do the good that they have begun to practice purely through fear of punishment, and may thus succeed in finally winning virtue. This discipline, based on the fear of punishment, is the discipline of the law.[10]

In this manner we may understand both the dignity of the legal order and its intrinsic limitations. The law is a very efficient instrument for the moral progress of citizens, but it acts only from without. The public power does not cause the moral virtue of each person but favors it by means of the morality or public regulation of customs. It promotes, for example, the physical health of the population by means of hygiene, security by means of the police force and the administration of justice, knowledge by means of an organization of learning, buildings, and proper equipment, etc. Such are the "outside conditions" which the state must provide in its nature as the universal achiever of the common temporal good.

THE PLACE OF EDUCATION IN THE COMMON GOOD

First of all we must consider the place occupied by educational activity with relation to the common good. As has been said before, the temporal common good is formed in its strict sense by spiritual goods, since the nature of these allows them to be shared and held by an infinite number of individuals. This is the reason, let us remark in passing, why economic goods, being material, have not in themselves the status of common goods, since they are held in private, and it is only possible to include them as parts of the common temporal good insofar as they are means necessary for obtaining higher values.

This shows that the universal level activity occupies a place of absolute preeminence among the elements constituting the good of society. This will be even more evident if we consider the relationship existing between human happiness and the aim of the social order. In his *Nicomachean Ethics*,[11] Aristotle tries to pinpoint the definition of human happiness and analyses the different operations of man, from the most generic to the most specific, concluding that the human operation par excellence is the exercise of one's intelligence and, on a universal level, maintains that the perfection of man resides in a life lived in accordance with virtue, and above all, the most excellent among all virtues, wisdom. In the same work,[12] at the end of his exposition, the problem is posed of the superiority of either the speculative or the practical life (based on moral principles); Aristotle concludes by maintaining the superiority of the former. This doctrine has been totally taken over by Saint Thomas and presented in his *Summa Theologica*[13] and in all his moral teaching. But it is in the *Politics*[14] that Aristotle applies the preceding doctrine to the problem of the goal of the political society. Here he affirms that there is only one goal, for both the individual and society; such a goal can only be the speculative life, which is the most worthy of all, and to the achieving of which all others are directed as so many means.[15] Although it is not the task of this study to

enlarge upon this, it is necessary, however, to indicate briefly
the basis of this superiority. Its first root lies in the superiority
of the intelligence over the will, by reason of the loftiness of
the object of intelligence.[16] From this it follows that the speculative life is superior to the active life. If, on the other hand,
we take into account what has been stated in the preceding
section, that is, that the political society per se is regulated
towards the perfection of man (*bene vivere multitudinis*), we
conclude finally that knowledge or wisdom forms the most
essential element of the common temporal good, inasmuch as
it is the highest good to which man may aspire. For this reason
Saint Thomas says that for the perfection of human society it is
necessary that some give themselves over to the contemplative
life.[17]

The affirmation of these common notions occasions new
difficulties. Indeed, we already said that the state cannot cause
either moral or intellectual virtue in citizens, and must confine
itself to creating the necessary exterior conditions for the development and exercise of these virtues. The problem arises
when the state, in its capacity as director of the common good,
tries through all its resources to promote the intellectual life.
All activity of the state belongs to the "active life," using the
expression of Aristotle: it is a prudential activity concerned
with putting into effect the legal order, by means of which the
state coordinates individual actions to achieve the well-being
of the entire social body. Such a prudent activity, like all practical knowledge, presupposes speculative truth as its own norm
and measure.[18] But may the state make decisions concerning
intellectual life, the development of science and systems of
teaching, when its specific field of action is the active life?
Does this mean, perhaps, that what is on a lower plane regu-
lates and directs what is on a higher?

Historically, the myth of the educator-state envisioned by
a man such as Rousseau, among others, is nothing more than
the application of such a principle. However, and without for-
getting that there is in this a real subversion of values, one may

wonder what the state ultimately has to do in matters of education and intellectual life. As soon as these form part of the common political good, the state must protect and favor them to its maximum capacity. On the other hand, given that it is a question of a function higher than its proper field, the state cannot make any proper judgment in such matters, since it lacks competence. The key to the solution is found in a capital (and very little known) distinction made by Saint Thomas in his *Commentary on the Ethics* of Aristotle:[19]

> But political science dictates to a speculative science only as to *activity* (*ad usum*) but not concerning the specification of its proper activity (*ad determinationem*). Political science orders that some teach or learn geometry, and actions of this kind, insofar as they are voluntary, belong to the matter of ethics and can be ordered to the goal of human living. But the political ruler does not dictate to geometry what conclusions it should draw about a triangle, for this is not subject to the human will nor can it be ordered to human living, but it depends on the very nature of things. Therefore, he [Aristotle] says that political science ordains which science, both practical and speculative, should be studied in a state, who should study them, and for how long.

From this there follows the clear distinction between what is concerned with *putting into effect* (efficient causality), the proper field of public power, and what is concerned with *specification* (formal causality), which depends on the discipline itself. Thus the ruler may demand and order that the teaching of certain basic disciplines should be given to the population, but he would be going beyond the limit of his powers if he wished to determine by himself the content of each science and the intrinsic order of each of them. This is because each science has its own peculiar demands as to its object, principles, and method, and such things cannot be modified by a simple act of power. From this it follows that political power, since it is not competent in matters concerning the content of the education to be given, must be constantly advised by the experts in each discipline and must apply their conclusions in the working out of an integral educational system, suited to the possibilities and aspirations of the people. If the opposite were to occur, Plato's old error of the philosopher-king, or the no less serious error of the educator-king of modern socialism, would arise.

We may finally point out that the evolution of modern thought from the Renaissance until our own days has undermined the natural hierarchy which must exist between the theoretical order and the practical order. The superiority of contemplation, commonly accepted in ancient times and in the Middle Ages, has been radically reversed in recent centuries. We have only to remember Descartes who proposed the substitution of speculative knowledge by a "practical knowledge" permitting us to "become the lord and master of Nature," or Hobbes: "The end of all knowledge is power. . . . The end of all speculation is to allow some action" (*De Corpore*). In our days Marxism is seen as the radical dissolution of all absolute truth by denying that there is anything definite, lasting, or sacred. This subordination of theory to practice has facilitated the domination by modern states of the legitimate spheres of competence of intermediate bodies in educational matters. Thus, for example, we see that the state will encourage with huge subsidies certain investigations in the field of nuclear science, since in this a problem of defense and security is directly intermingled, but at the same time it neglects totally other less "practical" disciplines, such as philosophy, history, or poetry. Will the poet's turn come one day?

The function of the state in educational matters, as in the other fields, has been clearly transformed by the modern revolution. To re-channel this function properly into its supplementary activity with respect to the initiative of private persons, we must now consider the other basic principle of the social order which complements the superiority of the common good mentioned above. This other principle is none other than that of *subsidiarity*.

THE KEY PRINCIPLE: SUBSIDIARITY

When stating the broad outlines of just socio-economic order, Pius XI formulated clearly in *Quadragesimo Anno* what has been called the principle of subsidiarity. This principle constitutes a universal norm whose application is indispensable for every society desirous of carrying out its activities in constant progress within the proper field of the natural order. The importance of this key principle is explained in the very terms of the text:

> Above all the most important principle of the social philosophy must be preserved: that just as it is not lawful to take away from individuals what they may achieve with their own efforts and industry in order to hand it over to the community, so it is also unjust to reserve for a greater or higher society what lesser or lower communities may produce. And this constitutes both a grievous error and an upsetting of the proper order of society; because the natural object of any intervention of society itself is that of helping the members of the social body effectively, and not that of destroying them or absorbing them.[20]

We may resume the essential ideas contained in the text in the following three points:

1) To private persons and groups of a lower status must be left the tasks which they can carry out satisfactorily on their own initiative and responsibility;

2) The groups of superior status have as their only end the task of helping private persons and lower groups, supplanting them in what they cannot achieve on their own. Therefore, they must neither replace them nor destroy them;

3) The only case in which a group of superior status may replace another of a lower order, is when the latter lacks the indispensable elements (means and persons) to act effectively.

For a correct interpretation of the statement of the principle of subsidiarity, we must refer to the notion of "intermediary groups or bodies." Intermediate groups are all the associations, institutions, or entities existing in a society and situated between families and the state or public power. The families and intermediate groups are found within the social body as the cells and tissues respectively are found within a living organism. All these groups are formed of citizens and pursue partial objects by virtue of which their members come together and join their efforts. According to whether the goal pursued, the number of members and the magnitude of the means used by each group are more or less vital within the terms of the common political good, the greater or lesser importance of the group and its respective ranking within the social body will be calculated. Thus, for example, it is obvious that a confederation of labor unions fulfills a much more important function than a league of united philatelists"; by analogy, a province or region forms a unity of a greater hierarchical ranking than a municipality.

What the principle of subsidiarity strives to guarantee in the given instance is that the greater importance or power of a group, and principally the state, should not be detrimental to the activities which weaker social organisms can perfectly well carry out by themselves.

This principle is too often a matter of indifference to the contemporary mind. Are we not in the century of "socialization," of rationalizations, of interventionism and planification? It is enough, however, to reflect even momentarily upon the nature of this principle in order to discover its intimate connections with the very nature of man. Thus it is vitally important for the future of societies. The more deeply a principle is rooted in something essentially human, the more ignorance of this principle will entail the worst consequences. Precisely in the case on which we are commenting, we touch on not one essential element among many, but on the very root of man's personal dignity, a dignity which constitutes the basis of all human rights. Indeed, in what does the natural dignity of man consist? Saint Thomas explains this in a series of close-reasoned

chapters in his *Summa contra Gentiles*.[21] Man is a being endowed with reason, and by reason he may reach universal
concepts. Because he is *rational*, man is *free*, that is, he is the
cause of his own acts, since in being able to know an infinity of
objects, his will may choose between them as between so many
means to reach his fulfilment. It is by virtue of his rational
and free nature that man is a person responsible for his acts,
and reciprocally subject to rights and obligations. If his nature
is such, it is easy to understand that all limitations imposed on
a private individual relative to his initiative, his liberty, or his
responsibility, imply an attack on his personal dignity. From
this it follows that the greatest interest of a healthy society
resides in the maximum stimulation of individual or group
responsibility. Inversely, the greatest danger for the stability of
society lurks in all restrictions on the lawful competition and
independence of people and groups.

History has not had to wait for our century to show that
each time the principle of subsidiarity has been transgressed
in a society, that society has not been long in undergoing a
crisis, the victim of its own error. Thus, for example, the
Roman Empire, which was able to conquer the world precisely
under a policy of domination which respected local traditions,
languages, and religions, found itself in a crisis when the coun-
tryside was depopulated by the lure of urban pleasures, when
the birth-rate dropped, immorality ran high, and the heroic
generals changed into satraps who abused their magisterial
power to gain easy riches. The same fate befell the Carolingian
empire and, in more recent times, Tsarist Russia.

From the preceding, we may deduce that the activity of
the state is above all supplementary. Political power must respect all legitimate activities of the lower groups, taking care
not to usurp them unduly—a step that is easy, given the resources of the modern state. Its essential action must consist in
stimulating, coordinating, orientating, controlling what the social body does by itself. Such is the general principle, and it is
precisely on the level of educational activity that the supple-

mentary action of the state must be brought to bear most clearly and decisively.

This supplementary role of the state authority has, as we shall see later, its exceptions. The action of the state comes to the foreground whenever the lower groups do not possess or cannot in the future count upon the resources, means, and men of sufficient ability to confront in a proper manner certain activities important to social life. This is explained by John XXIII in his "Letter to the Grenoble Social Week":

> Taking under their intermediary bodies jurisdiction, the tasks of an excessively burdensome or complex nature, which cannot be carried out by persons or families, such groups thus release new potentialities, both individual and collective. *But this is so on condition that each one of these institutions remain at the level of its own competence, by offering its services to and not by imposing itself on the free choice of men.*[22]

If this is valid for the intermediate groups, it will be all the more valid for the state itself. This is to say that the state must intervene when the groups tend to go beyond their proper sphere of action and overreach themselves in their functions.

However, the state must display a great clarity of vision and a great spirit of service, since even in the case where it must, through circumstances, substitute for the action of the lower groups, it must always do so with the intention of simultaneously creating the conditions which facilitate the assumption of those tasks by the individuals themselves. It is easy to see nowadays how often the state simply dominates private autonomies for ideological reasons or reasons concerned purely with subjection, thus provoking incalculable evils and encouraging citizens' lack of enthusiasm for the common good:

> Unfortunately, it is not at present a question of hypotheses or mere foresight, since the sad reality is already before our eyes: wherever the demon of organisation invades or tyrannises the human spirit, suddenly the signs of an abnormal and false orientation of social progress are revealed. In numerous coun-

tries, the modern state is in the process of becoming a gigantic administrative machine. It reaches out its arms over all life. The entire range of the political, economic, social, intellectual realms, from birth until death, all this it desires to put under its administration. It should not be surprising, therefore, *if in this impersonal climate the cause of common good disappears in the conscience of individuals, and if the state loses its primordial character of the moral community of citizens.* Thus we discover the origin and starting point of the evolution which plunges modern man into anguish: his "depersonalisation." He is to a great extent deprived of his countenance and his name. In many of the most important activities in his life, *he is reduced to a mere object of the society, since society, in turn, is turned into an impersonal system, into a cold organisation of forces.*[23]

This subjugation of essential liberties and consciences by the modern state is not confined to the economic sphere but occurs at all the levels of existence. In this sense we must, in the light of this text, reflect on the problem of political democracies, as posed by Pius XII in his Christmas Message of 1944 (a theme which goes beyond the limits of the present study). Let us now continue to go more deeply into this vital question of the functions of the state by clearly distinguishing the tasks of the different educational agents.

THE AGENTS OF EDUCATION

We must now examine those whose delicate task it is to educate, and what is their field of action and their specific responsibility. The majority of writers agree in distinguishing three principal agents: the family, the church, and the state. To these we may add, for the completion of the list, the *intermediate groups,* that is to say, those institutions or associations existing between families and the public power. Granted that our goal is to determine with the greatest possible precision the competence of the state in educational matters, it is convenient to delineate beforehand the role of the other agents of education.

The family: To the family falls the responsibility for assuring the first education of children. Children belong primarily to their parents since they are the fruit of their mutual affection and, human love being the act of rational beings, this same love entails *responsibility*. Second, this dependence has its origin in the fact that being is the origin of acting, and acting the goal of being. Given that procreation is defined under the heading of being and not under that of the good as such, it follows that the task of procreation, given over to the family, inseparably includes the "starting off" of the child, his existence, that is, his education.[24] Third, since children are the result of the affection existing between man and wife, their parents tend naturally to care for them as something belonging to themselves, in virtue of an inclination of their nature, and to make the sacrifices which such a care presupposes.

It is especially important to emphasize the intimate connection existing between human procreation and education in times like our own when in certain countries the educational function is again given over to the state. As Chesterton said, "If the state desires to take over our children, let it begin by bearing them and giving them the breast." Indeed, human procreation can never be limited to the simple material communication of life, since the new being, unlike the animals, is without all goods, even those most essential for his survival, and, on the other hand, he cannot naturally carry out by himself the most elementary operations to assure his subsistence. This radical destitution supposes, in compensation, that the parents furnish his basic necessities and the progressive development of his powers of learning and will, that is to say, his intellectual and moral formation. This continues as long as his incapacity for being self-sufficient in his daily actions endures.[25] The clearest mark of this long period of subordination is shown by the positive law of all nations, in that they do not grant full legal status before the age of twenty-one.

Domestic society, inscribed within the order of procreation, is deeply rooted in human nature, consolidating an inclination common to man and to beast.[26] The putting into effect of a previous principle[27] assures man of a *private* stability, prior to that with which political society is concerned. In consequence, the family has the role of the basis and beginning of the social order; from this arises its *priority*, in relation to society.[28] Such a priority demands that family order and functions be carefully respected and guaranteed by the public power.[29] Even if, like all human institutions, the family must adapt itself to circumstances which are continually changing, this does not imply in any way that the state may arbitrarily reduce the family's rights.

History, both ancient and modern, shows clearly that every time that political power has attempted to weaken or modify the constitution of the family, the entire political society has suffered the consequences.

The respect due to the family, in its dual character as the starting-point of the social order and irreplaceable agent of education, was declared sacred in the Universal Declaration of Human Rights approved by the U. N. on December 10, 1948: "The family is the natural and fundamental element of society and has a right to the protection of society and state." Article 26 accords to parents "by priority, the right to choose the kind of education to be given to their children."

The Intermediate Bodies: We may also include the intermediate bodies as educational agents. Here would be professional teachers' associations at all levels, since inasmuch as they are given the mission of teaching in schools and universities, they must be the first to be consulted in everything which concerns teaching practice.

Moreover, the associations which bring together the members of the various liberal professions must exercise an active educational function in everything related to professional practice in its most contingent aspects, both in the recognition and in the granting of official titles.

The Church: Pope Pius XII has defined education in the following manner: "Education within the natural order has as its object and goal the development of the child to achieve a complete man; Christian education has as its object and goal the formation of the new man, reborn by baptism, in order to make a perfect Christian of him." This "new man" to whom the Pope refers is none other than the one described by Saint Paul, re-established in his dignity as the son of God through the merits of Christ's incarnation and called upon to participate in the divine life, by means of his insertion into the order of grace and his obedience to the divine will.

In this perspective, the Church appears as holding a divine mandate to educate men within the demands of the divine plan, developing in them the sense of supernatural realities, both in what concerns faith and what has to do with daily activity. The exercise of its educational mission must, in consequence, enjoy all the freedom necessary to it, a freedom which must be guaranteed by the public power. This impiles that, in virtue of the subordination of the temporal to the eternal, even the activities of Christians in the temporal sphere must conform to the needs of the eternal life. Saint Pius X has expressed this clearly:

> In whatever the Christian does, even in the sphere of earthly things, it is not lawful to neglect supernatural goods. On the contrary, in accordance with the precepts of *Christian* wisdom, he must direct all things toward the supreme good as the ultimate end. Moreover, all his actions, inasmuch as they are good or bad with reference to customs, that is, inasmuch as they conform or do not conform to natural and divine law, are subject to the judgment and jurisdiction of the Church.

The exercise of the educational mission of the Church must enjoy, consequently, all the liberty necessary for this exercise, a liberty which must be guaranteed by the public power.

Let us now consider the function of the state in matters of education. To do so, it is necessary to distinguish two funda-

mental levels, by considering first of all what the state is empowered to carry out in its condition as a principal agent, and,
second, what is its supplementary function.

THE ROLE OF THE STATE AS PRINCIPAL AGENT

We maintained previously that truth is the most noble and
important element in the political common good, since the end
of legal order, namely, to promote the virtuous life of the social
body and the practice of the moral virtues, presupposes the
knowledge of certain universal truths. From this follows the
obligation of the state, in its nature as the director or procurer
of the common good, to encourage the creation of a complete
system of education in accordance with the demands of the
present day and to exercise an effective control over this
system.

We have also considered the principal of subsidiarity as
the universal regulating norm of state activity in its relations
with families and intermediate bodies. This principle is reaffirmed by Pius XI in *Divini illius Magistri:* "The function of
the civil authority, is, thus, dual: to protect and promote and
not absorb the family and the individual or supplant them."

However, and even when the demands of subsidiarity are
faithfully respected, the state must still take over some extremely important tasks (and in these it assumes the character
not only of principal agent) which depend *exclusively* on its
competence. Let us briefly analyse these diverse fields of action
of the state.

In the first place, we must distinguish between intellectual
and technical education, moral education, and civic education.
These three spheres must be carefully separated, since each
one has its own demands.

In questions of intellectual and technical formation, the
state must organize by itself the training of the entire body of
civil servants and employees of the public administration at all

levels. It is also the exclusive task of the state to watch over the
satisfactory preparation of the personnel of the diplomatic
corps so that it may take upon itself the representation of the
interests of the nation in the field of international relations.
(An example of this is the Higher Institute of Public Administration in France). Nobody is ignorant of the vital importance
which this corps has for the obtaining of the political objectives of a country. Finally, it is also the exclusive task of the
public power to organise and train the security forces, both in
the sphere of the police and in that of national defense. The
army and the police obviously cannot be prepared in private
academies. Only the civil power is competent in that field
which is of vital importance for the security of the nation.

As far as moral education goes, the state has a most important function which it must not delegate to other bodies. The
promotion and maintenance of a high index of public morality
are given over directly to its jurisdiction. The vigilance of customs, a flexible but efficient control of public performances
insofar as the diffusion of ideas is concerned, demand from
authority an attitude of profound respect for the convictions of
people and groups, but at the same time a proper vigilance of
all that may undermine the very foundations of the social
order. Into this same field come the repression of all forms of
crime, prostitution, violence, drug-trafficking, alcoholism, etc.
This latter task, seemingly more negative than the ones previously described, must find its natural complement in a series
of enactments that have as their goal moral and social rehabili-
tation and the regulation of places of detention (pensions,
asylums, homes, orphanages, etc.). The organisation of an efficient service of social aid makes much easier this work of the
state for the redemption from moral wretchedness of more or
less extensive groups of the population.

Finally, as far as the civic education of the population is
concerned, it also falls to the public power before any private
group or institution to encourage a public conscience-
searching, a respect for and loyalty to national values, by

means of the diffusion of an objective account of national history, by encouraging the cult of duty and the spirit of sacrifice through works of public solidarity, military service, which is a school for patriotism, etc., and, especially by means of the constant example that civil servants and magistrates give to the population. In this we may point out the pedagogical function which lawmakers must carry out when they make known, by means of modern techniques, the ends, advantages, and conveniences which the adoption or the rejection of a certain proposed law will bring to the country.

THE ROLE OF THE STATE AS SECONDARY AGENT

After explaining the various educational tasks which are directly in the hands of the public power, it is useful to turn briefly to the state's supplementary function with relation to the activities of the other agents of education.

We have already stated that the family occupies a fundamental role in education; it is obvious, however, that if the parents relinquish their educational mission, it is the job of the state to assure for the children more satisfactory living conditions, so that their physical and spiritual development may continue without hindrance.

In the faithful application of the principle of subsidiarity, the state has, however, a most important supplementary function in order to surmount the difficulty arising from the natural limits of the intermediate bodies. Indeed, here we come into the really discretionary field where circumstances play a preponderant role, and must be analyzed in each particular case. We may say that the civil power must intervene to help those persons and groups which, enjoying the necessary competence, actively take on their educational mission. Government action is mainly an action of stimulation, control, and coordination of all the institutions and activities of private bodies. Granted that authority is defined in the sphere of execution, that is, the application of means to the end, the government must lay down, with the collaboration of experts, the essential framework of all educational bodies, their goals and necessities, both for future educators and students. Its essential preoccupation is not that of teaching for its own sake, since it is not competent to do this (except in the cases mentioned in the previous paragraph); it must not "administer" education but assume its "government," by respecting to the maximum the capacity, initiative, and responsibility of private individuals.

However, in the complex reality of our societies, there always remain some neglected groups or regions, whether it be because the individual initiative does not afford all the necessary guarantees of a serious purpose, or because their financial resources or their competence are excessively limited. In such cases, it is up to the public power to assume such tasks and care for such groups, in order to prevent the conversion of certain natural inequalities into unjust situations or backward situations which may hinder the progress of the entire community. The state may also create, outside the private sphere, a public sphere of education to guarantee the widest access to all groups of society, especially to those with fewer economic resources, so that all human potential may develop its capacities to the maximum. These activities must always be seen as supplementary aid, and not as the exercise of a right by the state. If this is respected in practice, the government will attempt, at the same time as it assumes these exceptional tasks, to remedy, as far as possible, the incapacity or lack of resources of the private groups in order to enable them to take up on their own what the government itself has had to organise and administer.

CONCLUSION

Thus we reach the end of this long discussion of the role of the state in matters of education. I believe that the importance of the subject, as well as its great complexity, demanded this consideration.

It only remains for us to underline the enormous importance of this function of the public power in our modern societies. Everybody realizes the vital role which the encouragement of education in all its forms has for the progress of peoples. Nobody is unaware, either, of the grave risk which is usually run when the functions of the civil authorities in this field are exaggerated. If we have taken the liberty of expounding certain principles of a very universal nature concerning the general action of the state, it is precisely because many of these regulating principles are, in fact, frequently unknown. The Church throughout the centuries has formed a corpus of doctrine in which the most basic demands of the human being are harmonized in an admirable synthesis with the demands pertaining to the supernatural order. Its labor of many centuries has been to state and diffuse these principles. Our only desire is that today, more than ever, such principles may not only be heeded but also spread and applied by all promoters of international peace and security.

GERMAIN G. GRISEZ

3: The Right to be Educated—
Philosophical Reflections

What is education? Certainly the concept embraces more than schooling, since the school is only one institution invented to accomplish the purpose of education. Then too, we must admit that not all schooling makes an authentic contribution to education. Sometimes the instrument fails to achieve its end.

Education is an aspect of human development. But the concept of the development of the person is wider than education, since much development occurs unsought as a by-product of activities done for their own sake. Moreover, development can be negative—for example, a person can be taught to lie, to violate the rights of others, and to indulge habits damaging to himself. One remembers the waifs in *Oliver Twist* who were trained in vices. Such development could hardly be called "education."

Education is the purposeful development of the human person. Development is the end in view, the objective intentionally pursued by education. At least the educator must aim at development. If the one who is being educated also aims at it, he begins to participate actively in the process of his own education. Self-education is a real possibility, not a contradiction in terms.

Education is a positive development of the person. Development is directed toward what is conceived to be the true end and good of the person. Human good is realized both in the individual and in the community. Education aims toward the betterment of persons and communities. Without a standard of human good, no education is possible. All education is implicitly dominated by a philosophy of man, an understanding of what man is and what he ought to become.

The development involved in education is not mere transient change. If two equally strong and healthy boys are sleeping, then it may be impossible to distinguish which of them has been trained in gymnastics and which has not been trained. But when the boys awaken, a simple test will answer the question; since the one who has been trained will have a ready ability for athletic feats, while the boy without training will lack such ability. Similarly, each field of knowledge presents the possibility of a ready ability. For example, to know a language is to have a ready ability to read, write, speak, and translate it. To know mathematics is to have a ready ability to solve mathematical problems. To know medicine is to have a ready ability to treat and cure diseases.

In its most general sense, then, education may be defined as a deliberate attempt to develop in a human person any ready ability that he can exercise for the true good of himself or others.

COMPLEXITY OF EDUCATION

In a very simple human culture there is little need for education. Children acquire the abilities they need spontaneously by imitation. Without a written language and division of labor, each couple incarnates the fullness of the culture, actuates it in their daily acts, and passes it on to their children without making any deliberate effort to do so.

With a division of labor beyond that found within each family, a problem presents itself. Either each separate task will be hereditary and the various aspects of the culture will become the property of different groups, or some deliberate effort will be made to pass on the various abilities to those who do not acquire them by spontaneous learning. To the extent that the latter solution is adopted, there is a beginning of primitive education.

As techniques become more sophisticated, education becomes more necessary. Simple and easily imitated techniques are gradually modified into complex, efficient, but difficult to imitate processes. At a certain point in this evolution, a stage is reached where the technique can no longer be acquired by direct imitation. First a ready ability for the simpler, less efficient forms of the technique must be gained. The first ability is a vehicle for transition to the more sophisticated ability of the evolved technique. To aim specifically at the transitional ability, using it merely as a stage in the process of development, is to engage in activity that is purely educational. However simple the culture, formal education begins at this point.

Sometimes the lack of a ready ability is not due to the complexity and difficulty of the behavior of those who exercise the ability. A small child cannot share in making decisions for the community, not because of technical difficulty, but because of his lack of sufficient knowledge, proper attitudes, and spiritual capacities. Not merely past experience, but also common cultural meanings must be transmitted symbolically by stories, legends, myths, rituals, and object lessons. The ability to act in a community presupposes and gathers into itself a whole host of meanings and values that belong to the spiritual dimension of the culture.

As time passes, man's acts become more and more significant in both dimensions. His technical acts gain greater and greater power through ever more complex instruments. The ready abilities for such acts become ever more difficult to acquire. Social acts gain greater and greater meaning through ever more complex and self-conscious extensions of spiritual culture. The gaining of the status of full membership in society becomes a task ever more difficult.

Thus as man progresses, the proportion of his life that

must be devoted to formal education grows greater and greater. The ready abilities take longer to acquire, but they are increasingly significant and indispensable. We may imagine the process of development reaching its ultimate limits when individuals will spend almost all their lives developing abilities which will be exercised only for a very brief time. Nevertheless, the few acts that will be performed will be so effective and so filled with human meaning that the life-long education needed to perform them will be worthwhile.

EDUCATION AND HUMAN LIFE

Looking at education in this way, one can see that denial of it is tantamount to denial of human life itself. Once culture reaches a level at which education is necessary; no one without it is able to participate in his community as a full member, for he lacks the ready abilities to perform the acts that are most effective and meaningful in his society. The denial to anyone of educational opportunity automatically limits his role in the society. He is, as it were, consigned to a certain earlier and lower level of cultural development and prevented from reaching the frontier of present-day life and activity. It is little wonder that a society that degrades certain groups always restricts the educational opportunity of those against whom discrimination is practiced. The right to education is the foundation of all the rights of the person to live as a free and equal member of his community.

Written language may not have been invented as an instrument of education. From one point of view, it presents a large and basic challenge to the more educated part of the community. Since the ready ability to read and write is a key to so many other abilities, those who are more educated can hardly feel that they are doing justice to those who lack this ability until every reasonable effort has been made to eliminate illiteracy. Whatever else belongs to the "elementary and fun-

damental" part of education, certainly instruction in reading
and writing belongs to it.

From another point of view, written language is the most
powerful instrument of education. Discoveries and thoughts
that are recorded are less likely to be lost, and they can be
spread widely and quickly. The past becomes more fixed, less
subject to revision; and hence genuine cumulative progress
becomes possible. The abstract symbols of language make possible a larger community of shared, human meanings and the
development of a social structure based on the intelligent ar-
ticulation of legally stabilized rights and duties. From written
language grows civilization. And civilization is a school, an
institutionalization of education.

In considering illiteracy, we would make a serious mistake
to imagine that the problem is simple. There are many levels
of ability to read and write. The mere ability to vocalize written phrases helpful for daily life is precious, but minimal. If
the written language is to attain its full power as an educational instrument, literacy of a rather high order must be the
aim of the general elementary education. Reading comprehen-
sion, including especially the logical analysis of argumentative
content, is necessary if the ability to read is to be used as a tool
in self-education. Moreover, even the most skillful reader
needs a good library.

The right to a free elementary education therefore includes
the right to instruction in reading and writing up to a solid
level of ability, and the right to use free public libraries.

Taken by itself, this conclusion is not very sweeping, for it
deals with the issue only at a general level. Further specifications may be introduced if a nation as a whole is economically
in advance of the most undeveloped peoples. For if there is
some margin of resources that can be used for more than minimal education, then it is a strict requirement of social justice
that these added resources be used with justice to every citizen. Each child to be educated must be regarded as a person
having an absolute dignity, as an irreducible bearer of value,

not merely as a potential contributor to some larger political, ideological, cosmic, or religious design.

Moreover, basic education is a good that must be distributed with equality, and any failure in equality of distribution demands restitution. This remains true even if the fault was committed at some time long past by one group in the society against another.

In the United States, for example, the grave injustice of Negro slavery, with all its associated evils, was practiced for centuries. Still today the children of this injustice—together with other groups in the population whose ancestors were also treated unjustly—suffer such great cultural deficiencies that a merely proportional allocation of educational resources is far from just. Yet it remains that the best schools are generally to be found in the most prosperous areas while the poorest schools are generally to be found where the children of injustice live.

In such a situation, the right of the culturally deprived to education certainly ought to mean their right to the best education available—the best school buildings; the best equipment; the best books; the most intelligent, best trained, and most experienced teachers. Of course, those who at present enjoy great and unjustly held advantages will say that such a proposal is unfair and impossible to put into practice. Nevertheless, if as much genius were used in finding ways to rectify injustice as is used in finding ways to do injustice and to rationalize it, a way surely could be found to achieve the restitution of education that has been unjustly withheld.

I have used the situation of the United States to illustrate this point. I use this illustration both because I am familiar with the American scene and because otherwise a citizen of another country might excuse himself by pointing out that I am insensitive to the tear gas in my own eye, and impolitely attentive to the speck in his. But having admitted the inadequacies of America's achievement in regard to social justice, I must point out that similar situations seem to exist everywhere in the world. For in every society there are the exploited. And everywhere those who profit from injustice receive a large part of that benefit in the form of a far larger than average share of educational opportunities.

A key in this matter is that we must not think in static terms about the possible. In the field of human action, what a small and poor heart finds impossible, a larger and better heart finds possible. Resources are not a fixed quantity; they can expand so that injustices can be rectified with only a temporary halt to the increasing advantages of the prosperous. If only the rich and the comfortable do not become richer and more comfortable, then justice can be done to the deprived. Moreover, while social justice in education is a matter of strict moral obligation, justice also is a worthwhile investment which will bear fruit in increased future productivity and in social stability.

In nations where it is possible, the right to basic education should be understood to include more than what is essential for making a living. If all of a man's activity is aimed at gaining the bare necessities of life, he has little chance to enter upon the endless creative process characteristic of advanced human culture. Obstacles of various kinds stand in the way of trying to communicate ultimate ideals and values in the common educational process. But there are fewer obstacles in the way of a better distribution of the chief instruments of the first steps toward self-transcendence. For these instruments are those of play and of esthetic experience, and neither ideological nor political conflicts need prevent the expansion of education to include them.

Play should include all kinds of games and sports—to be engaged in, not merely to be watched. If we use imagination in writing rules and setting qualifications, every child might find some form of play to which he could devote his self-discipline and in which he could excel. Accomplishment should receive public recognition, not only as a stimulus to effort, but even more because play, which is an adult's *recreation,* is a child's *work.*

Esthetic experiences also should be cultivated in a wide range of abilities to perform and to appreciate. How many who would have been great artists have never been discovered in childhood, have never been disciplined? To what loss to us all? How to combine freedom and discipline is the great question of modern life. The problem of the esthetic sphere is simpler: how to unite creativity with high standards of excellence. Yet it seems certain that a life lacking esthetic cultivation is not well disposed to receive the higher and more complex cultivation of moral and spiritual discipline.

EDUCATION ACCORDING TO MERIT

Beyond the elementary or fundamental level of education, the right to technical and professional education should be according to merit—that is, according to individual ability. The proposition seems self-evidently true, but its meaning is far from clear.

A young person whose parents were not themselves technically and professionally trained is likely to seem less able to profit from such training himself, even if his native ability is high. Does an educational system simply accept applicants on the basis of developed qualification, or must an attempt be made to equalize advantages? If the former, technical and professional education can produce something of a new elite class, even in a "classless" democratic society. If an attempt is to be made to equalize the position of young people from less advantaged backgrounds, the demand of justice in education presupposes a transformation in society that will permit all children to profit from an equal wealth of cultural experiences. No civilized society has attempted such equalization.

Another problem arises from the indefiniteness of the concept of the "technical and professional." If only a few established areas are recognized, competition for education will be limited to those areas. If, on the other hand, the aim is to find some area in which *every* student can be given a technical or professional education, then the number of fields must be expanded indefinitely.

A related problem concerns standards within established fields. An area such as medicine may be well organized with very high educational standards. The result may be a shortage of persons able to exercise limited medical skills.

Although this last problem is complex in the concrete order of political and social action, it is comparatively simple conceptually. Many persons of limited ability could be trained to exercise certain medical skills. Undoubtedly, their work would not be as satisfactory as that of a fully trained physician. But such medical care could be superior to no medical care at all. Accordingly, the principle of a right to professional training according to merit seems to imply that some who are not now admitted for such training—for example, in medicine—probably should be given access to it. Even if they were less able and standards were somewhat lowered, the result could be justified so long as the end for which the profession exists were better served on the whole.

A solution to the other problems seems to presuppose some theory of justice by which to balance the rights of the individual and the welfare of the community as a whole. The right to education is not an immunity, and so its corresponding duty requires performance, not mere avoidance. To fulfill such a right, society must allocate some part of the available resources, which are always inadequate to demand.

Of course there are some forms of technical and professional education that have an unquestioned social value. In these cases, the allocation for education can be viewed as an investment. The ready ability developed by education is a capital asset for the society. As long as the productivity of this form of investment is greater than that of possible alternatives, the expenditure is justified in purely economic terms, and no conflict between individual rights and social welfare arises. Thus dentists and elementary school teachers are educated, because their training is a sound investment.

But what of the technical and professional education required to engage in space exploration, historical research, or philosophic speculation? Clearly, each society estimates according to its own sense of values the extent to which there is a right to education in such fields. If an educational program does not terminate in a ready ability for some activity that is already socially valued, then any claim to a right to such education is not likely to be honored.

Such discrimination on the part of society may seem reasonable enough, and perhaps it is. Yet at some point the perspective must shift, or individual persons will become mere cogs in the social machine. This point is illustrated very clearly by the problem of hard-core unemployment.

As technology progresses, unskilled and semi-skilled workers are more and more replaced by automatic machines. Of course, the quantity of output is not fixed, and the machines themselves must be manufactured; thus automation creates many new jobs. But the new positions require ever-rising qualifications. Not everyone is naturally apt to be an engineer. Fewer and fewer people having special natural aptitudes developed by longer and longer technical education are producing the increasing output in a more and more efficient way. What is to become of the displaced unskilled and semi-skilled workers?

Some can be retrained for other tasks. In many cases, there is no lack of native ability. An imaginative and vigorous effort at education can restore these displaced persons to the dignity of productive work. Such an approach is necessary not only within each nation, but also on a world-wide basis. The developed, technologically advanced nations are displacing the citizens of undeveloped nations from their economic roles.

Measures which stave off starvation are not sufficient to meet the standards of justice. A person ought not to be condemned to misery merely because he committed the sin of being born in an undeveloped land. Those who have resources owe him technical education. Men of every nation have the

right to share in the dignity of productive work. The universal-
ization of opportunity for technical education is far more
urgent than further technical advances.

More serious is the problem of the increasing proportion of
persons who cannot be trained for any productive role. There
always has been a small group of such persons—individuals of
very low intelligence, the physically disabled, and those suffering from other severe handicaps. The boundaries of this group
are socially defined, however. Advancing technology seems to
be tending to increase the size of the group. The tasks required by more sophisticated technology are more complex,
require more education, education for which a smaller proportion is apt.

A static approach to this problem will mean that society
will regard this group as an increasingly large dead-weight. If
human life is respected, the weight will be dragged, though
reluctantly. If respect for life falters, the temptation will grow
strong to practice euthanasia on such useless individuals.

A dynamic approach to the problem would seek to alter its
conditions through education, not only of those displaced by
advancing technology, but also of those consuming goods and
services. Although material goods are closely linked to technological development, services are related less directly to it.
Anything one individual can do for another may be a valuable
service if the human significance of the act is appreciated by
the one who receives it. In a world made more and more
impersonal by technology, inventiveness is needed to find new
ways in which those lacking aptitude for professional and
technical work can preserve their personal dignity while offering services to others. Education must teach the value of service by instilling the ready ability to appreciate what even the
least able of us can offer.

We may imagine a band of travelers crossing a trackless
desert. A few are far ahead and making rapid progress, while
others straggle behind, and some are barely crawling through
the hot sand. Such is mankind. The primary task of profes-

sional and technical education is not to accelerate the progress of all, for then their relative positions would become even more widely separated. Rather, education should be used to draw the band together. The pace of the stragglers must be improved. None may be left behind. Even those who cannot continue the march must be brought along. Their contribution could be to cheer the rest with good humor and to remind us all of where the trek is headed—lest in the haste to make progress everyone forget this most essential point.

EDUCATION BY PARENTS

The primary right to decide what sort of education shall be given is assigned to the parents. Why to the parents? Why not to the larger community, which also has an interest in the matter?

The answer to this question lies in the manner in which persons originate. Our understanding is distorted by individualistic and mechanistic images which conceal the real continuity in the process by which persons emerge from persons.

Even from a purely biological point of view, the new person is not a new beginning of human life. The living substance of the father and the living substance of the mother join to form the beginning of the new individual. At first the new life is most intimately united with that from which it has been formed. Then, gradually, step by step the new organism grows apart, distinguishing and separating itself from its mother. Birth is merely a memorable moment in a long, slow process of separation. Even after birth the life of the infant is closely united for some months with that of his mother.

The complexities of the process of sexual generation should not blind us to the essentials. Human life comes from human life, just as truly as life comes from life in the simple organisms that reproduce by a straight-forward process of fission.

Psychic and spiritual life also arises from pre-existing life.

Parents not only become one flesh in their children; they also become in them one mind and one heart. To be a father, to be a mother is more than physical reproduction. The parent not only must give the beginnings of physiological life, but he must give all the beginnings—at least, the beginning of all the beginnings. Parents must provide for their children the ready ability to educate themselves or to receive education from others.

Here, once more, we see why the right to education is so fundamental. To refuse education is to strangle new life in its beginnings. The right to education and the right to life are inseparably linked. Education is the psychic and spiritual equivalent of conception. To withhold education is to commit a kind of psychic and spiritual abortion.

Thus education belongs to procreation as its psychic and spiritual aspect. Parents are naturally concerned with the education of their children, because the children are sparks from the fire of the parents' own life, sparks that will burn on when the parents themselves have died.

While the child is unable to exercise his freedom and depends upon someone's care for the beginning of his life, the responsibility and the right naturally falls to the parents, because the psychic and spiritual life of the child is most closely united with the life of his parents until the child achieves independent personhood by distinguishing himself from them. The emerging person cannot be interfered with by outsiders to any greater extent than any other member of the community may be interfered with by another, because the child may be resolved into two functions: his identity with his parents and his independent personhood. To the extent that the child is one with his parents, no one may interfere with the existence of the child any more than he may interfere with the existence of the parents themselves. To the extent that the child is an independent person, he is a self, a free and equal member of society. He himself can determine the directions his own education will take.

EDUCATION AND AUTHORITY

But to say that the parents, or the person himself when he becomes capable, have the primary right and responsibility in regard to education is not to deny that within the educational process itself there is need for legitimate authority. One cannot learn anything from another unless he is willing to be led. Even if one reads a book, he must accept at its true value the authority of the author. Between the lack of an ability and the acquisition of it is a void that can be traversed only by trust. The teacher is a better judge of how to learn, because the teacher knows and the student does not. Educational anarchists, who would exclude all authority from learning and leave everything to the spontaneity of the children, confuse the ideal of autonomy which may be achieved at the end of education with the condition of the human person who comes to be from another, and after not having been at all.

Thus the fundamental commitments that will determine the kind of person the child will be must be reserved to the parents. Not every detail of the educational process, but the kind of education the children will receive is for the parents to decide. The state may seek to remove children from the influence of their parents, to impose a system of values and a meaning of life that the parents do not accept. This is the sort of interference which violates the basic right of the parents to control the education of their children. Coming to be from their parents, children must begin life in the likeness of their parents' psychic and spiritual selfhood, not according to the pattern of some utopian or scientific blueprint for a better humanity.

The point is worth stressing because it is fundamentally important. Over and over again those who have set out, confident in their blueprint, to remake mankind have sought to seize control of education. If only the children were brought up as the dreamers and planners desire, then their entire scheme could be a success. Thus there is a totalitarian effort to break the continuity of human life. The parents are regarded as mere suppliers of a human raw material to be shaped and formed into the new humanity in the educational factories of the state.

EDUCATION AS "PRODUCTION"

The conception of education as a form of production is insidious and widespread. It appears wearing only a thin disguise in the least likely places. Again and again in modern times liberal social reformers have turned hopefully to the schools. The "openness" and "flexibility" of young minds offer the hope that reforms resisted by the caution and rigidity of the older generation can be brought about by the proper cultivation of a new outlook in young people. Those who make a profession of condemning indoctrination seem to be insensitive to the fact that they also make use of it whenever they seek to accomplish social changes by turning young minds and hearts against the beliefs and attitudes of their parents.

The concept of education as production also appears in some efforts to develop "scientific" pedagogy. Medicine often serves as a model. As medicine has achieved scientific status by basing itself upon chemistry and biology and by utilizing the experimental method proper to science, so it is thought that education can achieve scientific status by basing itself upon psychology and sociology and by engaging in pseudo-scientific experimentation.

The difficulty with this project is that education should be concerned with the reality of the integral human person, and man transcends the determinacy of nature. He is not merely what is already given, for he *exists*—his being is creative self-determination. The self comes to be through its own effort, through its own acts, through its own ingenuity or dullness, through its own choices and omissions. Man is the only creature who makes history, for the person composes his life and is author of the material of his own biography.

Psychology has attained scientific status precisely to the extent that it has abstracted from the existential reality of man and has concentrated on aspects of human life that are common to man and other animals or on aspects in which man fails to achieve his potentiality for freedom and falls into the causally determined patterns of neurosis and other forms of psychic disease. Of what is uniquely human and truly personal there is no science of psychology, although there are philosophical anthropologies which emphasize the characteristics of the person. These anthropologies do not provide a basis for a scientific pedagogy, but they do point the way toward an appreciation of the unique dignity of individual lives.

Similar remarks can be made concerning sociology. The sociologists have developed techniques for describing with some degree of accuracy certain aspects of society. But the techniques of sociology are most effective when the data collected are most abstracted from human meaning—for example, a compilation of demographic statistics. When sociologists enter into more sensitive territory, their conclusions tend either to pretentious statement of the obvious and trivial or to deceptive clarification of the arguable and ambiguous.

Surely in "sciences" of psychology and sociology there is little ground for pedagogy. Little ground, but some. For there are aspects in which education is not dealing with the person as *person*. A public authority needs to know how many seats must be made available in order to provide them when they will be needed. More significant, empirical psychology is gradually revealing the possibilities and limitations of the human organism for various forms of learning. But such matters are not the areas in which occur the great battles of educational theory and practice. In these conflicts, science has little to contribute. The real issues invariably concern philosophical assumptions about the nature of man and the ideals of human existence.

In a field such as medicine, a great part of the work is purely technical, and the decisions concerning policy can safely be left to those who have technical expertise. The ends of the medical profession are generally well understood and agreed upon by both the medical profession and the public. In a field such as law, a great part of the work is not technical, and thus decisions concerning policy cannot be left entirely to experts. The entire public has a stake in the making of law and in its execution. Education is nearer to law than it is to medicine.

EXPERIMENTATION IN EDUCATION

For this reason, the public at large, and especially parents, should not relinquish the right to a role in forming educational policy for the community. When psychological and sociological jargon is used to create a seeming technical expertise, the "layman" should not timidly admit his incompetence to judge. Of course, there is such a thing as expertness about the technique of teaching reading, for example; and those who have not studied the matter would overreach themselves if they attempted to criticize technicalities of method. But there is not any expertness on questions such as the extent to which an established culture should be preserved, or whether boys and girls should be mixed together and given the same educational experiences, or what general theory of pedagogy should be adopted. Here teachers and officials overreach themselves if they attempt to reserve for "expert" determinations such questions of educational policy, questions concerning which the judgments of parents are as likely to be sound and have more claim to be followed.

Extensive efforts to make use of the experimental method in education often mean a false reduction of education to technique. Experiment has its place primarily in the technical field;

it can be applied only in an analogous and restricted sense in the existential domain.

In strict experimentation, the experimental material must be expendable. That is why medical experiments that cannot be performed on human beings can be done on animals. In education one can never take the attitude that the person who is developing through the educational process is an expendable sample. If experimentation with the human body must be strictly limited, how much more strictly must we limit human experimentation involving the mind and soul.

Again, in strict experimentation it is essential that generalization be possible. Unless the experiment is really typical of a general class, no significant application can be made of the results. In education the more one approaches the existential center of the personality the less generalization is possible, and the more the uniqueness of the person dominates the reality. Pedagogy which has a real basis in generalization will have to keep its distance from the creative center of personal self-determination.

Then too, strict experimentation requires that one have a very clear understanding beforehand of what is being sought by the experiment. Accurate means of determining if the expected result has been forthcoming are also necessary. In education "experiments" often are undertaken with little or no idea of the precise result that is sought and with no means to measure many important effects. Or at times, the entire educational process is subverted by the requirements of the experimental technique, since only factors that are readily measurable are considered valuable. Whatever the educationists may wish, the most easily tested kinds of learning always have an advantage over the acquisition of more subtle values in a regime dominated by experiment.

Experimentation has a limited role in education, because some strictly technical problems of methods can be investigated in this way. Even here, there should be a cautious re-

gard for the fact that although the teacher or the investigator
may have a new class to work with every year, the children
who have been subjected to a new technique must live with its
good and bad effects. Thus changes in education should be
introduced cautiously with the conviction that the new factor
is simply better and with the intention that it should be permanent. Of course, if the results lead to a different judgment, then
a further change or a return to the old pattern may be war-
ranted. Such cautious change can be called "experiment," provided the word is used in a merely analogous and restricted
sense.

NORMS AND VALUES IN EDUCATION

If the right to education implies a right not to be treated as a
subject for experimentation or as raw material for the production of some model of humanity designed by the overconfi-
dence of social engineers, that is because the person exists as a
self-determining source of creatively free activity. The right to
education is the right to human education, not merely to training for a social role.

But if as human persons we are self-determining, that does
not mean we can make ourselves out of nothing or that we
exist with no reference to realities that antecede us and transcend us. Here we touch upon the most critical problem of
contemporary philosophy: how to reconcile the originality of
human existence with objective norms and values. We cannot
deal with this problem here. The question is too important and
too difficult to be handled incidentally near the end of a brief
essay on another topic.

But it is certain that there are some objective norms and
values and that the education to which every person has a
right is an introduction to the appreciation of them as much as
it is an introduction to the world of facts. If one could educate
a child omitting altogether any introduction to a world of val-

ues, it would be a grave wrong to do so, for his life would be robbed of meaning. In fact, no education is possible that does not include inculcation of values. The only question is whether the values to which the child is introduced are authentic and integral or partially illusory and more or less mutilated.

Some have imagined that the whole problem can be evaded by allowing the child to develop his own sense of values through his own experience and to make and alter his own commitments as he wishes. The errors in this view are many. To begin with, this approach itself embodies certain values on which it puts an extreme estimate—for example, the values of personal experience and individual freedom. Then too, allowing the child to learn by his own experience in this most important area seems to depreciate its significance even in comparison with matters such as diet and hygiene where a similar approach is not followed. Finally, a child cannot learn the lessons of experience in a situation where he is shielded by his parents and society—as he certainly will be in any advanced culture—from suffering the full effects of his choices. If the child is to learn by living, then the initiation of his acts cannot be free while the results are cushioned by responsible intervention.

Thus it is fitting that a declaration of the right to education also assert that education should inculcate a respect for the rights of others, an attitude of cooperation toward the efforts of men to establish an international community, and a love of peace. The child may not understand immediately from his own limited experience how important these values are. But mankind as a whole has gained some insight by painful experience, by reflection, and by criticism. No one can be forced to accept and commit himself to values, but no one developing toward the moment of full responsibility and commitment should be deprived of an introduction to basic and important values such as these.

However, a difficulty arises because every system of education presupposes an entire world view, not merely a few values concerning which there is very common agreement. Some systems of education are religious. They embody an outlook and system of values determined by a fundamental conception of God and of man's relationship to him. Other systems of education are not religious. They embody an immanentist view of the world and a system of values determined by a concept of integral personality, or self-conscious authenticity, or loving interpersonal relations.

I do not wish to argue here which of these approaches to education might be correct. In fact, I think any of them can become a fanaticism and that an ideal outlook would include many limited values, none identified as the absolute good. But my point is that any system of education is committed and that at least implicitly it inculcates its commitment. There is no such thing as educational neutrality. The only way to be neutral is to avoid personal relationships altogether, but no one can teach another without relating to him on some basis or other.

Some have imagined that an official position of neutrality can be maintained with regard to ultimate questions. The schools would teach only what is objective, while parents and churches would supply whatever else they might wish. But the very determination of what is to be considered objective presupposes an evaluation. What is more important, this manner of resolving the problem may do more to form the minds of children than anything that could be said. Though it is oversimple to say that the medium is the message, perhaps it is true that the system is the evaluation.

The system of education must give reasons for studying and it must teach students some way of dealing with conflicts within themselves and of establishing relations with teachers and fellow students. The inescapable moral aspect of the educational process itself must be conceived by teachers and school officials within some ultimate framework that gives a meaning to human life as a whole. A so-called "neutral" system will in fact be dominated by the religious (or areligious) outlook which happens to have the support of a consensus of those determining educational policy. Neutrality will obtain only in regard to the relatively insignificant issues that adherents to the consensus are willing and able to compromise among themselves. Such a neutral system will not be neutral in regard to the worldviews of those who differ radically from the common ground of the consensus.

The right to education and the right of parents to determine the kind of education thus implies a duty of the community to fully respect the plurality of ultimate value-systems among its citizens. The imposition of a single public school system clearly violates the basic rights of all who do not fully adhere to the consensus embodied in that system. The mere toleration of free schools does not fully satisfy the rights of those who do not accept the common, secular philosophy of life. Only when every philosophy of life is treated on a par will the right to education be fully met. The community of course can require that certain abilities be inculcated. That is the reasonable meaning of saying that elementary education should be "compulsory." But the duty of the community to supply education will only be fully met when the public recognizes and acts on the basis of the equal right to public support of every parent for the kind of education he chooses for his children.

RELIGIOUS EDUCATION

The right to education includes a right to religious education. For whatever else religion may be, it is a subject matter that involves several ready abilities that belong to a full and ultimately happy human existence.

Yet religious education is not merely a matter of information. The primary modality of religious education is neither to inform nor to form, but to challenge. The religious teacher preaches a message which conveys a vocation and demands a response. The individual himself must determine his reaction: either to accept the message and to respond to the vocation or to reject the message and to turn away.

In this domain the duty to educate does not fall upon civil society. Freedom of religion, however, does require that civil society maintain the conditions in which religious education is possible. Those who believe—as well as those who disbelieve, for disbelief too is a religious commitment—can then freely present to one another what they hold.

Perhaps partly because of the excesses and the failures of religious teachers in the past, many men of our day fear religious education as if it would detract something from what is properly human. This is a mistake. Religious teaching cannot contravene man's freedom, because religion gains its effectiveness only by being willingly accepted. Religious belief need not take man's heart away from the tasks of humanity, for faith adds new dimensions of meaning and urgency to the fulfillment of these tasks.

Thus, the right to education and the right to religious freedom meet and complement one another. There is no question about the right of those who wish to limit their worldview to an immanent and humanistic perspective to accept such restrictions. But, at the same time, there should be no question that those who see in the whole of human life a divine pedagogy by which man is raised to share in the life of God have a right to believe in that for which they hope, and to fulfill in their charity their life's mission of communicating to others the gift in which their own hearts rejoice: the ready ability to search for God.

CATHERINE SCHAEFER

4: Catholic Influence
on the Universal Declaration

Pope John XXIII characterized the adoption by the United Nations of the Universal Declaration of Human Rights as "an act of the highest importance for the political-juridical organization of all the world's peoples."

Why? Obviously because it places human rights and duties —respect for man as God made him—at the core of world order, or what Pope Pius XII called (December 6, 1953)[1] that "higher community of men, willed by the Creator and rooted in the unity of their common origin, nature and final destiny." Thus it reflects a millennial norm and goal of Christian social teaching. In such teaching, based on the natural moral law, it is "the complete man, the human person, the image of God" who is "the subject, the foundation, and the end of social order" (Pius XII, February 20, 1946.)[2]

The multiple relations of "the complete man"—and the rights and duties they engender—plainly imply smaller human communities for which the state and the organized world society must also be concerned. Christian teaching, with its emphasis on love as well as justice, on truth as well as freedom, has devoted itself—insofar as human and temporal society is concerned—to the totality of these relationships.

This "treasury of Christian thinking on the right ordering of society" (John XXIII, Easter, 1963),[3] later so lucidly synthesized in *Pacem in Terris*,[4] found many authoritative expres-

sions in the period immediately preceding formation of the
United Nations and the formulation of the Universal Declaration. These were the guide and inspiration of Catholics who in
the first place labored for the idea of a Declaration and later
sought to achieve a view, within the Declaration, of "the complete man" in relation to his various rights.

This chapter will endeavor to present some of these efforts
in the light of personal recollection based on association during
crucial years with the Catholic Association for International
Peace and the National Catholic Welfare Conference and as
the representative of the International Union of Catholic
Womens Leagues to the Economic and Social Council of the
United Nations.

BIRTH OF AN IDEA

It is impossible to consider the idea either of a Universal Declaration of Human Rights or of the United Nations which
adopted and proclaimed it apart from the evils to which they
were humanity's reaction. These were world war and genocide,
precipitated by a brutal philosophy and active policy of atheistic racism on the part of a totalitarian state—Nazi Germany.
National Socialism itself rose in a world climate of excessive
individualism, secularist nationalism, and imperialism on the
one hand and, on the other, of a militant international Communism, atheistic and materialistic, under the aegis of a totalitarian state. It was a climate of failure to organize for world
social justice in freedom in which one World War and a world
wide depression had already occurred.

The destruction of free institutions and associations, including those of the churches, of education and the press, and
arbitrary interference with the rights and institution of the
family were necessary preludes to full realization of the Nazi
reign of horror in which human life, dignity, freedom, and
equality were equally violated.

Such barbarities in revolting the world's conscience stimulated concern not only with the meaning of the human person, but for some international means by which men's rights could be ensured on an international level. The League of Nations, which foundered on the rocks of nationalism, had secured nondiscrimination clauses in minority treaties following World War I, and a Convention on eradicating slavery had been concluded under its auspices. It had also issued a Charter on the Rights of the Child. But it had never concerned itself formally, systematically or organically with human rights. The International Labor Organization, its allied organization, however, had in a limited way broken ground on concrete protection of rights and conditions of workers through international conventions arrived at by tripartite (government-employer-worker) cooperation. Fittingly enough, the ILO was able to continue its existence (and to some extent its activities) during the war years from a base in Canada when it was everywhere acknowledged that the predominantly political League of Nations had died and could not be resurrected in its old form.

The relationship that should exist between a world organization, human rights, and human cooperation was pointed out by Pius XII in a discourse to the Minister of Haiti (November 10, 1939)[5] in which he advocated

a stable, fruitful organization such as is desired by men of good will, an organization which, respecting the rights of God, will be able to assure the reciprocal independence of nations large and small, to impose fidelity to agreements loyally agreed upon, and to safeguard the sound liberty and dignity of the human person in each one's efforts towards the prosperity of all . . .

Earlier, in response to the specific situation, Pius XI in his Encyclical on Atheistic Communism (March 19, 1937) reminded the world that man "has been endowed by God with many and varied prerogatives; the right to life, to bodily integrity, to the necessary means of existence; the right to tend toward his ultimate goal in the path marked out for him by God; the right of association and the right to possess and use property . . . "

Pius XII began his constant emphasis on the God-given nature of fundamental human rights in his first encyclical *Summi Pontificatus* (October 20, 1939) which dealt with the function of the state. There, for instance, he stressed that "man and the family are by nature anterior to the state and that the Creator has given to both of them powers and rights."

His wartime Christmas messages consistently dealt with conditions for peace and the rights of peoples, including the necessity of an international organization.[6] The 1942 message related the achievement of peace with

> respect for, and the practical realization of the following fundamental personal rights:
> The right to maintain and develop one's corporal, intellectual, and moral life and especially the right to religious formation and education; the right to worship God in private and public and to carry on religious works of charity; the right to marry and to achieve the aims of married life; the right to conjugal and domestic society; the right to work, as the indispensable means towards the maintenance of family life; the right to free choice of a state of life, and hence, too, of the priesthood or religious life; the right to the use of material goods in keeping with his duties and social limitations.

These rights, Pius XII stated, should be guaranteed by a juridical order in every state:

> A constitution conformable to the Divine will gives a man a right to juridical security and accordingly grants him a sphere of rights immune from all arbitrary attack . . . this supposes a tribunal and a judge taking their direction from law carefully defined; clear legal principles which cannot be upset by unwarranted appeal to supposed popular sentiment or by merely utilitarian considerations; and recognition of the principle that the State and its officials are under the obligation of revising

and withdrawing measures incompatible with the liberty, the property, the honor, and the health of individuals.

It should be recalled that these and similar statements were being made during a devastating war. Most of Europe was either a battle ground or under occupation. In addition to sharing the general heightened sense of responsibility of U.S. citizens for bringing about conditions for a just peace, American Catholics felt a particular obligation to seek realization of the principles being so unceasingly advocated by the Holy Father in his concern for all peoples. As an indication of this concern, a special committee of the American bishops, under the leadership of the late Cardinal Stritch of Chicago, was set up to give maximum publicity and study to the Pope's peace messages.

In 1941, the Catholic Association for International Peace* discussed "America's Peace Aims" at its national conference. Its Committee report of that title asserted that in organizing the world for peace "the rights of man and of peoples must be defined and recognized, and an institutional way established to ensure human rights." In a draft "International Bill of Rights," it enumerated rights of a political, economic, religious, and social nature. The CAIP *World Society* report of 1942 likewise urged the United Nations (a wartime coalition of 26 nations) to form "a special committee on human rights and means of their protection," to "draw up an international bill of rights and provide a way to correct violations," as part of over-all plans of a world organization for peace and justice.

"America's Peace Aims" had stressed the importance of the role of intermediate non-governmental organizations in the development of a just social order and as a vital safeguard of rights in the following statement:

* An organization of American Catholic scholars formed in 1927 to study international affairs, and particularly America's role therein in the light of Christian social teaching.

One point requires emphasis. This is the right of free non-governmental associations to handle matters that they can care for apart from government and to cooperate with government in work which government does in these fields. This right goes close to the heart of the crisis of our time. Without it, there is only government and the individual is a kind of slave regardless of legal affirmations of rights.

The year 1943 saw an intensification of study by many groups in the United States on methods of safeguarding human rights on the basis of apparent promises from official sources.

President Roosevelt had delivered his famous "Four Freedoms" speech in January 1941; and on August 14, 1941, President Roosevelt and Prime Minister Churchill had issued the Atlantic Charter as a statement of common principles. The latter enunciated the right of peoples to choose their form of government and the hope that the peace would assure "that all men in all lands may live out their lives in freedom from fear and want," in the framework of a system of international security and world social justice.

Archbishop Mooney, Chairman of the Administrative Board of the National Catholic Welfare Conference, writing to President Roosevelt on December 22 of that year, urged official confirmation of respect for principles of human rights in international policy.[7]

The United Nations Pact, signed by the 26 allied nations in Washington on January 1, 1942, had tied the achievement of human rights to victory in the following considerandum: "Being convinced that complete victory over their enemies is essential to defend life, liberty, independence, and religious freedom, and to preserve human rights and justice in their own lands as well as in other lands."

A group of eminent Protestants, Jews, and Catholics, including the Chairman of the Administrative Board of the National Catholic Welfare Conference, agreed in 1943 to a set of principles which were described by the Catholic signatories as "the minimum requirements of a peace which Christians can endorse as fair to all men . . ."

Beginning with the affirmation that "the organization of a just peace depends upon practical recognition of the fact that not only individuals but nations, states, and international society are subject to the sovereignty of God and to the moral law which comes from God . . ." these principles stipulated that

> The dignity of the human person as the image of God must be set forth in all its essential implications in an international declaration of rights and be vindicated by the positive action of national governments and international organizations. States as well as individuals must repudiate racial, religious, or other discrimination in violation of these rights.

Known as the *Pattern for Peace*,[8] the principles were the object of a nation-wide crash discussion campaign which penetrated beyond the strictly religious community.

In the same sense, the Bishops of the United States devoted their annual statement in 1943 to "The Dignity of the Human Person." However, when on October 9, 1944, the representatives of the United States, the United Kingdom, the Soviet Union and the Republic of China issued the Dumbarton Oaks proposals on an international organization to maintain international peace, the latter contained only one mention of human rights in a section devoted to International Economic and Social Cooperation. The inadequacy of this approach was pointed out in the intense debate over the proposals which followed in the United States.

Attention to the vital importance of human rights was called for in a 1944 statement on "Man and the Peace" by the American Bishops, and·in 1945 the Bishops formally urged an Inter-Nation Bill of Rights in the proposed new organization.

The three religious groups which had issued "Pattern for Peace," formulated another, "Goals of San Francisco," prior to the UN organization conference. The Charter (of an international peace organization), this statement held, "should contain an international bill of rights and provide a commission or commissions to protect and further the rights and liberties of the individual and of racial, religious, and cultural groups, especially those uprooted by war or oppression.

HUMAN RIGHTS: A PURPOSE OF
WORLD COMMUNITY

Religious groups, which included the National Catholic Welfare Conference and the Catholic Association for International Peace, as well as other active segments of American non-governmental life, were afforded an opportunity to press for this goal when the U.S. Government invited 48 non-governmental organizations as consultants to serve its delegation to the San Francisco organizing Conference in 1945.

In this they were in harmony with the Latin American States. The latter, at a meeting in Chapultepec early in 1945, had solemnly declared that one of the main purposes of the new organization of the United Nations should be the elaboration of a method of protecting human rights. The Inter-American Juridical Committee (in which, incidentally, a former president of the Catholic Association for International Peace, Dr. Charles G. Fenwick, figured prominently) was charged with drawing up a draft Declaration. This was adopted by the American States at Bogota in 1948, prior to the completion of the Universal Declaration of Human Rights.

Although Panama at San Francisco had provided a "Declaration of Essential Human Rights" (prepared by a Committee of the American Law Institute) for integration into the Charter, and other Latin American delegates had urged inclusion of specific rights, none of these proposals was accepted. The work of the U.S. "consultant" organizations was decisive not only in the emphasis given throughout the Charter to

Human Rights, but in that it secured United States Government leadership to press for establishment of a human rights commission by specific terms of the Charter.

There is specific mention of human rights in the Preamble and 7 articles of the United Nations Charter. Seven other articles relate to the exercise of function by various organs of the United Nations involving human rights.

Another article (71), which had its genesis in recommendations of the Consultants group, provided that the Economic and Social Council might consult competent international nongovernmental organizations on matters within its jurisdiction. The importance of this provision was to be demonstrated in the elaboration of the Universal Declaration.

Over and above general nondiscrimination clauses, there is specific mention of the equality of men and women in the Preamble of the Charter. This was the result of efforts by members of the Inter-American Commission of Women (an official organ of the then Pan American Union) present at San Francisco. In this they had the support of the U.S. consultant organizations through the intermediary of women's groups represented.

Significantly, and as a departure from established diplomatic custom, the Charter Préamble opens with the words "*We the Peoples* of the United Nations." The Preamble reaffirms "faith in fundamental human rights, in the dignity and worth of the human person, in the equal rights of men and women and of nations large and small," and determines "to promote social progress and better standards of life in larger freedom."

A principal purpose of the UN is stated in Article 1 to be the achievement of international cooperation "in promoting and encouraging respect for human rights and for fundamental freedoms for all without distinction as to race, sex, language, or religion." Under Article 55, the UN has the duty to promote "universal respect for and observance of human rights and fundamental freedoms for all without distinction as to race, sex, language, or religion." In Article 56, States Members pledge to fulfill this duty by joint and separate action in cooperation with the UN.

In articles defining functions, the General Assembly is given prime responsibility to initiate studies and make recommendations to assist in the realization of human rights and fundamental freedoms for all without distinction as to race, sex, language, or religion; and the Economic and Social Council, acting under the General Assembly may "make recommendations for the purpose of promoting respect for, and observance of, human rights and fundamental freedoms for all." Under Article 68, the Economic and Social Council is enjoined to set up a commission "for the promotion of human rights." (This is the only commission specifically designated in the Charter.)

Other relevant articles deal with the obligations of the trusteeship system set up in the Charter to encourage respect for human rights, through specific means including petition from inhabitants of trust territories, and with the obligations of administering powers of non-self-governing territories to promote the well-being of inhabitants of these territories and to ensure their just treatment and protection against abuses.

DRAFTING OF THE DECLARATION

Article 68 (providing for a Commission on Human Rights under the Economic and Social Council) was a key provision, not only for drafting a declaration of human rights, which it was understood would be its first task, but for implementing all other references in the Charter to promoting human rights. To assist the Commission in its tasks, the Economic and Social Council in 1946 approved establishment of sub-commissions on Prevention of Discrimination and Protection of Minorities, on Freedom of Information, and on the Status of Women; the last was later given the status of a full Commission.

When the Commission on Human Rights held its first session at Lake Success in January 1947, it consisted of eighteen distinguished personalities who, however, represented their governments and as such had been elected by the Economic and Social Council. Some were freer of restrictive governmental policies than others. Coming from various geographical areas with different problems and different cultural histories and the product of various philosophical systems or religious teachings, they brought their different approaches to a task on the importance of which all agreed. The different approach was most marked between the communist view of the State as the great protector—the perfect sum of all its parts—particularly of social rights, and the concern of Western representatives for personal, political, and civil rights and freedoms.

The Commission, through working parties, embarked simultaneously on the preparation of a three-part "Bill of Rights"—a Declaration which would provide "recognition" of certain basic rights, and a Covenant which would ensure legal protection of such rights by the voluntary accession of governments and international implementation measures by which the Covenant could be enforced in case of violations. Priority was given to completing the Declaration. The Commission Secretariat had assembled drafts of declarations drawn up by international and national groups, including the American Institute of International Law, the (U.S.) Commission to Study the Organization of Peace, and the Catholic Association for International Peace; and it had itself prepared a draft for the Commission.

After the Commission had begun meeting, the National Catholic Welfare Conference released to the public the draft of a Declaration it had earlier submitted to the United States State Department. It received wide comment in the press and full copies were made available to all Commission members through the Office of UN Affairs, which NCWC had established in New York the previous October.

A concise formulation of perennial principles expressed in

recent Papal statements as regards 1) rights of the human person, 2) rights pertaining to the family 3) the domestic rights of states, and 4) the rights of states in the international community, the NCWC Declaration[9] did not, however, pretend to be exhaustive. The enumeration of rights under each category was introduced by the phrase: "Among these rights are:"

These quotations from the General Preamble indicate the specific as well as the universal social context in which rights are situated:

> God, the creator of the human race, has charged man with obligations from his personal dignity, from his immortal destiny, and from his relationships as a social being. These obligations are in reference to the creator, to himself, to his family and fellowmen, to the State, and to the community of States. For the fulfillment of these obligations man is endowed with certain natural, inalienable rights. These obligations and rights form the substance of the natural moral law which can be known by reason.
>
> Obligations and rights are correlative. At all times the obligation to respect the rights of others operates against the arbitrary use of rights.
>
> Suitable opportunity to discharge fundamental obligations in the various and separate situations of life is a right which cannot be justly denied. For man's use God has provided the basic resources of this world.
>
> The unity of the human race under God is not broken by geographical distance or by diversity of civilization, culture, and economy, and the adequate use of the world's resources by all peoples is not to be denied because of these factors.

Rights pertaining to the family are listed as:

PREAMBLE
The family is the natural and fundamental group unit of society and is endowed by the Creator with inalienable rights antecedent to all positive law. The family does not exist for the State, but on the other hand is not independent. Among these rights are:

1) The right to marry, to establish a home, and beget children.

2) The right to economic security sufficient for the stability and independence of the family.

3) The right to the protection of maternity.

4) The right to educate the children.

5) The right to maintain, if necessary by public protection and assistance, adequate standards of child welfare within the family circle.

6) The right to assistance, through community services in the education and care of the children.

7) The right to housing adapted to the needs and functions of family life.

8) The right to immunity of the home from search and trespass.

9) The right to protection against immoral conditions in the community.

In preliminary general discussion of the Secretariat draft some Commission members referred directly to the NCWC Declaration. For instance, M. Lebeau of Belgium, on February 4, spoke on the total relationships of man as a human person emphasized in the NCWC draft which he found lacking in the Secretariat draft. He cited particularly the attention to the family given in the former. Dr. René Cassin of France, without direct allusion, at this time also expressed his desire to include the concept of the unity of the human race in the UN Declaration.

The report of the drafting committee appointed by the Commission at its first session contained, however, only one reference to the family. This occurred in an alternative text which had been proposed by the United Kingdom delegate but had not been discussed. It would have ensured the right of parents to determine what religious teaching a minor should receive. (Although not accepted in the article on religious freedom which does refer, however, to the freedom to teach, the substance of this proposal is implied in a paragraph on the rights of parents in the final text of the article on education.)

The United States encouraged comments from American non-governmental organizations on this first draft and on all succeeding drafts.

The Catholic Association for International Peace, for example, submitted to the State Department at least three sets of critiques and proposals during the various drafting stages. The National Council of Catholic Women also transmitted proposals.

Essentially the same function was performed on an international level by two Catholic international organizations which had been admitted in July 1947 to consultative status with the Economic and Social Council under Article 71 of the UN Charter. These organizations were the International Union of Catholic Women's Leagues (now known as World Union of Catholic Women's Organizations) which then had its headquarters in the Netherlands, and the Catholic International Union of Social Service, with headquarters in Brussels. They participated actively in the consultative process during the second and third sessions of the Commission at Geneva and Lake Success respectively, prior to final consideration and adoption of the Declaration by the UN General Assembly in Paris, December 10, 1948.

The consultative process involving officially sanctioned discussion with individual delegates, formal oral interventions and written memoranda, covered a wide range of comments and proposals in relation to various drafts of the Declaration. Other international organizations active at this time included the Commission of the Churches on International Affairs of the World Council of Churches (which concerned itself especially with the article on freedom of religion), and several Jewish organizations—Agudas Israel, World Jewish Congress, Consultative Conference of Jewish Organizations, and the Coordinating Board of Jewish Organizations. The International Federation of Christian Trade Unions, which based its social philosophy on Christian social teaching and made its contributions accordingly, along with other large international economic organizations (the Communist and the Free Trade Union organizations, cooperatives, chambers of commerce, etc.), enjoyed superior status, and was thus able to speak directly to the drafting committees.

The formulation of the NCWC Declaration assisted the Catholic organizations both national and international in their various proposals and criticisms, which covered nearly all of the personal and social rights enumerated in the NCWC draft. Some of these rights were of course almost universally accepted from the beginning, and others found numerous explications.

The emphasis here will be on Catholic organizations' efforts in relation to the family—the basic human community— in which few others were initially interested. However, to indicate the general scope of the work of such organizations the NCWC text on personal and social rights furnishes a brief guide.

PREAMBLE

The dignity of man, created in the image of God, obligates him to live in accordance with law imposed by God. Consequently, he is endowed as an individual and as a member of society with rights which are inalienable.

Among these rights are:

1) The right to life and bodily integrity from the moment of conception regardless of physical or mental condition, except in just punishment for crime.

2) The right to serve and worship God in private and in public.

3) The right to religious formation through education and association.

4) The right to personal liberty under just law.

5) The right to the equal protection of just law regardless of sex, nationality, color, or creed.

6) The right to freedom of expression, of information and of communication in accordance with truth and justice.

7) The right to choose and freely to maintain a state of life, married or single, lay or religious.

8) The right to education suitable for the maintenance and development of man's dignity as a human person.

9) The right to petition the government for redress of grievances.

10) The right to a nationality.

11) The right of access to the means of livelihood, by migration if necessary.

12) The right of association and peaceable assembly.

13) The right to work and choose one's occupation.

14) The right to personal ownership, use and disposal of property subject to the rights of others and to limitations in the interest of the general welfare.

15) The right to a living wage.

16) The right to collective bargaining.

17) The right to associate by industries and professions to obtain economic justice and the general welfare.

18) The right to assistance from society, if necessary from the State, in distress of person or family.

RIGHTS OF THE FAMILY[10]

It would be impossible here to even list the problems touching the family which arose in drafting various articles of the Universal Declaration, e.g., that of abortion in connection with a Catholic proposal on the right to life "from the moment of conception." Only articles will be mentioned which finally, directly refer to the family.

By the end of its second session in Geneva Dec. 2-17, 1947, the Commission had referred to the family in two articles—one on the freedom from arbitrary interference with privacy, family, etc.; the other on the right to work and to compensation looking to "a family living standard." In addition, a special article was devoted entirely to marriage and the family. The latter was an elaboration of the drafting committee's text on the right of everyone to marry.

A brief history of this family article, its vicissitudes and emendations, may be of interest.

At the Drafting Committee's First Session (May-June, 1967), referring to the Secretariat draft provision on the right of everyone to marry according to the law, the Russian delegate M. Koreysky had pointed out that in some countries women were subjected to discrimination in the exercise of this right. The matter was referred to the Sub-Committee on Prevention of Discrimination and the Commission on the Status of Women for recommendations.

Even though such recommendations had not yet been made, at the second session in Geneva the Russian delegate suggested the Commission itself should formulate an article on marriage which would stress the principle of equality of men and women in this regard as well as special protection of maternity and childhood by the State.

The U.S. delegate indicated that equality should apply also at dissolution of marriage. Mlle J. de Romer of the International Union of Catholic Women's Leagues and August Van Istandael of the IFCTU both opposed the introduction of this concept into the Declaration, urging the Commission to content itself with a general statement on the equality of the spouses in relation to marriage. The text adopted—on the basis of a Philippine proposal—stated that men and women enjoy equal freedom to contract marriage in conformity with the law and that marriage and the family should be protected by the State and society. On the proposal of Dr. Charles Malik of Lebanon this text was preceded by a statement he admits was inspired by the NCWC formulation,[11] which had been called to his attention by the representative of the World Union of Catholic Women's Organizations: namely, "The family deriving from marriage is the natural and fundamental unit of society." Dr. Malik reserved his right to reintroduce a second sentence, rejected by the Commission, to the effect that "the family is endowed by the Creator with inalienable rights antecedent to all positive law and as such it shall be protected by the State and society."

When the drafting committee met again at Lake Success,

May 3, 1948, to review the Geneva text, objection was raised to retaining any part of the family article on grounds that "motherhood and childhood" were guaranteed special care and assistance in another article. This was the position of the United States, which as a later vote showed, was fearful that the State would be led to assume *too* protective a role in relation to the family. Russia was opposed to any mention of "the nature" of the family or to the assertion that it derives from marriage, holding that the family takes many forms. Egypt likewise objected to the phrase "deriving from marriage" as discriminating against children born out of wedlock. Despite an appeal by Dr. Malik for special recognition of the rights of the family as such, his amendment mentioning the Creator—to which Russia took exception—was roundly defeated, and the Drafting Committee likewise deleted the earlier reference to the family as the fundamental unit of society. The latter paragraph was, however, restored at the end of the marriage-family article by the Commission itself at its Third Session (May 24-June 18, 1947). Belgium introduced a new text; the United States made an alternative proposal, and agreement was finally reached on a formulation by Dr. Cassin of France. This read: "The family, which is the natural and fundamental group unit of society, is entitled to protection."

Russia at the General Assembly meeting in Paris succeeded in adding the words "by society and the State" to this text. Freedom of consent of the spouses and full age were other new elements inserted in the marriage article at the third session.

The question of the equality of partners at "dissolution" of marriage was then formally raised by the representative of the Commission on the Status of Women when it submitted its recommendations. The particular term "dissolution" had been arrived at in the hope it would satisfy those who did not accept divorce in view of the fact that women were discriminated against legally and in other ways when marriage was terminated by death as well as by separation or divorce, in the very determination of which under certain legal systems wives had no voice.

Ignoring the suggested terminology, Russia formally proposed to recognize equality of the right to "divorce" as well as to contract marriage. This proposal was rejected after a statement by the representative of the International Union of Catholic Women's Leagues that such mention would seem to advance the idea of divorce. In a declaration intended to incorporate ideals to which all nations should aspire, this was, therefore, offensive to the conscience of millions of women, she said. However, the same formulation was reintroduced by Russia in the Third (Social) Committee discussion at the General Assembly in Paris and there adopted. Thanks to the efforts of M. Cassin of France, the style committee changed the term "divorce" to "dissolution", a word which admits of the various interpretations noted above.

The article as finally incorporated in the Declaration reads:

1. Men and women of full age, without limitation due to race nationality or religion, have the right to marry and to found a family. They are entitled to equal rights as to marriage, during marriage and at its dissolution.

2. Marriage shall be entered into only with the free and full consent of the intending spouses.

3. The family is the natural and fundamental group unit of society and is entitled to protection by society and the state.

Four other articles in the Final Declaration contain references to the family. These are:

Article 12 which guarantees protection against arbitrary interference with privacy, *family*, home or correspondence, etc.;

Article 23 (3) which enunciates the worker's right to just and favorable remuneration ensuring for self and *family* an existence worthy of human dignity and supplemented if necessary by other means of social protection.

Article 28, which deals with the right to a standard of

living (including housing etc.) adequate for the health and well-being of self *and family;* protection of motherhood and childhood and equal social protection for all children whether born in or out of wedlock.

Article 26 on education which in its third paragraph assures that "parents have a prior right to choose the kind of education that shall be given to their children."

The guarantee of parents' rights in the education article was not given without considerable difficulty. Recognition of the parents' rights and duties in respect of their children's education, particularly their religious education had been urged repeatedly by Catholic communications. Among these were comprehensive memoranda covering other rights as well, submitted by the International Union of Catholic Women's Leagues on May 4, 1948.

An amendment to the draft education article which would have provided such assurance was proposed by Lebanon to the Commission's Third Session (May 1948). In a statement to the Commission the representative of the International Union of Catholic Women's Leagues, while recognizing the rights and duties of the State in providing education facilities and setting standards, called attention to the danger that the then formulation that "fundamental education shall be free and compulsory" might be interpreted as a mandate for state monopoly in the absence of explicit guarantees of parental rights. Following debate, in which it was contended by the United States, among others, that the rights of parents were safeguarded elsewhere in the Declaration and that there are limits to parental control, the amendment was defeated. The principle, however, was resurrected in the General Assembly Committee at Paris by the Netherlands representative, Rev. J.C.F. Beaufort, O.F.M. His amendment was later withdrawn in favor of the new and more acceptable Lebanese formulation which was finally adopted.

Once the Declaration was adopted as a "common standard of achievement," with consequent impact on the future decisions and working programs of the U.N. and its agencies, as well as for the legislation and practice of member states and the Constitutions of "new" states, the Commission on Human Rights devoted its immediate energies to completing the two Covenants—one on Political and Civil Rights and the other on Economic and Social Rights.

Non-governmental organizations continued to make recommendations. Thus in 1949, Protestant, Catholic, and Jewish organizations supported—with no success at that particular time—a proposal to include in the article on Religious Freedom assurance for the rights of parents to determine the kind of religious education their children should receive.

Such recommendations were made over a span of many years. For example, detailed statements on the family, the rights of children, and the status of women were sent by the International Union of Catholic Women's Leagues in 1949 to various organs of the United Nations concerned with human rights. Quoting from the last named statement in 1953, the representative of this organization urged the Commission on the Status of Women to forego mention of "dissolution" of marriage in its recommendations for the Covenant. She suggested instead a formulation first advanced by St. John's Alliance (a Catholic organization dedicated to securing equal rights for women): "All persons shall have equality before the law in all matrimonial matters."

At the time only the Draft Covenants on Economic and Social Rights, which it was expected would be implemented only by cooperative social action, included mention of the family. The IUCWL intervention asked the Status of Women Commission to press for a guarantee of essential marriage and family rights in the Draft Covenant on Civil and Political Rights as well and suggested the following formulation:

1. "Men and women of full age have the right to marry and found a family and rear their children. Marriage shall be entered into only with the full and free consent of the intending spouses."

2. All persons shall have equality before the law in all matrimonial matters.

3. The family deriving from marriage is the natural and fundamental group unit of society and is entitled to protection by society and the State.

4. Parents have the prior right to determine the education of their children.

5. Parents have the right to maintain, if necessary, by public protection and assistance, adequate standards of child welfare within the family circle.

As it happened the United Nations took 19 years to complete and adopt the Covenants, despite the fact that by 1954 the Commission on Human Rights had finished its draft—with consultation from an increasing number of non-governmental organizations—of the two Covenants (One on Civil and Political Rights, the other on Economic and Social Rights), together with appropriate measures of implementation for each.

The deteriorating political atmosphere among the Great Powers and the increasingly manifested differences of approach to the meaning of international commitment to human rights protection had, among other reasons, prompted the United States in 1953 to state that it would not support the Covenants. Its proposals for an educational program based on the Declaration were therefore adopted by the Human Rights Commission. This program consisted of examination of national reports on progress and problems, advisory services (fellowships and seminars), and global studies on the actual state of particular rights.

Largely but not entirely as a result of such studies, a certain multiplication of declarations and conventions dealing with particular rights occurred pending a more favorable outlook for the Covenants. These activities promoted dialogue and a deeper common understanding, especially among representatives of the many "new" nations, of the meaning of particular rights, which proved helpful in their discussion of articles of the Covenants bit by bit over the years by the General

Assembly. Moreover, the adoption of interim measures, for example on the family, affected the drafting of relevant articles in the Covenants. In this category are such instruments as the Declaration on the Rights of the Child, the Convention on Free Consent Minimum Age and Registration of Marriage, and the UNESCO Convention on the Elimination of Discrimination in Education, which stemmed from a "global study" (to which a number of Catholic international organizations had contributed) by the Sub-Commission on the Prevention of Discrimination and Protection of Minorities. (The latter recognizes the rights of parents with regard to the education of their children.)

No less than the influence of the Declaration was that of rapid change, which had led Pope Pius XII in his Christmas message, 1945, to call for greater and better public conditions so the family could continue to exist and develop as an economic, juridic, moral and religious unit. The number of nongovernmental organizations concerned with the family in all of its roles had increased, directly or indirectly, not merely in the realm of local action, but in relation to the various studies and projects on which the UN had embarked after the Declaration. For instance, the International Union of Family Organizations at its General Assembly in Brussels in 1951 had adopted a comprehensive "Bill of Rights of the Family," which pays tribute "to the value and scope of the articles concerning the Family contained in the Universal Declaration of Human Rights." In addition to explicating rights which have already been mentioned here, the last article of this "bill" declares that "Families as such have a right to be represented on the official and other bodies responsible for giving advice to or managing social, economic and cultural institutions."

As early as 1950, there were United Nations efforts to redraft the "Charter of the Child," which the League of Nations had adopted in 1924 at urging from the International Union of Child Welfare. Eventually it was decided that the Human Rights Commission would draft a "Declaration" on the subject, based on the Universal Declaration of Human Rights. The Declaration on the Rights of the Child adopted by the General Assembly in 1959 had benefited considerably from recommendations of non-governmental organizations, including the International Catholic Child Bureau and the International Union of Catholic Women's Leagues. While dedicated to the rights of all children, whether born in or out of wedlock, as against the human community as a whole, this Declaration stresses the right of children to a family milieu, to love, affection, and care. The right of the child to an education which will promote the full development of his personality "physically, morally, spiritually and socially" is recognized to be first of all the responsibility of parents.

In 1951, following a study tour in Africa, a representative of the World Union of Catholic Women's Organizations, Dr. Alba Zizzamia, had urged the Commission on the Status of Women in its consideration of women in dependent territories to make recommendations leading to legal standards on freedom of consent, minimum age, and civil registration of marriage in those territories—all of which would tend to promote and protect monogamous marriage. She urged also that the Commission recommend that the right of parental authority be legally recognized for the true father and mother.

The resulting recommendations of the Commission led, through a study of conditions in such dependent territories for which the WUCWO submitted most comprehensive information, to eventual adoption of a Convention on the subject of Free Consent to, Minimum Age, and Registration of Marriages.

RIGHTS OF THE FAMILY IN THE COVENANTS

Under each of the two International Covenants on Human Rights adopted by the General Assembly in 1966, special protection and guarantees for the family are provided. Due largely to the efforts of religious organizations—Jewish and

Protestant as well as Catholic—significant precisions of the Declaration were made in Article 18 of the Convention on Civil and Political Rights, which deals with the right to freedom of thought, conscience, and religion. Thus paragraph 2 provides that "No one shall be subject to coercion which would impair his freedom to have or to adopt a religion or belief of his choice," and under paragraph 4 "The States Parties to the present Covenant undertake to have respect for the liberty of parents, and, when applicable, legal guardians to ensure the religious and moral education of their children in conformity with their own convictions."

Article 23 of that Covenant covers the substance of the marriage and family article (16) of the Declaration and attempts to safeguard the child against consequences of "dissolution" of marriage: "States Parties to the present Covenant shall take appropriate steps to ensure equality of rights and responsibilities of spouses as to marriage, during marriage and at its dissolution. In the case of dissolution, provision shall be made for the necessary protection of any children.

The rights of all children are specifically guaranteed in Article 24:

1. "Every child shall have, without any discrimination as to race, color, sex, language, religion, national or social origin, property or birth, the right to such measures of protection as are required by his status as a minor, on the part of his family, society and the State."

2. Every child shall be registered immediately after birth and shall have a name.

3. Every child has the right to acquire a nationality.

In the Covenant on Economic and Social Rights, Article 7 would assure to everyone just and favorable conditions of work, in particular fair wages, equal pay for equal work, and a decent living for themselves and their families in accordance with the provisions of the present Covenant, safe and healthy working conditions, equal promotion opportunities, rest, leisure, and limitation of working hours.

Article 10 of the Covenant on Economic and Social Rights is devoted to the family.

1. The widest possible protection and assistance should be accorded to the family, which is the natural and fundamental group unit of society, particularly for its establishment and while it is responsible for the care and education of dependent children. Marriage must be entered into with the free consent of the intending spouses.

2. Special protection should be accorded to mothers during a reasonable period before and after childbirth. During such period working mothers should be accorded paid leave or leave with adequate social security benefits.

3. Special measures of protection and assistance should be taken on behalf of all children and young persons without any discrimination for reasons of parentage or other conditions. Children and young persons should be protected from economic and social exploitation. Their employment in work harmful to their morals or health or dangerous to life or likely to hamper their normal development should be punishable by law. States should also set age limits below which the paid employment of child labour should be prohibited and punishable by law.

Under Article 11, States Parties to the Covenant recognize the right of everyone to an adequate standard of living for himself and his family, including adequate food, clothing, and housing, and to the continuous improvement of living conditions. The Article also calls for appropriate actions from these states to ensure the realization of this right, recognizing to this effect the essential importance of international cooperation based on free consent, "particularly as regards improvement of methods of production, conservation and distribution of food by making full use of technical and scientific knowledge."

In Article 13, which deals with the right of everyone to education, a special paragraph (3) provides that

The States Parties to the present Covenant undertake to have respect for the liberty of parents, and, when applicable, legal guardians to choose for their children schools, other than those established by the public authorities, which conform to such minimum educational standards as may be laid down or approved by the State and to ensure the religious and moral education of their children in conformity with their own convictions.

No part of this article shall be construed so as to interfere with the liberty of individuals and bodies to establish and direct educational institutions, subject always to the observance of the principles that education shall be directed to the full development of the human personality and the sense of its dignity and shall strengthen the respect for human rights and fundamental freedoms; that it shall enable all persons to participate effectively in a free society, promote understanding, tolerance and friendship among all nations and all racial, ethnic or religious groups, and further the activities of the United Nations for the maintenance of peace, and to the requirement that the education given in such institutions shall conform to such minimum standards, as may be laid down by the State.

CONCLUSION

From the preceding consideration of articles connected with family rights, the contribution made thereto by principles of Catholic social teaching is evident.

The value of this contribution is attested to by its continually reevaluated acceptance in the social policy and the practical programs of the UN and its Specialized Agencies, no less than by increasing attention to the principles involved in national policies. Even the United States is beginning to sense, in relation to its welfare policy, the practical consequences for human rights and social progress of helping the natural, monogamous family perform its own functions and exercise its own rights.

The family is a "school of deeper humanity" (*Gaudium et Spes*)[12] where one "finds his true identity" (*Populorum Progressio*)—where "the various generations come together and help one another to grow wiser and harmonize personal rights with the other requirements of social life" (*Gaudium et Spes*).

Important as this contribution of Christian thinking is to the articles of Declaration, it should not be isolated from the comprehensive aim of the similarly inspired efforts to obtain recognition and respect for the dignity, freedom, and rights of the "complete man" in all his relations, especially that of his own destiny.

Pope John's appraisal of the Declaration itself is an index of the extent to which this aim was realized:

> In it, in the most solemn form the dignity of a person is acknowledged to all human beings. And as a consequence, there is proclaimed as a fundamental right the right of free movement in the search for truth and in the attainment of moral good and justice, and also the right to a dignified life, while other rights connected with those mentioned are also proclaimed . . . It is our earnest wish . . . that the day may come when every human being may find [in an improved United Nations] an effective safeguard for his rights which derive directly from his dignity as a person, and which are therefore universal, inviolable and inalienable rights.[13]

The completion of the Covenants is an initial step towards the realization of this wish. Their ratification by governments is a necessary next step.

Yet, whatever the legal or judicial measures for protecting men's rights on the national and the international level, it remains obvious that Christians living the social teaching of the Church are called to continuously vitalize the principles in the Declaration.

Only by active love and cooperation in freedom, truth, and justice, can men themselves through many kinds of association fully realize human rights and human progress.

CORNELIUS F. MURPHY, JR.

5: Is the Parental Right to Educate Protected by International Law?

In discussing the international aspects of the parental right to educate, the first consideration is to evaluate the juridical status of the relevant documents that bear upon the problem. How, for example, should one characterize the Universal Declaration of Human Rights which proclaims the values in question? Is it law? If not, is it merely exhortatory? To what extent are decision makers, national and international, obliged to consider its meaning? These questions are important. The answers to them can affect, in a substantial way, the actions of legislatures and courts throughout the world as they become increasingly involved in the difficult political and legal problems which have humanistic overtones.

UNIVERSAL JURIDICAL STATUS
OF THE DECLARATION

The Universal Declaration of Human Rights was adopted by the General Assembly of the United Nations on Dec. 10, 1948. After recognizing in its Preamble a relationship between the acknowledgement of human rights and the establishment of peace, the Assembly reminded the member states of their pledge to promote human rights and further proclaimed:

(T)his Universal Declaration of Human Rights [is] a com-

103

mon standard of achievement for all peoples and all nations, to the end that every individual and every organ of society, keeping this Declaration constantly in mind, shall strive by teaching and education to promote respect for these rights and freedoms and by progressive measures, national and international, to secure their universal and effective recognition and observance, both among the peoples of Member States themselves and among the peoples of territories under their jurisdiction.

Article 26 of the Declaration enumerates the rights concerned with education:

1. Everyone has the right to education. Education shall be free, at least in the elementary and fundamental stages. Elementary education shall be compulsory. Technical and professional education shall be made generally available and higher education shall be equally accessible to all on the basis of merit.

2. Education shall be directed to the full development of the human personality and to the strengthening of respect for human rights and fundamental freedoms. It shall promote understanding, tolerance, and friendship among all nations, racial or religious groups, and shall further the activities of the United Nations for the maintenance of peace.

3. Parents have a prior right to choose the kind of education that shall be given to their children.

Can these provisions be characterized as law? If by law is meant a positive rule emanating from a political superior and susceptible of coercive implementation, the answer must be in the negative. The decentralized character of contemporary international society, with the absence of supranational authority, makes it impossible to conceive of the Declarations as constituting a legal norm. This is so because the General Assembly does not possess any general legislative competence; and outside the enforcement machinery of the Security Council, there is no international power empowered to impose legal rules upon the nation states.

While the Declaration does not have the status of a positive rule of international law, it is inaccurate to characterize it, as Kelsen does, as being completely without legal effect.[1] The Declaration cannot be viewed in isolation; it must be considered in the light of the Charter of the United Nations. While there is no provision for the enforcement of human rights, the Charter does contain express obligations to promote those rights.[2] Moreover, there is a very real interaction between moral standards and the process of legal decision making. Mr. Justice Cardoza of the U.S. Supreme Court has amply demonstrated that the making of judicial decisions is unintelligible unless adequate attention is given to the profound interaction between law and morals.[3] At the international level, writers have shown how the process of deciding important questions both within and outside the United Nations is significantly influenced by technically non-legal, essentially moral standards such as the Declaration of Human Rights.[4]

Thus, while the Declaration of Human Rights is not a positive rule of international law, it by no means follows that its provisions, including those concerned with education, can be ignored by officials within national communities who must make decisions that effect the values which the Declaration seeks to protect. Those who have the responsibility of decision cannot ignore the relevance of the provisions of the Declaration on the excuse that it is not, strictly speaking, a legal document. For while its items may not be positive law, they are

. . . something more compelling than a simple expression of faith. The issue is, of course, bound up with the broader question of the legal effect of resolutions of the General Assembly. In this regard, compiling a list of sources of international law may be somewhat useless. It would, perhaps, be more satisfactory to approach the problem by asking what rule a candid mind would choose as "most in conformity with reason and justice for the solution of any particular controversy." The sources of law are hardly more than limitations on choice. They are matters which it would be unreasonable or inconvenient not to consult. This is, I suggest, the position of the provisions of the Universal Declaration, namely, the expression of the collective opinion of a large community which, in a case where choice is open, it would be unreasonable not to consider. They are not necessarily rules of decision but are surely the stuff of which decisions are made.[5]

THE PROPOSED COVENANTS ON HUMAN RIGHTS

There are other international documents which must be considered in connection with this essay. On Dec. 16, 1966, the United Nations adopted and opened for signature two Human Rights Covenants, one on Economic, Social, and Political Rights, and a Covenant on Civil and Political Rights. These covenants, designed to implement the United Nations general program concerning human values, contain particularizations of the general aspirations of the Declaration of Human Rights.[6] The Covenant on Economic, Social, and Cultural Rights contains the following specifications with regard to education:

ARTICLE 13.

1. The States Parties to the present Covenant recognize the right of everyone to education. They agree that education shall be directed to the full development of the human personality and the sense of its dignity, and shall strengthen the respect for human rights and fundamental freedoms. They further agree that education shall enable all persons to participate effectively in a free society, promote understanding, tolerance and friendship among all nations and all racial, ethnic, or religious groups, and further the activities of the United Nations for the maintenance of peace.

. . . .

3. The States Parties to the present Covenant undertake to have respect for the liberty of parents and, when applicable, legal guardians, to choose for their children schools, other than those established by the public authorities, which conform to such minimum educational standards as may be laid down or

approved by the State and to ensure the religious and moral education of their children in conformity with their own convictions.

Of itself, this document is not a legal obligation. It cannot become juristically effective until ratified by a minimum number of states, and then its positive legal quality obtains only between the signatories. Few nations have actually signed the document, and it is doubtful whether the major states will do so. In the United States there is considerable debate whether such an agreement is within the constitutional treaty-making power. In addition, there is apprehension both here and in other countries that such an obligation would seriously infringe upon domestic jurisdiction.

From the perspective of political philosophy it is doubtful whether international treaties are the best vehicle for the promotion of human rights. As the goal is human freedom, the means of accomplishment should, as far as possible, be characterized by volition. It is preferable that the perfections of human dignity grow organically as the cumulative effect of national legislative, executive, and judicial decisions rather than have the requirements of human freedom achieved as the begrudged consequence of an international treaty obligation.

This shift in emphasis turns attention towards the domestic law of the countries of the world community as a possible source of concrete meaning for the human values in question. Such an approach is not novel in international law. In situations where the interaction of states, by custom or treaty, is not a sufficient guide to the solution of an international issue, jurists draw upon comparative legal developments or the standards of legal justice as they have evolved through national legal systems. For example, when the question concerns the international responsibility of states for injuries to aliens, the international standard of justice includes the principles of justice recognized by states having "reasonably developed legal systems."[7]

Such a survey of the domestic law of the world community

yields a meager harvest. There are no uniformities; legal norms within the nations cover a wide range of possible implementations of Article 26 of the Declaration from flat statements such as Article VI of the Constitution of Chad that "public education shall be secular,"[8] to the requirement of the law of Somalia that the teaching of Islam shall be compulsory for pupils of Islamic faith in primary and secondary state schools.[9] Parental rights with respect to their children are recognized in various decrees;[10] but the available information is either cast in too general terms to be helpful, or, as in the case of the United States, crucial questions have not yet been definitively resolved.[11]

However, in spite of disappointing results, the fact of considering comparative possibilities gives us a starting point for reflection upon the content which should be given to the abstractions of the Declaration. The focus upon developments within the national legal systems makes concentration upon the growth of the law within a particular country a legitimate aspect of research. On the other hand, the cosmopolitan atmosphere which comparative analysis evokes is a reminder that in the realm of universal values the search must not rest within any one national system.

DEVELOPMENTS IN THE UNITED STATES

Since there are no universal legal norms or uniform national laws fixing the meaning of the Declaration provisions, it is legitimate to examine as a starting point developments with which one is familiar. In the United States, recent litigation and legislation has been devoted to educational issues which are framed in First Amendment terms.[12] Courts and legislatures have been deeply involved with working out the meaning of both the Separation and Free Exercise provisions in the context of education, and it is clear that their final resolution in this country will have a profound effect upon the development of the law in other parts of the world. Thus, in analyzing the international aspects of Article 26 of the Declaration, it is important to evaluate the constitutional drama being worked out in this country.

First Amendment issues involving religion and education tend to fall into two general categories: problems of religious influence in the public schools and governmental assistance to parochial or sectarian education. The dimensions of Free Exercise as well as Separation have been involved in both aspects, although greater attention has been given in the two areas to an analysis in terms of Establishment.

At first glance it would seem that only the second set of issues—those dealing with aid to sectarian education—would come within the scope of this essay. Parochial school assistance directly involves the parental right to choose as envisioned by the Declaration. But parental right concerns something more than the choice of isolated individuals. It broadens out into the right of the people: the extent to which the human society, as distinguished from its impersonal agent, the state, has a right to direct the destiny of the entire educational system in both its public and private aspects. We shall return to these distinctions; suffice at this point to note that it is important for a full understanding of what is at stake to view the issues in terms of the role that religion will play in both public and private education.

To conceive the problems in terms of these two sets of issues is also justified in the light of historical development. In the United States the internal dialectic of these problems has indicated that they are in fact profoundly interconnected. The decisions of the Supreme Court of the United States dealing with religion in the public schools—beginning with McCollum v. Board of Education[13] and culminating with the Bible Reading Cases[14]—have increased emphasis on the value of church-related schools. In the main, it has been Catholic parents who have viewed the secularization of public education as pointing up the need for sectarian institutions, but, as the Court has intensified its efforts to abolish religion from public education, Jewish and Protestant groups have also indicated some alarm.[15] These developments have brought into sharp focus the role of the sectarian schools in the education of man and the specific constitutional issue of the compatibility of aid to sectarian schools with requirements of the First Amendment.

This national experience throws light on complexities which the Universal Declaration of Human Rights fails to articulate. Article 26 of the Declaration is silent on the role of religion in public education. Subsequent developments, such as the proposed covenant, place emphasis on religious education as an independent phenomena so that the relevance of religion in public schools is virtually ignored. This perhaps reflects the practical politics of the problem, a hypothesis which is confirmed in the social experience of the United States, where religious leaders' passionate concern with parochial education is matched by their ignorance of the religious problems raised within secular institutions. In this respect the American legal experience is instructive, for it demonstrates the pervasiveness of the religion issue in a manner which is too often missed by those most directly responsible for the education of the human person.

To what extent can developments within the United States be reconciled with the human rights program of the United Nations? Does the decisional pattern indicate that the Universal Declaration of Human Rights was genuinely considered in the process of decision?

It is difficult to uncover the universal aspects of a national law since the determinations depend proximately upon constitutional provisions unique to the history and traditions of a particular people. But, in some measure, the decisions are transnational, especially to the extent that they raise questions of the institutional competence of the governmental organ responsible for the results. For there is a significant link between the growth of human values and the antecedent right of people to choose the procedures through which the substance of its value system shall be determined. Rights of self government, which the Declaration also affirms,[16] surely include the idea that governmental agencies should act within the boundaries of competency conferred upon them by the people.

Some of the Supreme Court decisions concerned with the role of religion in education have been sharply criticized by jurists and philosophers whose objective competence is beyond question.

For example, to the extent that the decisions relied on a historical interpretation of the First Amendment, they have been severely criticized as being an inaccurate representation of original meaning. The famous legal historian, Mark De Wolfe Howe, stated the objection with considerable candor when he wrote:

> In recent years the Court has decided a number of important cases relating to church and state and, in each of the cases, has alleged that the command of history, not the preference of the justices, has brought the Court to its decision. I believe that in the matters at issue the Court has too often pretended that the dictates of the nation's history, rather than the mandates of its own will, compelled a particular decision. By superficial and purposive interpretations of the past, the Court has dishonored the arts of the historian and degraded the talents of the lawyer . . .[17]

Similar criticisms have been leveled at the Court because of the manner in which the Court has, in these decisions, dispensed with requirements which have been traditionally considered as essential to the exercise of *judicial* power. One element that has caused particular concern is the looseness with which the Court has treated the essential question of whether the complaining party has suffered an injury from the practices of which it is complaining. In the Bible reading cases, for example, the Court assumed that the result of the practice would necessarily have a coercively injurious effect even if the complaining students were permitted to be excused. Professor Sidney Hook, who is otherwise sympathetic to the trend of the decisions, has said of these assumptions that:

[On] the face of it, it seems singularly implausible to assert that a child's religious freedom is being violated when specific exemption is provided for him merely on the request of his parents. We are here dealing with questions of psychological fact that cannot be deduced merely from legal, or abstract psychological, principles. Once the facts in the case are challenged, only inquiry can settle them.

*   *   *

The reason offered by the father of the children in the Abington schools who was a plaintiff in the case that reached the Supreme Court, for *not* requesting his children to be excused from hearing the Bible read—something he could very well have done—will hardly bear examination. He contends that had he done so, his children would have been labeled "odd balls" by their teachers and fellow students. They might have been regarded as "atheists," even "communists!"

This explanation is questionable on its very face, aside from the gratuitous charge about the attitude of his children's teachers. Fearful of making his children conspicuous by invoking a perfectly legal exemption, this parent makes them a thousand times more conspicuous! He brings a legal action that puts his children in the national limelight, an action that can be construed as an effort to *prevent* his children's friends and associates from listening to Bible verses in the school. Which action is more likely to make Mr. Schempp's children appear "odd balls" and to generate resentment against them among their peer groups—the invocation by the children of an exemption that invades no one else's right to listen or not listen, or the bringing of a legal action which would make *Mr. Schempp's* conscience the bar to the right of millions to have their children listen to Bible verses?[18]

The cumulative effect of these criticisms is to highlight the fact that the decisional pattern in question is as much the expression of a theory of democracy as it is the necessary consequence of litigation. There is a certain inevitability to this, given the proclivity of the American people to call upon the Supreme Court to resolve all great and significant national issues. Nevertheless, it is legitimate to evaluate the soundness of the prevailing ideologies, especially as we must measure them against the supranational standards embodied in Universal Declaration of Human Rights. We may ask whether the orientation reflects a true humanism, responsive to the deepest exigencies of the human person which the state, as a member of the United Nations, has a solemn duty to promote.

SECULAR HUMANISM

The tendency of this constitutional development in the United States reflects a philosophy of secular democracy or humanism. Its judicial formula is that the state must be neutral in matters of religion: a prohibition of religion as a standard of classification either to confer benefits or to impose burdens.[19] One implication of this standard is that religious exercises are impermissible on public-school property, belief and observance of religious practices being essentially a private matter. Whether it precludes all assistance, directly or indirectly, to church-related education is still in doubt; but if secularism in its purest form prevails, its attitude would seem to exclude any form of assistance.

The proponents of this thesis argue that secularism faithfully reflects the deepest exigencies of democracy. The argument takes several forms, but certain predominant characteristics emerge and become susceptible of analysis. The root justification for the theory is that it accurately reflects the will of the people.[20] This is a formidable point, and it deserves closer attention than it usually receives. Moving beyond the fallibilities of historical interpretation, its central feature is the idea that the people *believe* in secular democracy; the Court, in developing the policy through litigation, is merely articulating the deepest aspirations of the body politic. How can this assertion be tested?

One method of a socio-empiric nature would be to measure the pronouncement against the reactions of persons affected. Partisan expressions of acquiescence in, or rejection of, the religion decisions were numerous, and it is doubtful whether they can, on either side, be considered as authentic reflections of the people's will. But some of the reactions were suggestive of a deep incongruity between what the Court has asserted to be the aspirations of the people and the feelings which actually reside in the depths of American life. That the Court's view of democracy does not coincide with what the people actually adhere to was profoundly implied by the reflections of a prominent Protestant theologian, Dr. Paul Ramsey, on the impact of the prayer and bible-reading decisions:

> The American way of voluntary religious associations certainly expresses the profoundest religious reasons for proscribing coercion for cause of conscience or religious faith. The notion of the church as a "gathered" sect is certainly one great strand in the American religious heritage. But sectarianism and voluntaryism as *religious* principles were always, without knowing it, dependent upon the cultural formation of almost-Christians within Christendom, and most American denominations have known this and been concerned about it. They have known that if we are "a religious people," this has been not only because of what goes on within voluntary religious associations themselves (though that is the heart of the matter), but also because "we are a religious people whose institutions presuppose a Supreme Being," and because these institutions have not been without consequence in traditioning this religious premise to the coming generations.
>
> The unprecedented situation today is that all denominations have become sects in relation to each other, to the state, and to the lesser social institutions that comprise the fabric of community relations in the United States. Voluntaryism is all that is judged to be needed to form a religious person or to make him possible (along with theological references to the ultimate mystery of God's dealing with men). In between voluntaryism as a social principle and God's grace as a theological principle, the cultural formation of a possibly religious people is squeezed out. The prayer decisions signal the final end of the Constantinian era, and Christianity (or religion) has likely been conducted to its exit from determinative influence upon the institutions of society at the point where it entered.

Perhaps necessarily so, in a pluralistic society. But this raises the crucial question: How on earth can a Christian or a Jew sing the Lord's song in a pluralistic land? The likelihood is that increasingly he will not and that in increasing numbers his children will not. This should enable us to understand why religious people (who want the church, not the state, to be the church, but who feel obliged to keep the land from becoming a land of strangers) have reason to be concerned about the Court's decision. As citizens they must search for another possible solution before reluctantly agreeing with that judgment.[21]

The suggestion that the Court is imposing a fictitious secularism upon a believing society is further advanced when the new democracy is examined in the light of political and social theory. The possibility of persuading a people that an imaginative way of life is truly their own depends, in large measure, upon the assumptions of political theory on which the argument is based. In the realm of religion in public life, the possibility of identifying secular humanism with the people's aspirations is facilitated when the dogma is advanced as an integral ingredient of civil peace. Mr. Justice Douglas, a leading advocate of secularism, is explicit on this point:

> To those who are the products of the free society of the Western world the secular state is an advanced form of government, offering special rewards.
>
> Our choice of the secular state was a philosophical choice as well as one founded on bitter experiences. The creation of the Board of Education in New York goes back to 1842, when the legislature, unable to divide public education funds among quarreling and envious sects, created a public-school system in which no religious sectarian doctrine or tenet should be taught, inculcated, or practiced. Had we not lived in communities where there was a multiplicity of sects, we might have followed a different path.[22]

That there is divergence between the political choices implied in this statement and the actual attitudes of the citizenry towards these questions should be obvious. Boards of Education in New York and elsewhere would not have pre-

scribed prayer and Bible reading in public schools if the issue
had been as conclusively settled as Mr. Justice Douglas asserts.
But the importance of this argument runs deeper than these
inconsistencies. Divergencies between social mores and legal
standards can be explained in terms of constitutional requirements; what the people wish to do in fact is not the equivalent
of what the Constitution means. The statement of policy is
more significant for the assumptions about the structure of
democratic society which it suggests. For the argument passes
beyond constitutional interpretation and fixes its ultimate justification upon a theory of government. What is being suggested
is that the people, insofar as religious issues are concerned, are
unable to live peacefully together. Consequently, they have
transferred to the Court their rights of self-government, thus
leaving those who wield this ultimate political power free to
develop the boundaries of religion and government—a process
whose acceptance is guaranteed by reminding the people of
their proclivities to violence.[23]

It is impossible to reconcile these Hobbesian postulates
with the deepest meaning of democratic government. The
people have not conveyed their right to govern to the
Court or to anyone else. The right of self-government, which
the Declaration on Human Rights asserts, is a moral power
inherent in the people. It can be *participated in,* but it is
nontransferable. Surely, by the adoption of a written constitution, the people have restricted their political choices; but that
is not the ultimately decisive issue. Any assertion that they
have completely divested themselves of *all* choices can be defended only on the basis of a theory of government insuffi-
ciently aware of the moral basis of democracy.[24]

Justice Douglas' quotation also reflects some assumptions
about the human person which deserve examination. For it
reflects an anomoly in the secularist attitude towards the
capacities of human person. In one sense the secularist is a
champion of human dignity and freedom, but this ontological
optimism is offset by a pessimistic attitude about the capacity

of the human person for self-improvement. The civil peace argument is premised on the assumption that because at one point in history people were incapable of peacefully resolving a type of issue, they are perpetually incapacitated from settling these problems with any measure of mutual self-respect and tranquility.

This attitude of transposing historical facts into moral theories is difficult to reconcile with the inner meaning of personality. If governments, including courts, are genuinely committed to the development of the human person, they should be willing to attribute to people some capacity for self-improvement. For to be a person assumes some ability to rise above our more destructive tendencies and to live in society in a spirit of peace and good will.

Finally, it may be asked, what emerged from the developments of secularism with respect to the exigencies and deepest needs of the human person? How responsive is the advocacy of secularism to the standard of the Declaration that "education shall be directed to the full development of the human person"?

In many respects secular humanism has an exalted conception of personality Its advocates have passionately promoted the emancipation of man by stressing the value of free intellectual inquiry and have insisted on the demands of academic freedom and the independence of the human spirit. But in its insistence that religion is a purely private affair—either inappropriate for the atmosphere of public education or of no governmental concern in its private manifestations—it fails to come to grips with the deepest needs of personality.

What is lacking is a just appreciation of the transcendental aspirations of the human spirit, its need to inquire into ultimate questions of origin and destiny. Secularism misses this point because it conceives of man as completely self-sufficient, absolutely autonomous. It is a closed humanism because its internal dynamism excludes any final end; it has lost the most profound meaning of ultimate purpose. What it fails to see is the essential ordination of the human person *to know God,* through reason to understand him as the cause of being and of knowing him in his intimate life through the illumination of revelation. It is the educational process which stimulates these ultimate quests, and it is within an educational milieu that these needs must be given their fullest scope.[25] To relegate them completely to the realm of private affairs, or to classify them as at best matters of individual devotion, is to fail to grasp the deep exigencies of human personality.

The insistence that religion is of no concern of the state, especially where it interacts with public or private processes of education, may seem a safeguard of human freedom, but its real significance lies deeper. Secular democracy does not advance the person; it rather champions the isolated individual, shut up in himself, who dismisses supratemporal concerns as irrelevant to his perfection.[26]

What is needed is an open humanism, which treats the human being as a person, with all the transcendental aspiration which personality implies:

> And what is that if not the fully-rounded development of the whole man and of all men? A humanism closed in on itself, and not open to the values of the spirit and to God who is their source, could achieve apparent success. True, man can organise the world apart from God, but "without God man can organise it in the end only to man's detriment. An isolated humanism is an inhuman humanism." There is no true humanism but that which is open to the Absolute and is conscious of a vocation which gives human life its true meaning. Far from being the ultimate measure of all things, man can only realise himself by reaching beyond himself. As Pascal has said so well, "Man infinitely surpasses man."[27]

Only then will a person's rights in the realm of education, both public and sectarian, receive the full implementation to which the Universal Declaration of Human Rights aspires and which the states of the international community are committed to achieve.

NEIL MC CLUSKEY

6: Catholic Americans and the Future of the Public School*

The attitude of the American Catholic community toward the state supported public school has fluctuated widely over the nearly two centuries of our national existence. This should cause no surprise. Since the public school mirrors society, it reflects a changing countenance. It has meant something different for each generation of Americans. However, what has divided and confused Catholic approaches to public education has been the absence of a rounded philosophy of education. Had there been a coherent and consistent theory of the school and its relation to profane learning, technical and professional skills, religious formation and civic education, the Catholic community might have entered fully into the public school movement, if not from the beginning, at least before the close of the nineteenth century, lent it strength and inspiration, and worked to achieve its own distinctive educational aims in other ways.

Indeed, though there has always been an abundance of episcopal and papal statements on education written in the most eloquent of terms, the arguments for Catholic schooling are invariably aimed at the ultimate goal of education with accompanying insistence on the need for religious training. The escatological and theological may illuminate a philosophy

* This chapter will appear in *Catholic Education Faces Its Future*, by Neil McCluskey, © by Doubleday & Company, Inc. Used by special arrangement.

of education; they can never substitute for it. Still, given the hostile climate in which the American Catholic Church grew to maturity, it is understandable how things happened the way they did; and it is easy to sympathize with the uneasiness Catholic Church leadership has nearly always felt *vis-à-vis* the state school.

Even less was the nineteenth century a time when a set of values could be quietly absorbed through the traditional Catholic home. The industrial and social revolutions were progressively shattering the order of the past. The unencumbered piety of the European village or country parish was not transplantable. For the young it was fast disappearing behind the smoke and bustle of the raw new cities and towns. Catholic leadership came to hope that the parish school would play surrogate for the agencies which during the age of devotion have kept men loyal and obedient to the Church. For the first time in history, the school was asked to become what it had never been: the primary guardian and tutor of the Catholic faith. The schools were established, accordingly, in response to the Church's pastoral concern. If a single theme characterizes the collective pronouncements of the American hierarchy on education over the past one hundred years, it has been the insistence that education was primarily moral training and religious formation to be achieved through the separate confessional schools. So true is this that the questions must be asked: was the school expected to replace the priest and the parish in fulfilling Christ's commission to teach or, even more fundamental, was the school expected to assume the natural obligation of parents to prepare their young for admission into the Christian community?

FACTORS THAT CONDITIONED
CATHOLIC ATTITUDES

Social and religious factors have conditioned the Catholic attitude toward the public school. Chief among them was reaction to Protestant anti-Catholicism and the defense mechanisms to which this gave rise. Inseparable from and only second to Protestant-Catholic tension was Catholic perplexity in face of the drive for mass education, which, with its mystical vision of the public school as the unique fount of America's greatness, seemed to smack so strongly of Protestantism itself. When Justice Robert H. Jackson of the U.S. Supreme Court wrote in his dissent in the 1947 New Jersey bus case that "our public school, if not a product of Protestantism, at least is more consistent with it than with the Catholic culture and scheme of values," he was only voicing a sober truth.

A third factor was the conservative reaction here and abroad to a Europe rocked to its Christian foundations by successive waves of revolution from the end of the eighteenth century onwards, beginning with the French Revolution itself. And equally to be weighed in an analysis of the social forces which shaped Catholic attitudes toward public education was the inability of traditional Europe and official Rome to comprehend the distinctive genius of the American experience.

That segment of leadership in the American Church which early saw how, freed from the social and political encumbrances of its tired past, the Church could take on renewed life and wax strong in the New World setting was engulfed by reactionary forces. The traditions of Catholic Europe ran counter to much of what the young country was beginning to stand for—opportunity for all (including state-supported education), the end of class privilege (including a favored position for the Church), a trust in the new science to ameliorate man's lot on earth (including encouragement for independent thought and initiative). Perhaps what Church leadership in Latin Europe found hardest to accept was the political philosophy so boldly expressed by one of America's greatest churchmen, John Ireland, when he stated: ". . . I say that government of the people, by the people, and for the people is, more than any other, the polity under which the Catholic Church, the Church of the people, breathes air most congenial to her mind and heart."[1] He and like-minded American bishops were at last discredited and their influence neutralized by the phantom of "Americanism," a heresy which never truly existed nor, for that matter, has ever been completely laid to rest in the minds of nervous officials of the Vatican Curia.

Conveniently, the school situation in the United States can be divided into three periods which have preceded the amorphous present. They are: from colonial times until 1840; from then down to roughly 1900; from then until 1965. These divisions will be made more meaningful in pursuit of the text.

FROM COLONIAL TIMES TO 1840

In tracing the origins of the American public school one characterization stands out. Early Americans looked upon the schools as "the children of the church." Nowhere was this description more accurate than in the colonies of New England. The school was considered simply the normal means for inculcating loyalty to the sponsoring confessional group. Literacy was virtue for it gave a person access to the word of God, thereby binding him to the Scripture-inspired community covenant. The oldest piece of public legislation on schools is the famous "Old Deluder" Act of 1647, tightly linking the school and religious formation.

> It being one cheife piect of ye ould deluder, Satan, to keepe men from the knowledge of ye Scriptures, as in formr times by keeping ym in an unknown tongue, so in these lattr times by pswading from ye use of tongues . . .[2]

So the Act would thwart the devil by requiring each township of 50 householders or more to appoint a teacher and set up a school.

During the century and a half of the colonial period, the religious tensions of the colonies were a faithful mirror of the social situation in the European mother countries, notably England. While there were a few Roman Catholic families of prominence and affluence, Catholics generally lived their lives outside the cultural and political activities of the community. The Church as such existed in the shadows with next-to-no organization and without strong leadership. A rigid penal code laid heavy disabilities on Catholics, depriving them of freedom to worship together, to take part in public life, and to educate their children. The Catholic child was an undersirable alien in the rudimentary colonial school, and yet his parents were liable to a heavy fine if they sent him out of the colonies for his education. Catholics themselves were barred from teaching or establishing schools. By 1704 even Catholic-founded Maryland had passed "An Act to Prevent the Growth of Popery," among whose bristling provisions was one which threatened to deport any Catholic who should keep school, board students, or instruct children.

The Revolution and its successful outcome eased many of the more onerous disabilities on Catholics, but only four States in their constitutional conventions gave them political equality with Protestants. As the established Protestant churches began to lose, at least *de jure*, their privileged status, distinctive articles of belief and particular features of church organization were de-emphasized, and believers of divided allegiance discovered more and more in common. This development was a decisive factor in the success of the public school movement by making this common endeavor possible among Protestant factions.

Since the community-sponsored schools belonged to everyone, any pattern of education, especially in its moral and spiritual aspects, could become a socially divisive issue. Some doctrinal common ground had to be found which would satisfy a spectrum of religious beliefs, ranging from liberal Unitarian to the most unswerving Congregationalist. It took imagination and diplomacy to effect the necessary compromise that would unite the community in supporting a common school. The movement found its leader in Horace Mann.

However, during the first struggling years of the public

school movement in Massachusetts, religious traditionalists and conservatives alike turned their anger on Mann, who held the position of secretary to the Board of Education of the Commonwealth between 1837 and 1848. They charged that he was reducing the place of religion in the school, divorcing religion and education, and creating godless institutions. Throughout his career he repeatedly had to defend himself from such charges. His stock reply was to point out to his critics that he had always acted on the principle that in a Christian nation Christianity should hold an honored place in the schools. Admittedly his own idea of Christianity was vague and almost indistinguishable from Unitarianism. In any event he had a point which gave many observers pause. Children should be given "so much religious instruction as is compatible with the rights of others and with the genius of our government."[3] However, it was the responsibility of parents, he said, to give children "any special and peculiar instruction with respect both to politics and theology," and "at last, when the children arrive at years of maturity . . . commend them to that inviolable prerogative of private judgment and of self-direction, which in a Protestant and a Republican country, is the acknowledged birthright of every human being."[4]

Mann's program called, accordingly, for a kind of Christian religion which should not be identifiable with the distinctive tenets of Congregationalist or Methodist or Episcopal or Baptist faith. The cornerstone of Mann's religion was the Bible, the great symbol and source of Protestant Christianity. Though "our Public Schools are not theological seminaries, is admitted," he wrote in his final *Annual Report,* yet "our system . . . welcomes the religion of the Bible, and in receiving the Bible, it allows it to do what it is allowed to do in no other system—to speak for itself."[5] As long as the Bible remained in the school, the school was Christian. Granted the times, any other approach but Mann's nonsectarian, biblically-based compromise would probably have meant the end of the common school movement.

In agreement with philosophers of education from Plato to Dewey, the American people have looked upon the schools as the main channel for the transmission of the national ethos or public philosophy undergirding their society. It has always been assumed that the common school had a large, if not the largest, part in the development of the American character in inculcating moral and spiritual values, in laying the ethical basis of character in the child. The social context of early America lent itself to an operative consensus regarding the religious roots of the nation's political patrimony. Even after this consensus no longer held, the United States of America considered itself a Christian nation, not in the sense that any general or specific understanding of Christianity was the established religion, but rather that the overwhelming bulk of the citizenry continued to profess some formal or nominal allegiance to the Christian tradition.

Provided the public school did not favor any special church or sect, it remained pretty well free to inculcate the generally agreed-upon moral and religious truths found in the common Bible. Despite creedal differences, people agreed that moral and spiritual values were rooted in some kind of transcendent value system. American democracy was presumed to be drawing its strength from a collective awareness that there was a divine value stamped upon man and that the ultimate guarantee of the rights of man defined in America's first political documents was the Almighty Creator of mankind.

In the historic working out of Horace Mann's compromise, the unavoidable became the inevitable. In the effort to remain "neutral," at first among warring Protestant sects and later between Protestant and Catholic, the educational process in the schools turned "secular," at least officially, for the compromise approach bore the seeds of its own dissolution. The area of agreed-upon tenets contracted inexorably, leaving almost nobody happy with the state of things. The only group which seemed to benefit was that which held a minimum of positive doctrine or none at all.

THE MIDDLE PERIOD

Historically the American public school descended from the common schools of New England without reference to non-Protestant groups, but in time these too had to be reckoned with. In the first decades of the nineteenth century, the total number of Catholics, while not negligible, was certainly not significant.[6] Consequently, each Catholic family had to face the dilemma of placing its children in a religiously hostile environment or of depriving them of the educational preparation essential to economic and social advancement. There was no American Civil Liberties Union to fight what today would be judged a blatant infringement of religious liberty—nor did that public think such an organization necessary. As Robert D. Cross has put it:

> To the eighteenth-century American, the Roman Catholic Church was pure evil—an affront against God and an international conspiracy against legitimate government. To the gilded age, it was an object of distrust because of its startling growth, of dislike because of its religious error, and of distaste because of the cultural backwardness with which it was usually associated.[7]

As the American public increasingly accepted and then enthusiastically supported the public school movement, the Catholic community was torn. Heretofore, the Church's commitment to formal education had been slight. Society generally regarded education beyond the rudiments as the prerogative of the upper classes or the gateway to the professions. When in 1785 Bishop John Carroll wrote to Rome, mentioning a new college in Philadelphia and two other proposed schools in Maryland to which Catholics could be admitted, he was talking about classical academies not under Church control. In fact, he expressed the hope "that some educated there will embrace the ecclesiastical state. We think accordingly of establishing a Seminary in which they can be trained to the life of learning suited to that state."[8] He wrote in another letter that the object dearest to his heart was "the establishment of a school, and afterwards of a Seminary for young clergymen."[9]

At the same time Carroll was working in 1786 with the Jesuits to establish "George-Town College," he was cooperating with Patrick Allison and William West, both Protestant ministers, to establish a nonsectarian college in Baltimore to prepare young men for the learned professions. That no general program for Catholic education was intended is clear from the pioneer bishop's pastoral letter of 1792 to the Catholic people of the United States. Referring to the opening of Georgetown, he writes:

> I earnestly wish, dear brethren, that as many of you, as are able, would send your sons to this school of letters and virtue. I know and lament, that the expense will be too great for many families, and that their children must be deprived of the immediate benefit of this institution. . . .[10]

And in 1829, the Catholic bishops spoke in the same vein of the luxury of Catholic schooling:

> How well would it be, if your means and opportunities permitted, were you at this period to commit your children to the care of those whom we have for their special fitness, placed over our seminaries and our female religious institutions?[11]

The public school of the ante-bellum period, however, was not only Protestant oriented, but most often belligerently so. The textbooks were shot through and through with derogatory references to things Catholic. The widely-used New England Primer with its stern injunction: "Child, behold that Man of Sin, the *Pope*, worthy of thy utmost hatred," is simply a graphic case in point.[12]

Catholic leaders were forced into a defensive posture. The school question and other long accumulated problems brought the seven bishops of the United States together in 1829 for the first of the seven Provincial Councils of Baltimore, covering the interval between that year and 1849. Their joint letter to

American Catholics urged the necessity for Catholic schools to preserve the faith of Catholic boys and girls, particularly from poor families. The textbooks were a sore point. "The schoolboy can scarcely find a book," the bishops said, "in which some one or more of our institutions or practices is not exhibited for otherwise than it really is, and greatly to our disadvantage."[13]

Nor had things improved by 1840, the year of the fourth council. The bishops put it baldly: "Since it is evident that the nature of public education in many of these provinces is so developed that it serves heresy, [and] the minds of Catholic youth are little by little imbued with false principles of sects, we warn pastors that they must see to the Christian and Catholic education of Catholic youths with all the zeal they have, . . ."[14]

They urged pastors to protest what were still widespread practices; Catholic pupils in the public schools were required to join in reading the Protestant Bible, in reciting Protestant prayers, and in singing Protestant hymns. The bishops' letter again singled out the textbooks, saying: "We can scarcely point out a book in general use in the ordinary schools or even in higher seminaries, wherein covert and insidious efforts are not made to misrepresent our principles, to distort our tenets, to vilify our practices and to bring contempt upon our Church and its members."[15]

They voiced concern over the plight of parents for whom it is "no easy matter to preserve the faith of your children in the midst of so many difficulties." The letter tries to explain why Catholics wanted their own schools:

> It is not then because of any unkind feeling to our fellow-citizens, it is not through any reluctance on our part, to contribute whatever little we can to the prosperity of what are called the common institutions of the country, that we are always better pleased to have a separate system of education for the children of our communion. . . .[16]

But attempts at compromise or conciliation by Catholics resulted in the "painful experience that in any common effort it was always expected that our distinctive principles of religious belief and practice should be yielded to the demands of those who thought proper to charge us with error. . . ."[17] The dismay of the Old World-oriented bishops, uneasy and torn over certain liberal assumptions underlying the public school movement, is voiced in their next words: "and because we saw with great pain the differences which an attempt to combine and conciliate principles, which we have never been able to reconcile, has produced in a distant Church which has always been found faithful."[18]

The Catholic community sought to remedy the situation in several ways. They asked that the offending passages be deleted from the common textbooks; they asked that Catholic children be excused from the daily prescribed reading of the King James Bible. They asked that a fair portion of their own school tax money be returned to help support separate Catholic schools.

The textbook situation did slowly improve and by stages the more abusive references disappeared. The Bible, however, was looked upon by most Americans as the moral Gibraltar of the Republic, and it was simply inconceivable that the schools of a God-fearing nation could exist without it. In fact, powerful legal support for retention of reading from the Protestant Bible was supplied by an 1854 decision of the Maine Supreme Court, affirming the right of a school district to require the practice.[19] In a number of cities there was tension and strife consequent upon the caning or expulsion of Catholic pupils who refused to take part in what they steadfastly believed to be a Protestant religious exercise. It was only in 1890 that the Wisconsin Supreme Court in the much-agitated Edgerton Bible case reversed the earlier precedent and ruled the Bible a sectarian book.

In today's more open and sophisticated society we find it hard to conceive of this fanaticism on the part of numbers of Catholics and bigotry on the part of many Protestants over an issue which our generation would consider trifling. After all, it is still the Bible whether garbed in the English of King James or of Douai College. Yet it is easy to forget that during the centuries of religious conflict following the breakup of Western Christian unity, things of small significance in themselves grew into towering symbols of division—like the vernacular *versus* Latin, or a right-left or a left-right axis in making the sign of the cross, or even down to the inclusion or deletion in the Lord's Prayer of the words: "For thine is the kingdom, and the power, and the glory."

Quarrels over different translations of the Bible were serious enough, but a larger bone of contention was in the unguided reading of the Scriptures themselves. In 1840 a spokesman for Archbishop John Hughes of New York voiced the Catholic objection:

> The Holy Scriptures are read every day, with the restriction that no specific tenets are to be inculcated. Here we find the great demarcating principles between the Catholic Church and the Sectaries introduced silently. The Catholic Church tells her children they must be taught by *authority*. The Sectaries say, read the Bible, judge for yourselves. The Protestant principle is therefore acted upon, slyly inculcated, and the schools are sectarian.[20]

The unabashedly Protestant orientation of the public schools, though generally diminishing as the nineteenth century closed, was then the principle reason that led the Catholic community to establish separate schools. A second reason, by no means exclusively Catholic, was a philosophy that judged formal schooling a subject beyond the competence of the State.

We of today are so used to the State's preponderant role in education that it is not easy to understand the strong feelings to the contrary entertained a century ago by many people. Today it is simply assumed that the State is the paramount educator and that private and religious groups play a supplementary role. In fact, there are contemporary educational leaders and philosophers of education who go even farther, arguing that the principal right to educate belongs to the State and that private groups sponsor schools by privilege of the State. This philosophy, though rare until comparatively recent times, has long had logistics if not logic on its side.

Leaders of the public school movement realized that the only solid basis for a republican form of government with broad suffrage was an informed and literate citizenry. Having rejected the monarchical and aristocratic forms of Old World government, the new pattern based on the consent of the governed could not long endure unless the people were educated to the level where they could participate intelligently in political and social decisions. Such was the incessant theme of educators like Horace Mann, Henry Barnard, Calvin Stowe, Samuel Galloway, Caleb Mills, and other leaders in the movement. Though the churches and private groups were multiplying schools, they were unable to provide education on the scale called for by the times. The public was beginning to demand that the State use its own resources to provide education for more children.

On the other hand, a large and influential cross-section of American society refused to see any direct role for the State in education. They could point for support to men like the British philosopher Herbert Spencer, who wrote: "In the same way that our definition of state duty forbids the State to administer religion or charity, so likewise does it forbid the State to administer education."[21]

If one argues that formal education is essentially a moral undertaking and that morality must have a religious basis, education would seem to be the more proper business of the churches, and mistrust of Caesar in the classroom becomes entirely understandable. It is against this background that some of the statements made by church leaders of past generations about state-controlled education should be interpreted. Bernard McQuaid, the fiery Bishop of Rochester, stated: "The

Catholic is unwilling to transfer the responsibility of the education of his children to the state. His conscience informs him that the state is an incompetent agent to fulfil his parental duties."[22] Writing in 1877, a Jesuit educator had this to say: "The State has the right and the duty to encourage good education; but its right to educate is but a Masonic invention."[23] Another critic went all the way with the bewildering charge "that the idea that the state has a right to teach . . . is not a Christian idea. It is a pagan one. . . ."[24]

As the traditional Protestant coloring of the public school faded under both Catholic and Protestant pressures, a handle emerged for the criticism that the schools were irreligious if not downright antireligious. Archbishop John Hughes, never distinguished for his tact and embittered over his failure to win tax support for the New York parochial schools, was one of the most hostile critics. His remark in 1852 that education as perpetrated in America was "Socialism, Red Republicanism, Universalism, Deism, Atheism, and Pantheism—anything, everything, but religionism and patriotism," was scarcely calculated to ease Protestant-Catholic tensions.[25]

On the other hand, Catholic leaders in many localities did try to take the hand extended them in good will by public school and community leaders. Occasionally a Catholic priest was even invited to serve on a local school board. An increasing number of Catholic young women became teachers in the public schools. However, until the deep Protestant animus toward the Roman Church, prevailing between 1830 and 1860, had been pretty well dissipated, rapport on any large scale was impossible. Bishops like John Ireland of St. Paul (1838-1918), John Lancaster Spalding of Peoria (1840-1916), and James Gibbons of Richmond and Baltimore (1834-1921) could and did exercise their social statesmanship only after Appomattox. The thought of these men was well-represented in the work of one scholar, Thomas Bouquillon, Belgian-born professor of moral science at the Catholic University of America. His pamphlet, *Education: To Whom Does It Belong?*, was a somewhat tardy explicitation of a principle implicit in Catholic dogma, namely, that within reasonable limits every State has the right to make use of the necessary means to achieve its legitimate ends in any sector of society. Still the pamphlet's appearance in 1891 caused consternation and drew heated rejoinders.

Bouquillon's adversaries could point to the long series of pastoral letters issued jointly by the American bishops in the discharge of their teaching office, not one of which gave the slightest hint that the State had any direct right in education. The most prestigious of these episcopal gatherings, the Third Plenary Council of Baltimore, at which sat fourteen archbishops and sixty bishops, wrote: "The three great educational agencies are the home, the Church, and the school"—with no mention of the State.

This traditional philosophy which permitted the State merely to substitute for parents delinquent in their duty of educating the child had hardened, no doubt, because of certain social changes that were remaking Western society. Social values, sanctions, even institutions themselves were perceptibly and imperceptibly shifting from the sacral to the secular order.

One radical departure was the State's encroachment on the regulation of marriage. From time immemorial the Church had had sole jurisdiction over the "sacred" bond of matrimony. Though marriage was considered simultaneously a contract and a sacrament, both were regulated within the sacral order. The State's jurisdiction extended simply to the civil aspects of marriage, for example, to the regulation of doweries, inheritances, legitimacy of succession, etc. Even following the sixteenth century breakup of Christian unity, the new churches and sects generally continued this division of ecclesiastical and civil jurisdictions. Luther alone of the major Protestant theologians parted company here and argued that the regulation of marriage was proper to the State, because it was *"ein weltlich Geschäft," "ein weltlich Ding"*—a secular business.

However, during the final years of the eighteenth century, the secularization of marriage was partially or wholly effected in every major country of the West. Church authority was set aside, and nations operated on the principle that the State had the principal if not the sole competence in marriage. The extreme occurred in the France of the 1790's. There the men of the Revolution organized a republican liturgy to replace the Catholic nuptial ceremonies. Robespierre pushed through the Convention a law which established the "Feast of Conjugal Love" on which day marital unions could be solemnized by the State.

The wonder is not small then, that men who recoiled from these changes would likewise entertain grave fears regarding education once it came under control of the State. Education and marriage are, in the nature of things, inseparably linked.

EFFORTS FOR TAX SUPPORT

Catholic efforts to obtain tax funds for separate schools as a solution to the school problem likewise failed. Swollen with the newly arrived immigrant population, New York City was the scene of the first important struggle by Catholics to obtain a proportionate share of the common school fund, and the outcome here went a long way toward establishing a national policy which has endured to the present day. Between 1795 and 1825, the State of New York had given financial aid to every educational institution in the City, practically all of which were operated by the churches. In 1805 the Free School Society was founded "for the education of such poor children as do not belong to, or are not provided for by any religious society." Shortly, it adopted another title, the "Public School Society," and soon became the dominant educational force in New York City. In 1825 a bill passed the State legislature, authorizing the city council to determine which schools should receive tax money. The next year the council decided that henceforth New York City's share of the state school fund should go exclusively to the nonsectarian Public School Society, except for minor grants to orphanages and mission schools.

Led by their colorful and combative Bishop (later Archbishop) John Hughes, the New York Catholics repeatedly urged the justice of their claims. The year 1840 marking the peak of Catholic activity was abetted by the support of Governor William H. Seward, who proposed that state money be used to establish schools under church auspices for immigrant children. A public petition was put before the board of aldermen. Speaking of his fellow citizens, the spokesman informed the board that as Catholics:

> They bear, and are willing to bear, their portion of every common burden; and feel themselves entitled to a participation in every common benefit. This participation, they regret to say, has been denied them for years back, in reference to common school education in the City of New York, except on conditions with which their conscience, and as they believe their duty to God, did not, and do not leave them at liberty to comply.[26]

It was not that local communities did not attempt to come to terms with the school problem. An early effort at compromise took place in Lowell, Massachusetts, which must have had some approval from the secretary of the State Board of Education, none other than Horace Mann himself. Between 1831 and 1852, Mann wrote in a letter, a "very intelligent committee," consisting of clergymen and laymen, entered into an arrangement with the Catholic priests and parents, "by which it was agreed that the teachers of their children should be Catholics."[27] These schools were part of the public school system and, as such, regulated by the district school committee like any other schools belonging to their jurisdiction. The plan was called "eminently successful" in 1837 by the school committee. By 1839 there were five schools enrolling 752 pupils under this arrangement.[28]

Similar arrangements were entered into in communities in at least ten states before the outbreak of the Civil War: Connecticut, Illinois, Indiana, Kentucky, Michigan, Mississippi, New Jersey, New York, Ohio, and Pennsylvania.[29] The objective was generally the same: to combine public and parochial schooling within a single institution. Actually, at one time or another, nearly every state in the Union has had some such plan in operation, at least briefly, for the benefit not merely of Catholic children, but for those of Presbyterian, Quaker, Lutheran, Mormon and other groups as well.[30]

The most notable pattern of compromise was one followed at Poughkeepsie, New York, and the small towns of Faribault and Stillwater in Minnesota. The key provisions of the plan were: (1) An existing parochial school in a heavily populated Catholic area is leased to the public school district; (2) the school board operates a "public" school in the parish-owned building, paying upkeep and salary costs; (3) all religious instruction or exercises are scheduled before or after the standard school hours; (4) with the Catholic pastor's approval, the school board appoints teachers and provides textbooks; (5) the school board retains complete control over examinations, promotions, and general policies.

The arrangement at Poughkeepsie worked smoothly for 25 years, beginning with 1873. It had the approval of the Archbishop of New York, Cardinal John McCloskey, and might have continued indefinitely; but, as will be seen later, in the aftermath of the school controversy of 1890-92, it fell a belated casualty. The Faribault-Stillwater arrangement was short-lived and was likewise a victim of the controversy which so closely involved its sponsor, Archbishop John Ireland.

RAPID GROWTH OF THE CATHOLIC CHURCH

During the middle decades of the century, the Catholic Church expanded rapidly. From the original ecclesiastical province of Baltimore, which was coterminous with the limits of the United States itself, were formed the Province of Oregon City (1846) and the Province of St. Louis (1847). By 1852, date of the First Plenary Council of Baltimore, Rome had erected three additional provinces: New Orleans, Cincinnati, and New York. From this Council the six archbishops and 35 suffragan bishops published a national pastoral, treating mainly of Church authority and education.

The document is hortatory in tone and betrays the anxiety of the pastors for their people. The Catholic Church felt itself under siege. Each of the preceding decades had had its ugly incidents which sent shock waves far and wide to frighten, to separate, to harden attitudes among American neighbors. The 1830's had seen the burning of the Charleston convent and the *Awful Disclosures* of Maria Monk. In the 1840's the Native American Party had provoked bloody riots in the streets of Philadelphia over Bible reading in the schools. The 1850's were to see the birth of the Know-Nothing Party, the anti-papal demonstrations which greeted the Pope's first representative, Archbishop Bedini, the tarring and feathering of the Jesuit John Bapst, the Massachusetts law for the inspection of convents, and the riots of Louisville's "Bloody Monday."[31]

The bishops urged fathers and mothers to watch over the purity of their children's faith and morals with jealous vigilance and to instill into their hearts principles of virtue and perfection. The lax parent was warned of the "terrible expectation of judgment that will fill his soul, should his children perish through his criminal neglect, or his obstinate refusal to be guided in the discharge of his paternal duties by the authority of God's Church."[32]

To avert such an evil, parents were to give children a Christian education, "that is, an education based on religious principles, accompanied by religious practices and always subordinate to religious influence." The faithful were warned against "false and delusive theories which are so prevalent, and which leave youth without religion." These educational philosophies leave youth "without anything to control the passions, promote the real happiness of the individual, and make society find in the increase of its members, a source of security and prosperity. Listen not to those who would persuade you that religion can be separated from secular instruction."[33]

Catholics were encouraged to establish and support Catholic schools. This worthy object would prevent Catholic children from becoming "involved in all the evils of an uncatholic education, evils too multiplied and too obvious to require that we should do more than raise our voices in solemn protest against the system from which they spring." In urging this duty, the bishops were following out the suggestion of Pope Pius IX in his encyclical letter of the preceding year, which urged bishops throughout the world to provide for the religious education of youth.[34]

The Civil War brought a lull to anti-Catholic activity and effectively broke the political power of the Know-Nothing Movement. Within a year of the war's end, 1866, the American Catholic bishops again gathered in plenary session at Baltimore to do their part in binding the nation's wounds. Two chapters of their pastoral letter were devoted to education. They repeated the admonition to establish and support parochial schools. They again expressed the conviction that "religious teaching and religious training should form part of every system of school education." The letter stated: "Every day's experience renders it evident, that to develop the intellect and store it with knowledge, while the heart and its affections are left without the control of religious principle, sustained by religious practices, is to mistake the nature and object of education. . . ."[35]

Here then was a philosophy or—perhaps more accurately —a theology of education which, beginning in mid-nineteenth century America, has long enjoyed almost the official patronage of the Catholic bishops. It was in sharp disagreement with the general philosophy of education that was rapidly replacing the non-sectarian Protestant orientation of the public schools of the 1830's and 1840's. The public school then felt itself responsible for the basic religious principles common to all creeds, that is, religious beliefs whose character was presumably not distinctive of any single Protestant sect. The public schools should now promote a knowledge and love of the great ethical principles which govern man's ideal relation to his fellows and which came out of the great Judaeo-Christian tradition. The Bible retained its privileged place, for Bible-reading would inspire students to a veneration of these principles and ideals. Increasingly, public school leaders used the phrase "moral and spiritual values" in place of "religious values." They were puzzled and annoyed at charges that the public schools were responsible for the increase in crime and delinquency. Whatever breakdown there might be in community morals, they argued, should be considered more the responsibility of the churches and homes than of the schools.

The Catholic bishops indirectly owned up to this responsibility in the same pastoral letter of their Second Plenary Council in a special chapter on "Catholic Protectories and Industrial Schools." "It is a melancholy fact, and a very humiliating avowal for us to make," they begin, "that a very large proportion of the idle and vicious youth of our principal cities are the children of Catholic parents."[36] The reason might be poverty or simply neglect, but there is an appalling ignorance by parents of "the true nature of education, and of their duties as Christian parents." A large number of Catholic parents are neglecting their duty of

> providing for the moral training of their offspring, or doing it in such an imperfect manner that day after day these unhappy children are caught in the commission of petty crimes . . . and day after day, are they transferred by hundreds from the sectarian reformatories in which they have been placed by the courts, to distant localities, where they are brought up in ignorance of, and most commonly hostility to, the religion in which they had been baptized.[37]

Once again, pastoral concern by Catholic leadership missed the critical issue. Is proper discipline of headstrong and wild youth within the family the "true nature of education?" Does moral training under devout Christian auspices within the home exhaust parental responsibility in education? Or hopefully, now, does a Catholic reformatory take over from inadequate parents (and pastors) to lead the errant sheep into the paths of gospel righteousness? Apparently these good men of 1866 thought so.

What is the solution? The bishops wanted to have established *Catholic* Protectories or Industrial Schools wherein "the youthful culprit may cease to do evil and learn to do good." They were happy that some dioceses had already begun to do this good work, and exhorted the clergy

> to bring this matter before their respective flocks, to endeavor to impress on Christian parents the duty of guarding their children from the evils above referred to, and to invite them to make persevering and effectual efforts for the establishment of Institutions, wherein, under the influence of religious teachers, the waywardness of youth may be corrected, and good seed planted in the soil in which, while men slept, the enemy had sowed tares.[38]

There is here an exaggerated faith in the Catholic school as the great sacrament of salvation, which was only matched by Protestant faith in the public school as the panacea for all of America's woes. Just how the "Catholic Protectories and Industrial Schools" were to become the solution to the staggering problems the nation faced in its first year after the bloodiest and bitterest war of its history, their excellencies did not detail. One can be excused for reflecting that there might have been more practical measures called for to combat the unemployment and violence and squalor and corruption in the urban America of 1866. True, it would be two more decades before a conscience-stricken public would respond to the prophetic voices of a Jacob Riis or Jane Addams or Ellen Gates Starr and begin to face ills of the industrial civilization whose grinding tenement misery was crushing the hopes and dreams and spirit of millions of new American Catholics. Largely cut off from the total community effort to cope with these problems, Catholic leadership would use the slender resources of the immigrant Church in the cause of "true education," by distracting the faithful from present ills and focusing eyes on the rewards and punishments of the afterlife through loyal adherence to the one true Church.

GROWTH OF THE PUBLIC SCHOOLS

After the Civil War popular education began to take wide hold, but it was only in 1880 that public school enrollment reached one million. Meanwhile the Catholic dilemma was not easing. The bishops were divided over the school question and remained so throughout the final three decades of the century. Perhaps too great an influence has been attributed to the Third Plenary Council of Baltimore (1884) in shaping the parochial school system. In the sense that this last and greatest of the national councils did formalize a firm policy concerning the rejection of the public school and commitment to the separate religious school, the Council's influence was paramount. Nevertheless there were earlier factors at work, none of them larger than the 1875 *Instruction of the Roman Congregation of the Propaganda* to the American bishops, which provided the essential material for the Baltimore school legislation of 1884.

Recent studies have made clearer the role played by a small group of all-out opponents of public education in eliciting this document from Rome.[39] Their leader was James A. McMaster, a convert and able writer, who edited the influential *New York Freeman's Journal* between 1847 and 1886. As an editor he had few peers, but his acid-dipped pen and strong prejudices left him few friends. In theological and political matters he was ultra-conservative, even reactionary. Just what prompted his crusade to keep Catholic children out of the public schools is not completely explicable. One historian speculates that it was his brooding over events in France after the Franco-Prussian War, in particular the violence against Catholicism in 1871 by the Paris Commune.[40]

In an editorial that July, McMaster declared war on the state school:

> Then we propose opening on the promoters of non-sectarian, non-dogmatic schooling, in this country. We will show all who follow us most rigorously, that they are working towards bringing on our country the calamities France has been suffering, and preparing torches for American cities such as have laid nearly one third *of Paris in ashes*.[41]

The next week he defended his "declaration of war," with an astonishing claim which, if only partly true, indicates the deep division over the school question among the American bishops. He states that for 23 years he had fought for independent Catholic schools without tax support from the State and that his position had been *"deprecated"* by nearly all the bishops and by most of the priests then in office—"as an idle, theory of exclusive Catholic education, that cannot be realized in this country &c. &c." The sole prelate he excepted was Bishop Ignatius Reynolds of Charleston.[42]

Writing on Feb. 17, 1872, McMaster presented his position in full. The editorial was entitled "Thesis on Catholic Duties toward Catholic Children," and reads in part:

> The *law* of the Catholic Church, promulgated and reiterated, in the Encyclicals of the Vicar of Christ—in which he has spoken to the Universal Church is not obscure. It condemns any, and every system of mental training for Catholic children, that is not under the supervision of approved Catholic teachers; or in which the continual influence of Catholic instruction is not exerted.
>
> . . . The *conclusion* which we propose is, that, considering the teaching of the Vicar of Christ, and of the general body of the Hierarchy believing with him, and teaching with him, the time has come for enforcing *everywhere,* the general law of the

Catholic Church, that Catholics must not send their children to any schools except Catholic schools!

Intermittently but with unflagging fervor, the editor pursued the battle. He gave fulsome praise and complete coverage to the pastorals of bishops who called for the building of schools and never hesitated even to scold the many bishops who were, he thought, dragging their feet on the issue. He urged that parents sending children to the public school be denied absolution. He bitterly attacked the Poughkeepsie Plan and other kinds of school compromise. Over and over he thundered editorially that the school question was no longer open, "for Rome has spoken!" All that remained was to obey:

> The argument about the evils, and the dangers of godless schools, has been ended, long since. The question is now, solely, about obeying the law of the Catholic Church!

> The *law of the Catholic Church* is, now, that it is *forbidden* to Catholics to send their children to any "schools from which the authority (that is the Priesthood in its teaching capacity) of the Catholic Church is excluded."[43]

Nor was he about to buy the so-called Sunday schools, which he contemptuously dismissed as "lazy pastors' soothing plasters." McMaster would settle for no less than "parochial day schools, under pious teachers."

Rome had certainly spoken. In a strong letter to the Archbishop of Freiburg in Breisgau, dated July 14, 1864, Pius IX protested the transfer of control of the public schools in the Grand Duchy of Baden from Church to State. McMaster was certain that what was bad for a Europe, whose moral strength was being drained away by Freemasons, socialists, and liberals, was equally bad for the United States of America. Twice McMaster printed the translated text of the Pope's letter. He reminded his readers that the very propositions condemning public education in the *Syllabus of Errors* of 1864 had been drawn from this source.

American Catholics, the bishops included, were too slow to

accept the promulgated law of the Church; so the New York crusader would appeal directly to the Pope to speed things along. Appeal he did. Through his strategically situated correspondent in Rome, Ella B. Edes, and a priest friend visiting there, Edmund DePauw of the Diocese of Ogdensburg, McMaster presented a letter of petition and formal *Memorandum*, dated Feb. 20, 1874, to the Sacred Congregation of Propaganda Fide.[44] The *Memorandum* asked two questions: (1) May Catholic parents send their children to non-Catholic state schools which have rejected the surveillance of the Catholic clergy? (2) Does Pius IX's letter to the Archbishop of Freiburg apply to the United States? It then added fifteen points to help clarify the issue, which in the grimmest possible terms depicted what was taking place in the American Church and especially what was happening to Catholic children in the public schools.

McMaster viewed the school issue in stark black and white. Writing to Miss Edes, he stated: "My thesis has always been that parents cannot *in any case whatever*, without violating their consciences as Catholics, send their children to *primary* school, in which the rudiments of intellectual development are imparted by non-Catholic teachers, or by Catholic teachers in schools which refuse the supervision of a Catholic priest."[45] And the basis for this sweeping statement? "I rest my argument formally," he wrote, "on the decretal letter, dated July 14, 1864 and addressed by the Holy Father to the Archbishop of Freiburg."

To reinforce the information supplied the cardinals of the Holy Office for their deliberation, McMaster supplied through Miss Edes Italian translations of news and articles from the *Freeman's Journal.* For example, one nightmarish article was "The Morality of the Public Schools in America."[46]

Action was rapidly forthcoming. April 10, 1874, seven weeks after the date of the McMaster petition, Cardinal Allesandro Franchi, prefect of the congregation, wrote to the archbishops of the United States. The letter opened with a

summary of the situation, obviously colored by the harshness
of the picture presented by the McMaster group:

> It has been reported to this Sacred Congregation that so serious
> are the evils which befall Catholic youth in the United States
> of North America as a result of their attendance at public
> schools which are not subject to the vigilance and inspection of
> ecclesiastical authority, that it can safely be said that there are
> in number more who thereafter fall into indifferentism and so
> lose their Faith, than there are who every year, by virtue of the
> zealous work of our missionaries, renounce the false religion
> that they used to practice and are received into the bosom of
> the Church.[47]

The money factor was then touched on. "It has furthermore been reported that parents send their children to the
aforesaid schools for reasons of small consequence, among
which this one is cited—that their Catholic schools demand
some small sum of money annually from the young people for
their education, whereas in the public schools the instruction is
provided at no cost whatsoever." This casual passing over of
what was certainly a crucial factor in the whole question must
have dismayed some of the bishops contemplating their impoverished immigrant flocks.

Cardinal Franchi went on to list five questions which the
congregation wanted answered:

> 1. Precisely for what reasons do the faithful permit their chil-
> dren to attend non-Catholic schools?
> 2. What sort of means are there whereby young people can
> more easily be kept away from schools of this sort?
> 3. What are the reasons why some up to now hold that sacra-
> mental absolution must be denied to Catholic parents who send
> their children to non-Catholic schools, whereas others think
> that absolution should be granted?
> 4. Whether by the denial of the sacraments it can be easily
> brought about that parents will not allow their children to
> attend such schools?
> 5. Finally, whether, and with what difficulties, could a remedy

of this sort be harmful, with due regard to the circumstances of places and persons?

In early May a group of prelates, including most of the archbishops, was assembled by Archbishop James Roosevelt Bayley of Baltimore to prepare a reply. They agreed to inform their suffragans of the content of the joint answer, leaving each bishop, who might disagree with the group, free to send his own answer to the congregation. Archbishop Bayley edited the final draft which represented an official position, considerably more moderate than that of the McMaster group.[48]

The bishops' answer began:

> First of all, it is to be noted that these public schools are not non-Catholic in the sense that they have in their very nature something which is directly and purposely opposed to the Catholic religion but are properly secular in which, to be sure, are handed down the elements of secular knowledge with the omission of all religious education.

The letter reviewed the efforts made by "all provincial councils and especially in the Baltimore Plenary Council held in 1866" to urge clergy and laity to build schools. It would be highly desirable that all Catholic children could be taught in their own schools, "for although secular schools are not opposed directly and purposely to the Catholic religion, and as a matter of fact Catholic teachers are often employed in them, nevertheless it must be admitted that not infrequently they are operated by their directors in a frame of mind opposed to the Catholic religion."

They doubted the wisdom of denying absolution to parents sending their children to public schools, even when such schools are available. There could be valid reasons, as would be explained in the body of the letter. They flatly denied that "there is always present in the public schools a serious and proximate danger of perversion, particularly in an area where Catholics live with non-Catholics in a mingled consortium of life."

The bishops then took up each of Cardinal Franchi's questions.

Why do Catholic parents patronize the public schools? A Catholic school is not always available, especially in rural areas and elsewhere where there is a scarcity of Catholics or a thin Catholic purse. Often the Catholic schools in the cities are too small to accommodate all the children. The next reason is an honest admission that "the literary instruction or training which has customarily been given in public schools sometimes —rather more often than not—surpassed the instruction which is given in Catholic schools, where sometimes at least the parents would desire more refined facilities." Moreover, "most Catholic schools, in fact, are considered somewhat inferior in rank, by reason of the impossibility of securing for them competent teachers. . . ." These are among the "serious considerations which persuade even devoted Catholics to prefer public schools to Catholic schools and in this manner make provision for the future of their children."

The first answer also takes care of the second question of the cardinal. The only remedy which can be safely employed to keep Catholic children from non-Catholic schools is to multiply the number of schools and get "the very best teachers for them." The bishops then brought up a point which has a contemporary ring:

> From the public treasury, the public schools have the wherewithal to offer far higher salaries to teachers than the directors of Catholic schools can provide, and as a consequence the directors of Catholic schools are unable to find any but less suitable teachers. Catholics indeed, who as a rule are poor, have to pay the government common taxes for the public schools, and in addition the funds necessary to maintain their own parochial schools must be provided by them.

To the third query, why there is a difference of opinion about the denial of absolution, the American bishops indicated that the point was met in the introductory statement. However, they added this warning "that absolution would have to be denied not only to parents, but also to Catholic members of the legislative assemblies by which public schools are established and supported in the individual states, and that it would forbid devout Catholics from taking part in assemblies of this sort to the considerable detriment of and even danger to Religion." Accordingly, they did not approve of indiscriminate denial of absolution to parents sending children to the public school, "but think that the decision should be made in individual cases in accordance with circumstances, with a special investigation of the care of the parents regarding the religious education of their children."

Their reply to the fourth query concerning the efficacy of denying absolution was pointed: ". . . We have already set forth the only means of achieving the end which we ought to have in view. Denial of the sacraments would only serve to exasperate feelings and stir up hatred against the Catholic religion among our non-Catholic fellow citizens." The fifth and final point of the Franchi letter, about the harm of denying the sacraments, they felt had been answered.

It took another year and a half before Rome sent its definitive decision to the American Church regarding the public school question. Incredibly enough, the Roman cardinals who framed the policy were far more influenced by the socio-religious picture presented them by McMaster than by the answer of the archbishops of the United States to Cardinal Franchi's letter. Some inkling of the episcopal feeling here can be conjectured from a line in a letter of reply from Bayley to Bishop Bernard McQuaid of Rochester who was concerned lest too strict a policy be laid down from Rome, denying absolution to parents. The Baltimore archbishop assured McQuaid that strong representation against such a policy would be in the joint letter and then indicated his awareness of where the pressure on Rome was originating. "McMaster is growing more & more dogmatic about this as well as other matters," he wrote. "He may abuse presbyterians [sic], but Presbyterianism is very deep in him. But before they send us any of their Procrustean rules from Rome, they had better inform us how it happens, that they absolve parents who send their children to the *present* Roman public school."[49]

The tone of the *Instruction* was set by its opening sentence: "The Sacred Congregation of Propaganda has been many times assured that for the Catholic children of the United States of America evils of the greatest kind are likely to result from the so-called public schools."[50] The *Instruction*, confirmed by Pius IX on Nov. 24, 1875, contained eight points.

The whole idea of the public school which excluded religious instruction was condemned as "most dangerous and opposed to Catholicity." Because then the children "can neither learn the rudiments of the faith nor be taught the precepts of the Church; hence they will lack that knowledge, of all else, necessary to man without which there is no leading a Christian life." This almost blind belief in the formative power of the school is astonishingly brought out in the reason their eminences advance: "For children are sent to these schools from their earliest years, almost from their cradle; at which age, it is admitted, the seeds sown of virtue or of vice take root. To allow this tender age to pass without religion is surely a great evil." One can honestly wonder if, in this philosophy of education, mother and father and family or parish are left any room to sow seeds of virtue and vice.

The nineteenth century defensive mentality of the Catholic Church, which moved it so far out of the mainstream of culture and civilization, dominates the next point of the *Instruction*.

Again, these schools being under no control of the Church, the teachers are selected from every sect indiscriminately; and this, while no proper precaution is taken to prevent them injuring the children, so that there is nothing to stop them from infusing into the young minds the seeds of error and vice. These evil results are certainly to be dreaded from the fact that in these schools, or at least in very many of them, children of both sexes must be in the same class and class-room and must sit side by side at the same desk. Every circumstance mentioned goes to show that the children are fearfully exposed to the danger of losing their faith and that their morals are not properly safeguarded.[51]

James McMaster had done his job well.

Now followed the third point: "Unless this danger of perversion can be rendered remote, instead of proximate, such schools cannot in conscience be used." An appropriate reference is here made to Pius IX's letter to the Archbishop of Freiburg, which had so well served McMaster, to the effect that what is here enjoined is simply a dictate of the natural as well as the divine law.

"It only remains then," continued the document, "for the prelates to use every means in their power to keep the flocks committed to their care from all contact with the public schools." So, Catholic schools were needed, and every effort must go toward multiplying and improving them. Teaching brotherhoods and sisterhoods are to be established. The obligation to support Catholic schools "should be especially brought to the attention of the more wealthy and influential Catholics and members of the legislature."

Point five simply reminded American Catholics that since there is no law preventing them from having their own schools, "it is therefore in the power of Catholics themselves to avert, with God's help, the dangers with which Catholicity is threatened from the public school system." The next item treated is the exception to the rule. Circumstances may sometimes permit parents to conscientiously send their children to the public schools. Whether there be sufficient cause in any particular case is to be left to the conscience and judgment of the local bishop. In general, if no school exists or if only an inferior school unsuited to the social condition of the family exists, public school attendance may be condoned.

Social strata were still part of the America of 1875. Several times the American bishops had cautioned ambitious parents against educating their children for stations in life they could never assume. Nor were the bishops the only Catholics who were not ready to adopt the Catholic school indiscriminately for all. One chancery official is quoted as observing that "when a pastor undertakes to erect a parochial school he meets with three classes of persons in his parish: the upper class which he cannot force, the middle class which he is able to force, and the poor people who are in favor of it."[52]

Christian training and instruction out of school hours is the burden of the seventh section. Pastors and parents are admonished to "spare no labor to give children thorough catechetical instructions, dwelling particularly on those truths of faith and morals which are called most in question by Protestants and unbelievers. Particularly must they "keep them from freedom and familiarity with those of the other school children whose company might be dangerous to their faith and morals, and absolutely away from the corrupt."

The final point, treating of the denial of absolution to parents, is diplomatically evasive, and is the one issue where Mc-Master lost out.

> Parents who neglect to give this necessary Christian training and instruction to their children, or who permit them to go to schools in which the ruin of their souls is inevitable, or finally, who send them to the public school without sufficient cause and without taking the necessary precautions to render the danger of perversion remote, and do so while there is a good and well-equipped Catholic school in the place, or the parents have the means to send them elsewhere to be educated—that such parents, if obstinate, cannot be absolved, is evident from the moral teaching of the Church.[53]

The *Instruction* of 1875 must remain one of the most curious documents in the history of the American Church. Two unusual aspects of it are the fact that it resulted from the initiative of the laity and assumed a reactionary and rigorous character despite the modifying representation of what was a fair consensus of the American bishops. The most remarkable circumstance surrounding this document, however, is the silent reception it got from the American hierarchy. There was no announcement of it. Little action immediately followed. Naturally it displeased those bishops who had pooled their thought in the letter sent to Rome by Archbishop Bayley. The *Instruction* seems to have been quietly buried until the preparations began for the Third Plenary Council of Baltimore.

In addition to the national assemblies of the bishops from which they had jointly addressed themselves to the school situation and other concerns, individual bishops and regional meetings of bishops had long been doing the same thing. Many dioceses had drawn up statutes ordering pastors to establish parish schools and parents to send their children to these institutions. Nowhere was this done with more exactness than in the Midwest, most particularly in dioceses where there was a heavy concentration of German Catholics. The German immigrant tended to lump together his language, his culture, and his religion. Moreover, he was suspicious and resentful of attempts to dilute his *Deutschtum,* whether by Americanizing bishops or Americanizing public schools.

Differing from his Irish brother, the German Catholic immigrant had not been forced from his homeland by grinding poverty and the spectre of starvation. He was usually better educated, notably in the possession of trade or farming skills, and had a more developed culture. Whereas the Irish who were crowded into the slum districts of Boston, New York, and Philadelphia had no affluent middle class on which the burden of supporting schools might fall; the Germans of St. Louis, Milwaukee, and Cincinnati did. Moreover, the German immigrant had far less poignant memories of hunger and oppression from the old country. He tended to regard his parish church and parish school as his closest ties to *die alte Heimat.* The flourishing German language press fostered this love as did the numerous cultural and fraternal societies dedicated to keeping his traditions fresh and green in the frequently hostile American environment. In large measure, these differences explain why the parochial school movement was pursued with greater *élan* among the German immigrant group in the Midwest, and later for pretty much the same reasons among the Polish Catholic community, than in the Mid-Atlantic or New England areas.

The second Provincial Council of Cincinnati had already ordered that all pastors of souls "under pain of mortal sin" were "to provide a Catholic school in every parish or congregation subject to them, where this can be done." The bishops of this region had much to do with the vigor of the decrees on the Catholic school of the Third Plenary Council of Baltimore, which at last opened on November 9, 1884.

THE THIRD BALTIMORE COUNCIL

This last of the plenary councils differed from its two predecessors, most notably in that the principal pressure to convoke the council came from Rome and in that the *schemata* of topics was controlled by the Congregation of the Propaganda. Rome's idea was to bring the "missionary" American Church into conformity with the discipline and structure of the older European Churches. Had the American bishops been more free to resolve the problems of the American Catholic community within a New World context, there would have been another history of the school question. In any event, one year prior to the opening of the Baltimore meeting, eleven archbishops and bishops were invited to Rome to plan the council's agenda with the advice and assistance of the Congregation of the Propaganda.

The 1875, *Instruction* and earlier published directives on mixed schools were among the *Capita Praecipua* in the center of the conference table around which the planning committee sat.[54] The Italian prelate who served as secretary dutifully recorded in the minutes for the session of Nov. 29, 1883:

The Most Reverend Archbishop of Baltimore declared to be most admirable both what was now proposed with regard to parochial schools and what had been previously prescribed by the Sacred Congregation in the Instruction already issued and he agreed that complete obedience was due in their fulfillment; he added that all difficulties in regard to those schools would be readily solved if the provisions of the Holy See would be observed.[55]

The minutes further record that the Archbishop of Oregon City, Charles J. Seghers, expressed concern over the insistence by some American prelates "that the council should enact a decree which would require, under penalty, that missioners should build parochial schools within a brief interval of time to be specified by the Holy See." In view of the difficulties, the cardinals replied that this measure did not seem expedient, but "that bishops should insist on the building of schools with appropriate attention to missioners who prove themselves culpably negligent." When Archbishop Michael Heiss of Milwaukee inquired "whether bishops could prohibit attendance at the public schools in order to prevent harm from coming to the parochial school," he received what he undoubtedly judged a surprising reply. Their Eminences said "that if this was the sole reason involved the bishops could not attach a penalty to their prohibition."

The penultimate step in preparing the council's agenda was to submit the work of the Roman committee to a committee comprising the archbishop and his suffragans of a province. The Province of Chicago was given the chapter on schools.[56] Having accepted the suggestions from Rome, they added that parish schools should be established wherever possible, but that they should be equal in quality to the public schools. Finally, a group of theologians drafted the legislation on education, laying down four rules which in substance, but after modifications, were voted by the council itself.

1. Near every church, when it does not already exist, a parochial school is to be erected within two years from the promulgation of this council, and to be kept up in the future, unless in the judgment of the bishop the erection and maintenance of the school is impossible.

2. A priest who is gravely negligent in erecting the school within the time or is gravely negligent in its maintenance after it is erected can and must be removed from that church.

3. The mission or parish which so neglects to aid the priest in erecting or maintaining the school, that on account of this supine negligence, the school cannot exist, is to be reprimanded by the bishop, and if it shall have been contumacious, it is to be given spiritual punishments.

4. All Catholic parents are bound to send their children to parochial schools, unless at home or in other Catholic schools, they provide sufficiently and fully for their Christian education, or on account of a good reason approved by the bishop, using meanwhile the necessary precautions and remedies, they are permitted to send them to other schools.[57]

The final wording of the decrees eliminated the threat of spiritual penalties, so America escaped the nightmare of an entire parish being placed under interdict or excommunication because a local bishop judged it seriously remiss in supporting the parish school.[58] The warmest debate was over the degree of parental obligation: should parents be exhorted or commanded to send their children to the Catholic school?

McQuaid of Rochester and the "German" bishops of the Midwest led one side of the debate. On the opposite side was Edward Fitzgerald of Little Rock. He did not see the public schools as the evil and dangerous places many of his confreres did, and so he was in total opposition to the entire decree. The priest's obligation extends only to the teaching of religion, he insisted. Once the children have been taught their catechism, the pastor's duty is done. No law binds parents to send a child to school to learn secular subjects. Here Fitzgerald was a minority voice. However, when it came to a proposal which would have denied absolution to parents remiss in their duty, the vote defeating the proposition was 37 to 32. Not even the *Instruction* of 1875 had gone so far, except that it did underscore the *natural* law obligation of parents not to seriously risk the spiritual well-being of their offspring by placing them in a serious and proximate occasion of moral harm. Whether placing a child in any given public school was to run this risk and incur the penalty, Rome never got around to ruling.

But what was meant by a "Catholic" school? Two bishops argued that it was one "which is subject to the authority of the bishop and to ecclesiastical inspection through the bishop." The Archbishop of Philadelphia affirmed that it was a Catholic school if, in addition to profane letters, Christian doctrine is also "taught by professing and practicing Catholics." Corrigan of New York gave the Roman understanding of the Catholic school as one wherein Christian doctrine was taught. It was Bishop Chatard's definition which came to be adopted, namely, that a Catholic school is one which the bishop has judged to be such.[59]

Whatever misgivings might have been in the minds of those bishops who remained unconvinced that their people could support the burden of what actually amounted to a second public school system for Catholic children or who felt that some kind of compromise with the state schools could have been entered into, the Third Council of Baltimore voted out four decrees in Title VI.

199. After full consideration of these matters, we conclude and decree:

I. That near every church a parish school, where one does not yet exist, is to be built and maintained *in perpetuum* within two years of the promulgation of this council, unless the bishop should decide that because of serious difficulties a delay may be granted.

II. A priest who within this time prevents the building or maintenance of a school through his serious neglect, or after repeated warnings by the bishop does not discharge his responsibility, deserves to be removed from the church.

III. The mission or parish which neglects to aid the priest in erecting or maintaining the school, that on account of this supine negligence, the school cannot exist, is to be reprimanded by the bishop and induced by more effective and prudent means to bring forth the necessary support.

IV. That all Catholic parents are bound to send their children to the parish school, unless it is evident that a sufficient training in religion is given either in their own homes, or in other Catholic schools; or when because of a sufficient reason, approved by the bishop, with all due precautions and safeguards, it is licit to send them to other schools. What constitutes a Catholic school is left to the decision of the bishop.[60]

EFFECTS OF THE COUNCIL

The decrees of Third Baltimore on the parochial school were never translated from their "glacial Latin text," but their thrust was carried in the long pastoral emanating from the council.[61] In the joint letter, Protestantism is no longer identified as the immediate foe. "In the great coming combat between truth and error, between Faith and Agnosticism, an important part of the fray must be borne by the laity, and woe to them if they are not well prepared." The moral and religious well-being of the people should be promoted to achieve a true civilization. "Take away religion from a people, and morality would soon follow." Without naming him or his book, Darwin and the *Origin of Species,* published twenty-five years earlier, are pointed to: "Civilization without religion would be a civilization of 'the struggle for existence, and the survival of the fittest,' in which cunning and strength would become the substitutes for principle, virtue, conscience, and duty." Education, therefore, must foster religion in order to foster civilization.

A key assumption behind this traditional position of the bishops is that religious knowledge and religious formation can take place *only* in the school—an assumption which by 1884 was being more and more abandoned by the Protestant churches.[62]

The pastoral confronts the point head on:

To shut religion out of the school, and keep it for home and the Church, is, logically, to train up a generation that will consider religion good for home and the Church, but not for the practical business of real life. But a more false and pernicious notion could not be imagined.[63]

Since the school is the principal tool fitting one for practical life, it "ought to be preeminently under the holy influence of religion." The bishops then warn that the avowed enemies of Christianity in some European countries are "banishing religion from the schools, in order gradually to eliminate it from among the people."

In the practical order, then, the Fathers of the council have two objects in view, "to multiply our schools, and to perfect them. We must multiply them till every Catholic child in the land shall have within its reach the means of education." Still the quality of Catholic education must be kept in mind. "We repudiate," they stated, "the idea that the Catholic school need be in any respect inferior to any other school whatsoever." There is a wistfulness clinging to these final words of exhortation:

> And if hitherto, in some places, our people have acted on the principle that it is better to have an imperfect Catholic school than to have none, let them now push their praiseworthy ambition still further, and not relax their efforts till their schools be elevated to the highest educational excellence.[64]

What happened after the council? What impact did the decrees have? Did the Baltimore legislation speed up the building of Catholic schools? This is the one thing we are certain did not happen. However, it should be kept in mind that the drive to establish separate schools had been well under way since the *Instruction* of 1875. The bishops who had pushed vigorously for schools continued to do so, and those who were unconvinced of the need did little more than they had been doing. It can be conjectured that most bishops, while agreeing with the ideal, threw their hands up at the sheer impossibility of the task. To put pressure on their impoverished flocks to multiply schools and to maintain them on a par with the free public schools called for great faith. That so many bishops and pastors did and that their people responded is evidence of the special loyalty the American Church has always had toward the Holy See. Many bishops still hoped for some kind of compromise, and even the "Germanizing" bishops promoted arrangements similar to the Faribault-Stillwater Plan.[65]

A study of the school statistics published each year in the *Catholic Directory* makes it plain that the immediate impact of the legislation was generally imperceptible.[66] Certainly, there was no dramatic increase by the end of the two-year period stipulated in the decree within which every parish was to put up a school. In 1884 there were 6,626 churches and 2,464 parochial schools enrolling 490,531 pupils. The corresponding figures for 1886 show 6,910 churches with 2,697 schools and 537,725 pupils. Some 233 new schools apparently were built and the percentage of churches with schools rose from 37 to 39. At the end of the two-year interval, 4,213 parishes still had not a school. True, the school population grew by ten per cent, but these were years of peak immigration which makes that gain less significant. Total enrollment increased steadily, rising from 490,531 in 1884 to 903,980 in 1900. But again it must be kept in mind that the Catholic population between 1880 and 1900 rose from 6,259,000 to 12,041,000, so that it is doubtful if as high a proportion of Catholic youngsters were in parochial schools in 1900 as in 1884. A more significant figure is the percentage of parishes that had or did erect schools during this 16-year span. The 1884 figure was 37 per cent; it peaked in 1891 at 44 per cent, dropped in 1895 and 1896 to 35 per cent, and at the start of the new century was at 36 per cent. Interestingly enough, the figure for 1968 is 57 per cent. Again, one might expect dioceses with a large German immigrant population to have a higher percentage of parishes with schools than others. On the contrary, no clear pattern of superiority emerges from a comparison of Milwaukee, St. Louis, and Cincinnati with Boston, Philadelphia, and New York.[67]

The state of the economy strongly influenced the capability of the Catholic community to build and sustain schools, and the last twenty-five years of the century are marked by the sharpest zigs and zags in the nation's economic history. What has been styled "the longest period of economic contraction in American history" occurred between 1873 and 1878. There was widespread unemployment, particularly among railroad builders, from 1882 to 1883, and until 1885 the economy remained in poor shape. A banking panic in 1893 resulted in the worst depression experienced by the American people up to that time.[68]

The school that "within two years" was to be built near every church was a strictly elementary institution with at most six grades, which satisfied the needs and ambitions of the overwhelming majority of Americans of that era. But needs heightened and ambitions broadened, so that more and more Americans began to lengthen their formal education. Until the high school movement swept over the country, secondary education was understood as an "academy" for girls or a "college" for boys. In fact, almost any formal schooling beyond the basic rudiments took place in a "college." Before the Civil War high schools were few and far between. In 1840 one might count about fifty, nearly half of which were in Massachusetts. The Chicago High School opened in 1856. Among the farming and working classes children were expected to earn their keep at an early age, and the idea of collecting taxes for free high schools for everybody was resisted as a downright luxury as well as an outrageous invasion of family right. What hastened the multiplication of these schools was the 1872 decision of the Michigan State Supreme Court, upholding the right of the city of Kalamazoo to levy additional taxes for a high school.

Four years prior to Third Baltimore, in 1880, three per cent of the youngsters of high-school age were enrolled in high schools. This figure represents approximately 110,000 pupils in about 800 schools. By 1890, when for the first time the U.S. Bureau of Education gathered complete statistics, the comparable totals were 202,969 pupils in 2,526 institutions, a rise to five per cent of the potential enrollment.[69] Catholics were slow to join the movement toward the four-year high school. The 581 Catholic academies and 83 Catholic colleges of 1884 provided whatever there was in secondary schooling. The colleges especially looked to their preparatory division (always by far the larger) for recruits and hence regarded the high schools as rivals. In 1900 there existed 183 Catholic colleges, all with preparatory departments. The first to drop its high school department and become a strictly four-year collegiate institution was Holy Cross College, in Worcester, Mass., and the year was 1914. These schools, conducted by religious orders and congregations, were financed through school fees and benefactions. As the high school movement spread, provision for Catholic high schools was more and more wanting. Again money was the problem. A continually higher proportion of Catholic youngsters were to be found in state-supported high schools —a situation hardly forseen by the conciliar fathers of Baltimore and a new problem.

COMPROMISE EFFORTS

At the 1889 convention of the National Educational Association in Nashville, Cardinal James Gibbons of Baltimore and Bishop John J. Keane, first rector of the newly opened Catholic University of America, gave addresses entitled "Should Americans Educate Their Children In Denominational Schools?" A paper by Edwin Mead of Boston, "Has the Parochial School Proper Place in America?" and a fourth, "Public and Parochial Schools," by John Jay of New York, represented a sharply divergent point of view. None the less, the two Catholic speakers judged the conference beneficial; a large and influential body of educators had heard a well argued presentation of the Catholic position, and certain valid questions had been raised relating to the place of the parochial school in the American context.

The next year Archbishop Ireland was invited to address the same national group when it met in his see city of St. Paul. A distinguished and forceful orator, John Ireland made a deep impression on his auditors with his call for a compromise approach, which would provide religious instruction for Catholic children while making parish schools a part of the public system. This pattern was already operative in two towns within Ireland's jurisdiction, Stillwater and Faribault. However, his address ignited a controversy among Catholic leaders that "was without parallel in American Catholic history, in point of extent, intensity, and bitterness of feeling."[70]

What did Ireland say that so infuriated some of his brother bishops and began a sharp escalation of the strife between progressive and conservative which would finally evoke strong papal intervention twice during the decade? He began his address to a strongly predominant Protestant audience by stating:

> I am a friend and an advocate of the state school. In the circumstances of the present time I uphold the parish school. I sincerely wish that the need for it did not exist. I would have all schools for the children of the people to be state schools.[71]

He dismissed as contemptuous the accusation that Catholics were bent on destroying the state school. He painstakingly set forth the grounds of Catholic opposition to the state schools and what steps could be taken to remove this opposition. The right of the state school to exist he considered a matter beyond the stage of discussion. In fact, he urged its necessity. Though parents have the primary right and function in education, "as things are, tens of thousands of children will not be instructed if parents solely remain in charge of the duty. . . . The State must come forward as an agent of instruction; else ignorance will prevail." Moreover, to achieve universal education the schools must be *free*.

> Free schools! Blest indeed is the nation whose vales and hillsides they adorn, and blest the generations upon whose souls

are poured their treasures! No tax is more legitimate than that which is levied in order to dispel mental darkness, and build up within the nation's bosom intelligent manhood and womanhood.

The Republic of the United States has solemnly affirmed its resolve that within its borders no clouds of ignorance shall settle upon the minds of the children of its people. In furnishing the means to accomplish this result its generosity knows no limit. The free school of America! Withered be the hand raised in sign of its destruction![72]

Can I be suspected of enmity to the state school [the prelate continued], because I would fain widen the expanse of its wings until all the children of the people find shelter beneath their cover?"

I turn to the denominational or parish school. It exists. I again express my regret that there is a necessity for its existence. In behalf of the state school I call upon my fellow-Americans to aid in the removal of this necessity.[73]

But the state school itself is laboring under a serious defect. As presently organized, this school tends to eliminate religion from the minds and hearts of the youth of the country. The state school is non-religious. In the absence of positive religion, the impressionable mind of the child comes to regard religion as irrelevant to his life because it is completely outside his school life. The father's long work day and the mother's unceasing round of household chores prevent parents from imparting religious instruction. An hour of Sunday instruction does not attract the child. Then Ireland enunciated his pivotal thesis:

Accidentally, it may be, and unintentionally, but, in fact, most certainly, the state school crowds out the Church. The teaching of religion is not a function of the State; but the State should, for the sake of its people, and for its own sake, permit and facilitate the teaching of religion by the Church. This the State does not do; rather, it hinders and prevents the work of the Church. The children of the masses are learning no religion.[74]

He offered the traditional rebuttal to counter the argument that the state school's function is simply to teach morals: "From the principles of religion morals derive power and vitality. Separated from a belief in God, and in the existence of the soul beyond the present life, morals are vague and weak commands which passion is not slow to scorn."[75] Nor was he willing to leave the schools to the secularists and unbelievers. He conceded their rights and had no desire to impose Christianity upon them. In turn, however, let them not impose the religion of secularism upon him and the American school. Nor is a common-denominator type of Christianity the answer. There is large dissatisfaction with the public school because it excludes religion, and the dissatisfaction will remain until the cause is removed. Ten million American Catholics cannot in conscience patronize the schools paid for by their taxes. This injustice is the more serious because "the ten millions are largely the poorer classes of the population, and they are sincerely and loyally desiring to obtain the benefits of the state school, if only the obstacles be removed."[76]

The archbishop then briefly sketched the compromise plan followed in Faribault and Stillwater and began his peroration. He protested against the charge that Catholics were the enemies of the nation's schools.

> Not one stone of the wondrous edifice which Americans have reared in their devotion to education would Catholics remove or permit to be removed. They would fain add to its splendor and majesty by putting side by side religious and secular instruction, neither of them interfering with the other, each of them borrowing from the other aid and dignity.[77]

He concluded with the proposal that in urging the Christian state school, Catholics were proving themselves the truest friends of the school and the State.

In a later letter to his good friend Gibbons defending his position on the public schools, Ireland repeated his contention that no absolute necessity for the parish school existed. They did not exist in Ireland and England, and they only came into existence in Belgium and France after "infidel governments had made the state school infidel."

> The necessity for parish schools is hypothetical—the necessity being not a direct result of the Church's mission, but a provision in certain cases for the protection of the faith. The Church is not established to teach writing and ciphering, but to teach morals and faith, and she teaches writing and ciphering only when otherwise morals and faith could not be taught.[78]

In 1890 there was widespread sympathy and support for this position among the American Catholic leadership. Despite the decrees of Baltimore, many bishops hoped for some sort of compromise. Nor was this attitude dictated only by economics, as much as this was a critical factor. "The burden upon our Catholics"—and Ireland's words could have been spoken by most of the hierarchy—"to maintain parish schools up to the required standard for all the children of the Church is almost unbearable." The true solution would be "to make the state school satisfactory to Catholic consciences, and to use it."

Leaders like Ireland and Gibbons were keenly aware of the value of these schools in assimiliating immigrant children and children of immigrants. They fully appreciated the need for compromise. Ideally, there should be parish schools, even though immigrant workers and farmers could not really support them. What concerned Ireland as a firm believer in the American philosophy was that these immigrant children needed the public school, as part of the process of becoming citizens of the great New World republic. Ireland's school stand drew to him the sharpest arrows of the opposition. Moreover, he had aroused bitter feelings among the defenders of *Deutschtum* because of his opposition to their foreign language schools and national parishes. During the fight in 1889 over the Bennett Law which would have required all schools in Wisconsin to conduct certain classes in English, he gave no support to the bishops of the Milwaukee Province who regarded the law as trespassing on Church and family right. Earlier along with Keane he used his considerable influence to have the Abbelen petition rejected.[79] This was a measure to have the national parishes established with full parochial rights. Ireland also used his weight in the defeat of the Lucerne *Memorials* which would have the pope appoint German bishops for America to care for German-speaking immigrants.[80]

The "American" bishops feared the results of parochial schools which tended to preserve European customs and foreign languages at the expense of American ways and the English language. They were also aware of the affection most Americans felt toward the public school and the resentment non-Catholics felt toward what seemed to be an official Catholic attitude of hostility, criticism, and boycott. In an 1890 letter to Leo XIII, Gibbons explained to the pope that the divisions between Catholics and their fellow citizens "are caused above all by the opposition against the system of national education which is attributed to us and which, more than any other thing, creates and maintains in the minds of the American people the conviction that the Catholic Church is opposed by principle to the institutions of the country and that a sincere Catholic cannot be a loyal citizen of the United States."[81]

For his part, Ireland deplored the harsh criticism of the public schools by some bishops. In fact, in those places the parish schools have done "more harm than good." He scoffed at the notion that the public schools were "hotbeds of vice" or that they taught unbelief or Protestantism. "Our public schools are better than those of France and Italy," he wrote, "and in those countries we hear no continuous anathemas."

Not every advocate of the secular nature of the school was an agnostic or unbeliever, although Catholic defenders of parochial education often lumped them together. A towering figure in the educational world was William Torrey Harris, superintendent of schools in St. Louis between 1868 and 1881, and U.S. Commissioner of Education from 1889 to 1906. He and like-minded thinkers were making acceptable the idea that, in the nature of things, the school was secular and incompetent to enter the area of religious education. No hostility toward religion or religious values was behind this philosophy, nor was there question of challenging the importance of religion in life. It rather concerned the most apt occasion for efficient instruction in religion and with safeguarding the rights of conscience in a pluralistic society. This last point, in turn, was an axiom deriving from the constitutional separation of Church and State.[82]

Harris' great friend, Bishop John Lancaster Spalding of Peoria, shared much of this thinking. "I am willing to assume and to accept as a fact," he said, "that our theological differences make it impossible to introduce the teaching of any religious creed into the public school. . . ."[83]

Cardinal Gibbons also tried to convince Rome that the absence of religious education in American public schools was not due to opposition of the continental variety. "The public spirit in this country," he said, "is fundamentally religious and there is everywhere a great respect for liberty of conscience well understood and in the legitimate sense of the word." However, the religious question had been set aside in the schools, he went on, in order not to offend the sentiments of the children and their parents; and the care of providing the religious education of the children was left to the Church and the Protestant sects.[84]

Evidently these representations did make an impression, if not permanent, at least for a few years. Pressed for a decision on the propriety of cooperating with the public school system along the lines of the Faribault-Stillwater arrangement, Rome returned a sphynx-like answer: "The sound decrees of the Baltimore Council as to parochial schools remaining fully in force, the agreement made by the Most Rev. Dr. John Ireland with regard to the Faribault and Stillwater schools, all the circumstances being taken into consideration, can be allowed." Instead of settling the issue, both sides at once interpreted the document in their own favor and claimed victory. Archbishop Corrigan announced in New York that the Faribault system had been condemned and that only the special exception was tolerated. To newspapermen Ireland said that his experiment had been completely vindicated and thought it could be adopted in those communities where similar circumstances prevailed.

Everything revolved around the meaning of the Latin phrase, *"tolerari potest."* Did the words mean toleration, permission, or approval? The "church-schools-at-any-price" group could be excused for their perplexity. How in the name of logic could the decrees of Title Six remain "fully in force" if Rome gave approbation to a compromise approach? For months the highly partisan press filled the sky with journalistic flak. The attacks took on an ugly note. Even high-ranking prelates took out after one another in print. Alarmed at this disedifying show, Pope Leo XIII sent a personal legate, Archbishop Francesco Satolli, to the yearly meeting of the archbishops with a set of fourteen propositions to clarify once and for all the school question. He was also instructed to try to ease the German-Irish antagonism which was in large part the source of the clash over the schools.

To the consternation and anger of the conservatives, the proposals seemed to allow greater cooperation with the state schools, all the while purporting to be upholding the legislation of Baltimore. The sixth proposition repeated the perennial truth that the Church holds for herself the right of teaching the truths of faith and the law of morals in order to bring up youth in the habits of a Christian life, but then adds, "Hence, absolutely and universally speaking, there is no repugnance in their learning the first elements and the higher branches of arts and the natural sciences in public schools, controlled by the State. . . ."[85] This was scarcely the tone of the *Instruction* of 1875, and what followed in the eighth proposition was not calculated to add to the repose of James McMaster who had been buried in 1886.

The separate Catholic schools in America were a necessity, said the document, because the public schools of 1892 were generally "a proximate danger to faith and morals" for three reasons: 1. They totally excluded religious teaching; 2. They used teachers selected indiscriminately from every sect; 3. They educated boys and girls together. But the proposition made haste to add—and this is where the conservatives felt they had been betrayed—that when these specific dangers to faith and morals disappear, "Then it is lawful for Catholic parents to send their children to these schools, to acquire the elements of letters and arts, provided the parents themselves do not neglect their most serious duty, and the pastors of souls put every effort to instruct the children and train them in all that pertains to Catholic worship and life." In other words, if pastors and parents did their job in giving religious education and formation, the state school could care for the secular side of things.

Bishop McCloskey of Louisville wrote Corrigan that the Satolli propositions would be "the death blow, to a certain extent, of our Catholic schools." McQuaid was even more aroused. He likewise wrote the New York archbishop:

> We are all in a nice pickle, thanks to Leo XIII and his delegate. Just as our arduous work of the last forty years was beginning to bear ample fruit, they arbitrarily upset the whole. If an enemy had done this! It is only a question of time, when present Roman legislation having wrought incalculable mischief, that we, school-children of the hierarchy, will again receive a lesson in our catechism from another Italian sent out to enlighten us.[86]

His letter to the pope, however, in which he took issue with nine of the propositions, was couched in more discreet language. Whether one agreed with him or not, McQuaid was a dedicated veteran of some forty-five years in the priesthood, twenty-five of them as a bishop, and he had a deep concern for the welfare of the people. His letter eloquently expressed the fears of many American bishops, and, as a matter of record, his thought within a matter of years replaced the conciliatory approach of the progressives on the school question. He wrote:

> What we have most to dread is not the direct teaching of the state schools, it is the indirect teaching which is the most insidious and the most dangerous. It is the moral atmosphere, the tone of thought permeating these schools that give cause for alarm. It is the indifferentism with regard to all religious beliefs we most of all fear. This is the dominant heresy that, imbibed in youth, can scarcely ever be eradicated.[87]

Simply look around our large towns and cities, he went on, to see how indifferentism has decimated the Protestant churches and be assured that it will do the same in our own. "Indifferentism with regard to all religions ends in infidelity."

However, for a few more years the progressive camp remained triumphant. The niceties of Vatican diplomacy did not bring the conflicting sides any closer, but the visit of Satolli did mute the public discussion. One historian of the period finds great significance in the decision from Rome.

> Instead of being forced to choose between an American culture bent on giving youth the finest possible secular education, and a Church which insisted that an inadequate parochial school, or no school at all, was better than a nonsectarian one, Catholics were freed to accept profitable compromises with the state schools, even while they worked to develop, under either state or Church auspices, a perfect Catholic educational system.[88]

In one way the school issue was simply an aspect of the larger Church-State problem, and much of the hostility between progressive and conservative stemmed from European and American attitudes toward society and its institutions. On the Continent the glorification of free enterprise, individual liberty, equal rights, and freedom of expression were, in the minds of most churchmen, associated with revolutionary-inspired attacks on the established order including the Roman Catholic Church. The loss of the Papal States and the flight from Rome of Pius IX during the *Risorgimento* quickly curdled any tendencies toward *liberalismo*. It was expecting too much, perhaps, for him and his successors to see beyond the troubles of Europe to the American scene and envision a situation much different politically and socially.

The confused quarrels among Catholics throughout the final decade of the nineteenth century, which culminated in Leo XIII's letter *Testem Benevolentiae,* condemned what was loosely called "Americanism." Despite the interpretation put upon it by some of the "German" bishops, the condemnation was not of American forms or social institutions, but was rather a repudiation of several theological doctrines.[89] However, by indirection the American political philosophy of separation of Church and State, the religious freedom guaranteed by the First Amendment, and the secularized state school all came under an official cloud. The Modernist troubles on the Continent called forth another condemnatory letter in 1907, *Pascendi Dominici Gregis,* from the new Pope Pius X. Here the faithful were explicitly warned that they "should approach any cooperation with the non-Catholic world with great caution." The climate of collaboration between Catholic and state schools chilled rapidly.

Conservative leaders had for long argued that somehow there was a basic incompatibility between full American citizenship and total adherence to the Catholic faith. Their hand was strengthened in the 1880's when the forces of nativism again banded together to form the American Protective Association. It was succeeded by the largest and most influential of these movements, the Ku Klux Klan. Founded in Georgia in 1915, the Klan enlisted millions of members in its campaign of vilification against Catholics, Jews, and the foreign-born. The 1928 presidential campaign of Governor Alfred E. Smith made it sadly plain that the virus of nativism could still burn at fever heat in the American body politic. It required another thirty-two years to show the world that loyalty to Catholicism is not an impediment to the fullest honor of citizenship—election to the presidency of the United States.

THE NEW CENTURY

As the new century opened, there was an enrollment in the Catholic schools of some 854,523 pupils, representing 5.2 per cent of the total sub-collegiate school population.[90] Fifty years later, it had reached 3,080,166 or 10.9 per cent of the total. In 1960 the figure was 5,622,366 and the percentage 13.4. The 1967-68 numbers are: 5,254,766 and 10.7 per cent. The explanation of this phenomenon is certainly in large part an economic one. As the American Catholic community became more affluent, it was able to respond to the exhortations of bishop and pastor to provide Catholic education for the young. The promulgation in 1918 of the *Code of Canon Law* provided the disciplinary motivation. For the most part the canons on education merely echo the assumptions and principles—in places in the actual wording—of the *Instruction* of 1875 and the decrees of the Third Plenary Council of Baltimore. The pivotal canon which laid down the Church's official attitude toward the state schools reads as follows:

> *Canon 1374.* Catholic children may not attend non-Catholic, neutral, or mixed schools, that is, those which are open also to non-Catholics. It is for the local bishop to decide, in accordance with the instructions of the Holy See, under what circumstances and with what precautions against the dangers of perversion, attendance at such schools may be allowed.[91]

Over and above the Canon Law of the universal Church, a large number of individual dioceses require, either through diocesan statute or episcopal order, attendance at a Catholic school. The last survey taken showed 55 dioceses in this category, but another nine had some restrictions or regulations governing attendance of Catholic children at public schools. Formal permission for this was needed in 38 dioceses. At that time, 1958, failure to send children to the Catholic school could result in the denial of absolution to negligent parents, but instances of enforcement of this penalty seemed to be so rare that they provided front page newspaper copy. Because even then almost no diocese had sufficient educational facilities to cope with the demand for Catholic schooling, these regulations were rarely enforced. The situation in recent years has been even more impossible.

Granted that the improved economic situation of Catholics generally and their loyalty to Church law played a considerable role in the great expansion of Catholic schools, desire for the schools remained the leading factor. As long as parents were confident that the neighborhood parochial school was the equal of the public school (and frequently the Catholic school was superior), they remained even anxious to patronize them. The choice between a Catholic and public high school was more difficult. On this level often the parish or diocesan institution suffered markedly in the comparison, especially in the new suburban areas. On the assumption that discipline was stricter in a Catholic high school, fathers and mothers thought it a safer place for daughters. Again parents often preferred the public high school if the plant facilities were decidedly superior or if the athletic program was more highly developed or if there were strong departments in music or art. Few dioceses have made adequate provision for the physically handicapped or mentally retarded pupil, so that the bulk of these youngsters always have gone to the public schools.

Many observers of the current scene feel that the enrollment in the Catholic elementary and secondary schools has peaked and will stay on a plateau for the foreseeable future. Certainly one no longer hears talk of "every Catholic child in a Catholic school." As a matter of record, the proportion of the nation's Catholic children that could be accommodated in these schools has not varied greatly over a 40-year period. About one half of the elementary school age group and about one third of the secondary school age group have attended Catholic schools, which conversely means that historically the majority of American Catholic youngsters have always been in the state schools.

Why has Catholic enrollment leveled off and actually de-

clined in some dioceses? The immediate answer is the improvement of the public school to the point where, in many
areas, the Catholic community is unable or unwilling to finance
competitive facilities. While they might be exhorted to do so
and probably have the financial resources if the burden were
spread evenly across the dioceses, many Catholics doubt the
necessity or advisability of a kindergarten to twelfth grade
Catholic education for their children. Everywhere there is increased awareness that religious education and spiritual formation for youngsters is the primary task, and that this must
include those in public as well as in parochial schools. The
post-Vatican II spirit has made a number of clergy and laity
aware of the need for a greater openness toward the non-
Catholic world and of their own responsibility for all the
nation's schools.

Despite the many unresolved problems that the future
holds, it is predictable that the new Catholic approach to the
state school will be more akin to the progressive attitude of the
1890's. This writer's opinion is that by the 1990's both the
present public school system and the Catholic system will be
replaced by one comprehensive public school system within
which the educational objectives of the Church can also be
realized. There will always be Catholic education, but there
will certainly be less Catholic *schooling*.

WILLIAM V. O'BRIEN

7: *American Catholic Higher Education and the Challenges of the Right to Know*

We are concerned here with the possible contribution of American Catholic universities to the achievement of the goals set forth in the articles relative to education contained in the International Declaration of Human Rights. It will be the contention of this study that American Catholic universities are in a position to make a very great, perhaps critical, contribution to the pursuit of these goals. But, it will be further argued, such a contribution is unlikely unless American Catholic educators firmly and realistically reassess their resources, their goals and their priorities.

In pursuing these lines of thought the following subjects will be explored:

1) The historical evolution of American Catholic higher education and its present status;

2) The decisions which American Catholic higher education must make now in order to adjust to the requirements of a global educational mission;

3) A projection of the main themes that might guide American Catholic universities in their efforts to make meaningful contributions to the quest for realization of the human right of education.

THE HISTORICAL EVOLUTION AND PRESENT STATUS OF CATHOLIC HIGHER EDUCATION IN THE UNITED STATES

It is commonplace to remark that American Catholic education at all levels, including that of the university, is undergoing an "identity crisis." Much of the debate about this crisis tends to be defeatist. It tends to conclude that American Catholic higher education has no real *raison d'être*, or that, given its present and predictable characteristics and limitations, it has no adequate and plausible goals it should continue to seek at great human and material expense and sacrifice. Alternatively, it is urged that American Catholic institutions of higher learning should be greatly reduced in number and that their areas of activity and responsibility should be drastically curtailed, partly by transfer to secular institutions, partly by transfer to other Catholic institutions.[1]

The present study does not seek to urge any particular blueprint for the future of American Catholic education generally or for Catholic higher education in particular. Rather, it seeks to identify the tasks that ought to be undertaken by higher institutions—of whatever kind—within the American Catholic education system. The sum total of these tasks relates to the achievement of the human right of "everyone" to education.

Catholic universities have the beginnings of a capacity to contribute to the achievement of a universal human right to education. But they are hampered by their historical evolution, viewpoints, and characteristics.

American Catholic universities, colleges, and seminaries developed during a historical period that witnessed the creation of a large, powerful system of Catholic higher education. But it was excessively limited in objectives and capabilities. The historical influences productive of this system are easily recalled. The American Catholic Church was overwhelmingly an immigrant church of hyphenated, often second- and third-class Americans. It survived and prospered against the grain of most of the prevailing forces of the American society.

American Catholic universities and colleges were conceived and developed as strongholds of the Catholic faith and its traditional teaching in an essentially alien society. The Catholic college was the place to which the good Catholic sent his children to protect them from the "dangerous" teachings prevalent in elite educational circles in Europe and the United States in the nineteenth and early twentieth centuries. More positively, the American Catholic institution of higher learning was valued as the guardian of the scholastic tradition; its substantive knowledge, its approach to life, and its concepts and techniques of education.[2]

As the twentieth century advanced, the Catholic university took on an increasingly important additional role, that of defender of Christianity and the West against godless communism and its insidious variants. It was rumored that dangerous influences from this source could be discerned within American society and higher education. The need to combat these influences was added to the mandate of the Catholic college and university to counter-balance or refute the older doctrines of aggressive Protestantism and atheistic or agnostic "scientism," the latter being increasingly a source of concern because of its supposed strangle-hold on the empirical social sciences. In short, there was so very much to combat and refute, so much to set right, that there was a grave temptation for the Catholic university or college to become excessively preoccupied with apologetics and ideological polemics. Lamentably, the image thereby created lingers on, to the detriment of American Catholic higher education and both the national and international societies it should be serving.

On the other hand, this defensive, self-righteous, literally ghetto, cast of American Catholic higher education was not altogether preferred by Catholics or without justification. For the American educational system as for the American society in general, Catholics and Catholic education were generally considered to be separate and far from equal. Few cared what Catholics learned or thought, except in circumstances wherein their beliefs proved to be politically or socially embarrassing, e.g., in such areas as laws and public policies concerning divorce, birth control, and censorship. That Catholic narrowness and inflexibility contributed in turn to this phenomenon is well-known. Mutual lack of respect and distrust between Catholic Americans and their compatriots abounded.

A convenient historical check-point for the situation at this time is the tawdry story of the defeat of Alfred E. Smith in the presidential election of 1928. Unfortunately, Smith seemed to confirm American Catholic educational and cultural stereotypes. In the background, evidence suggested that the only realm in which American Catholics should be taken seriously was that of politics. Not without good reason, there was deep-rooted suspicion about the morals and methods of American Catholic politicians. Moreover, the nightmarish visions of Vatican machinations and the revival in the New World of the Inquisition were taken far more seriously, or so it would appear, than any progress that American Catholic education, circa 1928, had made toward improving the usefulness of American Catholics to the nation.

Two developments began to change the situation somewhat. Interestingly enough, the first real impact of Catholic thought on the United States probably came without the knowing support of most of the country's Catholic colleges and universities and may well have been opposed by many of the leading figures in Catholic higher education at that time. This was the application of the social teaching of the popes and bishops, starting with Leo XIII, on economic and social questions. To resort to sociological jargon, a kind of "sub-culture" of American Catholic intellectuals, educators, and social activists emerged: men such as Msgr. John A. Ryan, Fr. Raymond A. McGowan, Fr. John LaFarge, S.J., and more recently, Fr. John F. Cronin, and Msgr. George G. Higgins. These individuals brought alive the social teaching of the Church on national issues through books, pamphlets, articles, syndicated columns, and personal activity; thus arousing the attention of influential figures in government, the judiciary, labor and management, politics, and journalism.

However, the relationship between this application of Catholic thought to the American scene and the goals, interests, sympathies, and policies of American Catholic universities seems to have been tenuous at best and strained at worst. But at least some of the promise of the revival in modern, relevant social theory as developed from the time of Leo XIII was beginning to be realized in a practical way in the United States. The first step had been taken to overcome the presumptions of irrelevance of Catholic thought to American life.

The second evidence of interest in Catholic thought in the United States took an almost opposite form, despite the intentions and hopes of its prophets and those Americans who welcomed their message. The revival of interest in traditional scholastic philosophy and political thought which resulted from the writings of European Catholics who lived in or visited the United States—Jacques Maritain, Étiene Gilson, Yves Simon, Heinrich Rommen—provided the first genuine breakthrough by Catholic thought into the inner sanctums of American intellectual and educational life. It became intellectually fashionable to welcome and discourse with these authoritative interpreters of the great classical and scholastic traditions of philosophy and political thought.

But these developments seem to have been destined to remain rather limited, academic, and theoretical. Despite the explicit efforts of such scholars as Maritain[3] to relate the great traditional principles to modern affairs and the enthusiastic attempts of such influential American educators as Robert Hutchins to support these efforts (e.g., in the realm of international law and organization), this renaissance of interest in modern scholastic-natural law thought seems to have had little discernible impact on intellectual, educational, and governing elites in the United States. It was as though American academic, intellectual, and political circles considered it sufficient to endorse an authoritative up-dating and clarification of several oft-maligned chapters in the history of Western intellectual and political development, without ascribing practical significance in the realm of educational and public affairs to the practical insights of these great Catholic scholars.

At this point it is important to acknowledge another reason for the limited impact of the neo-scholastic renaissance on American life. The Catholic universities themselves failed to grasp the opportunity to develop their own American school of Catholic political and social thought. It is significant that one associates serious interest in the relevance of this renaissance to contemporary problems with the University of Chicago. Today, as the great figures of the neo-scholastic revival are dying, one looks in vain for American replacements. With the exception of the work of problem-oriented scholars, such as Fr. Cronin and Msgr. Higgins and the late Fr. John Courtney Murray, S.J., who, for a variety of reasons, never became a central figure at an American Catholic university, one is hard pressed to mention American Catholic academicians who have produced through research, writing, and action responses to the challenge of the neo-scholastic revival to apply traditions of Catholic thought to modern problems.

Yet at precisely the time when this challenge was laid down, in the 1930s, '40s, and '50s, American Catholic higher education was growing in all directions, except in the direction of encouraging potential American Maritains. What, then, distinguished Catholic universities and colleges from their secular counterparts? It seems fair to say that these institutions, until quite recently, relied on their administration and image for their Catholic character and otherwise reproduced their secular counterparts with varying degrees of success.

Three characteristics became widespread if not universal in Catholic universities:

1) They established reasonably good professional schools,

particularly in law and medicine, which, however, had virtually no distinctive Catholic component to distinguish them from other professional schools.

2) They improved their programs in the arts and sciences on the undergraduate level and, in effect, instituted for the first time comparatively serious graduate studies in the arts and sciences. Here again, these achievements, valuable in themselves, remained almost entirely unrelated to the Catholic character of the institutions.

3) They continued to operate on the theory that the Catholic, or at least the normative, component of the education they offered could be insured by requiring all students to take theology and philosophy courses which were largely boiled-down versions of basic seminary courses. These courses were usually independent of other courses in the curriculum, and there was little if any emphasis on mutual relevance.

For many years the justifications advanced for Catholic universities were accepted at face value. Catholic medical and law schools were considered essential because of the many issues of individual and public morality which medical and legal studies raise. Additionally, of course, there was a historic tradition of religious administration of hospitals which led to a natural involvement in the establishment of medical schools. Some of the issues of private and public morality, deemed to be most important by the American Catholic Church, called for expertise in and intimate contact with the fields of medicine and law. There existed and there remains a real need for Catholic involvement in these professions.

Increasingly, the professional character of these institutions pushed aside the normative influences. A medical or law school is judged primarily on the percentage of its graduates who pass professional qualifying examinations' and who succeed in practice. Insistence on a course or two in medical ethics or, in the case of law schools, legal ethics and jurisprudence, wherein natural-law approaches are applauded and modern relativism denounced, seems to have meant very little

in terms of the overall professional education of students at
Catholic medical and law schools. This problem is well-known
to contemporary administrators of such schools, and imaginative efforts have been made to remedy the perfunctory character of explicitly moral or ethical components of professional
education.

American society has been greatly enriched by the thousands of well-qualified doctors and lawyers who happen to
have gone to Catholic professional schools. It has not, however, been enriched by more than a handful of scholars, pub-
licists, or activists who have been able to bring a distinctive
Catholic view to intellectual and public debates over medical
and legal issues. To take the field of law, with which the author is familiar, it is well-known that good law faculties, such
as those at Harvard and Yale, aspire to train Supreme Court
justices and great legal scholars, as well as successful lawyers.
They undertake to inspire and train men who will literally
shape the future of American society. Such aspirations have
not sufficiently caught the imagination of American Catholic
law schools. To be sure, there are problems of power and
wealth involved, but if Catholic thought has anything of importance to contribute to such professions as law and medicine
it should be more conspicuously studied and developed in professional schools whose existence is supposedly based on the
assumption that Catholic thought *does* have something unique
to say in these fields. Obviously, similar remarks could be
made about other Catholic professional schools, such as those
specializing in business, journalism, or international service.

To turn to undergraduate and graduate schools of arts and
sciences, we may combine the second and third characteristics
of Catholic universities distinguished above—namely, improvement in the technical quality of the education and disposition of the need to include an explicitly Catholic or normative component in the curriculum by requiring isolated courses
in theology and philosophy.

The era of Alfred E. Smith was used above as a reference

point in the history of American Catholicism. In 1928 serious graduate studies in the arts and sciences on American Catholic campuses did not compare with those at secular universities, if they existed at all. By the time that John F. Kennedy was elected president, this situation had changed. It had been changing before World War II; and the post-war period, with its bonanza of GI Bill students, saw a major breakthrough in the number, size, and scope of American Catholic graduate schools of arts and sciences. At the same time, undergraduate enrollments increased, and many new Catholic colleges were established or existing ones drastically transformed.

Two things in particular resulted from these related trends. First, the proportion of religious to laymen in the faculties of American Catholic colleges and universities changed. Soon the religious in the classroom became the exception, even in disciplines such as philosophy. Second, long overdue reforms occurred in Catholic universities. Doctorates from respectable institutions were required; participation in professional and scholarly activities was first encouraged and then increasingly demanded. This was all to the good, since it increased the level of education within each discipline offered and got more professors from Catholic campuses out into the world. But there was a price for this progress, a price very similar to that paid for maintaining Catholic professional schools.

Secular American universities had already experienced with concern the phenomenon of "discipline orientation" as distinguished from orientation in terms of institutions or problem areas or both. The discipline-oriented scholar tends to downgrade the importance of the broader institution of which his department is a part and of missions or problems that are not central to his technical disciplinary competence and prestige. He wants to be known as a competent economist, sociologist, or historian; and it may matter little to him whether he pursues this goal at Boston College, Southern Methodist, The University of Nebraska, or Swarthmore. Salary, working conditions, teaching load, ability to work on the kinds of problems which will bring recognition and advancement within his discipline, above all, are the factors which affect his career and his loyalties. Additionally, discipline-oriented scholars have a natural propensity to increase the size and complexity of their own departments and of those which relate particularly to their areas of professional interest.

This natural tendency among competent devotees to an academic discipline can often be channeled into productive directions at a large, affluent university where ample room, resources, and students to make everyone happy exist. Even at such universities, however, discipline orientation has produced problems and identity crises. But the identity crises are much more obvious and difficult in institutions such as the American Catholic universities which, first, have limited resources and, second, are supposed by definition to be guided by some central vision or corpus of goals. If Harvard or Berkeley can afford to have whole departments concerned with their disciplines, in effect, for their own sake, it seems clear that American Catholic universities cannot indulge in such luxuries.

Yet anyone familiar with contemporary Catholic universities can give examples of almost exclusive discipline orientation on the part of individual professors as well as of entire departments. It is at this point that the failure to integrate the normative with the empirical elements in Catholic education in the United States becomes most relevant. The fact of the matter is that, notwithstanding the claims made in the first pages of catalogues, in graduation addresses, and appeals to the alumni for funds, contemporary Catholic higher education lacks well-defined goals, based on some core concepts and aspirations, which can be placed above the goals of the various disciplines and professional schools that make up a Catholic university. Just as there are no American Catholic Maritains, there are apparently no American Catholic Robert Hutchins', a point made bluntly and appropriately by Dr. Hutchins himself in an address at Georgetown University.[4]

Neither theology nor philosophy are central disciplines, defining the broad outlines of Catholic approaches to education generally or to various areas of study and concern. They remain tagged on to a collection of professional and discipline-oriented courses and programs which are hardly distinguishable from their counterparts at public or non-Catholic private universities. In these circumstances, it is not surprising that American Catholic professional schools and undergraduate and graduate school departments in liberal arts accentuate what is professionally important and ignore or downgrade what might be necessary to the accomplishment of the goals of a particular Catholic university, to the Catholic Church in the United States, or to the universal Church.[5]

Meanwhile, ironically, the most competent Catholic scholars, including the best of the religious, increasingly settle in prestigious secular universities, to be joined later by whole seminaries. This leaves the American Catholic university faculties short of Catholic professors, usually without first-rate scholars who happen to be Catholics, and cut off from the seminaries where the faculties concerned with Catholic concepts should provide the cornerstones of Catholic universities in the first place.

As American Catholic universities are increasingly taken over by lay boards and administrators, as well as by university senates, the last vestige of distinctive character, namely the physical presence of religious in key administrative positions, will be gone; and, if present trends continue, American Catholic universities may become no more religious in their goals and orientation than such originally religious institutions as Princeton and Yale. To the extent that this occurs, present trends toward greatly increased avoidance of Catholic universities by American Catholic students will logically continue. In an age where there is an endless supply of students, almost any institution of higher learning can continue to operate. But in terms of Catholic commitment, why bother? And why continue to pretend that there is a distinct character to Catholic universities? This, as remarked at the outset, is the state of affairs in American Catholic higher education today, and everyone concerned is asking, "Where do we go from here"?[6]

THE GLOBAL MISSION OF AMERICAN CATHOLIC HIGHER EDUCATION

If the foregoing analysis is substantially correct, a profound reevaluation of the goals and forms of American Catholic education is needed. To be sure, reevaluations are already in progress. But, ironically, they tend to be limited to the terms of reference which Catholic higher education in the United States has historically set for itself, terms which virtually all critics agree are inadequate today. American Catholic higher education has been treated both by its defenders and its critics as a mere extension of the parochial school system. Thus studies of American higher education tend to concentrate on the effectiveness of Catholic education in helping students to retain and strengthen their faith while, at the same time, acquiring the benefits of a liberal arts or professional education. The overwhelming emphasis has been on personal morality and personal religious practice. Little emphasis has been given to the moral responsibilities of Catholics as citizens of the United States and of the world. What small portion of the *social* teaching of the Church that has been communicated has amounted to little more than a modest reiteration (usually belated) of secular "liberal" opinion on such subjects as race, international organization, and foreign aid. Such views are generally labeled "Catholic" if attributed to papal or other Catholic sources. But the content has usually been indistinguishable from the conventional wisdom prevailing among secular liberal elites.[7]

It is the contention of this paper that the concern of fortifying personal faith and religious practices ought not to be the primary goals of American Catholic institutions of higher education. To the extent that these institutions are concerned with the religious training of their students, they should consider this supplementary, certainly not central, to the goal of Catholic higher education. Viewed in this perspective, concern for religious formation does not differ greatly from the concerns of the Newman Club, the Confraternity of Christian Doctrine, adult education, and other programs. They are important concerns, but American Catholic higher education today is faced with even more important challenges. These challenges create priorities which a Catholic university, properly conceived, can meet more effectively than it can meet the need to maintain by traditional methods the personal faith and morality of its students. Furthermore, it is contended that personal faith and morality on American Catholic campuses will be benefited if these challenges are met.

The key to the challenges facing American Catholic higher education arise from the two identifications—"American" and "Catholic." The United States exercises enormous global power and influence. This power and influence obviously should be applied to the quest for a better, more peaceful, more stable, and more just international community. American Catholic universities should have something to say about the standards and approaches governing a more enlightened American contribution to this cause. It should be expected that some originality, based on the perspectives of Catholic social teaching, would be manifested. Thus far, international studies at Catholic universities have tended to alternate between the poles of sterile anti-communism and slavish repetition of the clichés and fads of secular internationalism to which are added an occasional reference to an encyclical. With the growing technical competence of scholars at American Catholic universities it should be possible to relate the social teaching of the Church to the foreign policies of the United States and to evaluate, critically if necessary, this social teaching. If any of this teaching lacks technical validity, feasibility, or relevance, there should be no hesitation about criticizing or correcting it. In fact, this should be considered a duty. On the other hand, if current encyclicals and other authoritative Catholic teaching prove to be substantially respectable in purely technical terms, e.g., the economics of development or the evolution of modern international law and organization, then their goals and standards should be vigorously applied to critiques of U.S. policy. Thus, American Catholic scholars owe it to their nation and their Church to deal with the global issues which a country such as the United States must confront.

At the same time, the narrow focus of much of the current debate over American Catholic higher education tends to ignore the unparalleled prestige and influence which the Catholic Church presently enjoys throughout the world. Much of this is due to the active role of the recent popes, leading bishops, and moralists, whose personal activities and initiatives have stirred the hopes of millions of people, many of whom are not even Christians. Where do these Catholic leaders get their ideas? Who helps them with their homework? Whose works are quoted and cited in their pronouncements?

After over twenty-five years of U. S. aid programs and enormous American experience in the fields of political, economic, and social development, Pope Paul VI issued his encyclical of March 26, 1967, *On the Development of Peoples*. A number of books, pastoral letters, and conference documents are cited in the encyclical—not a single one is by an American Catholic author. This is astounding! Is it because American Catholic higher education has not been doing the job it should in this field of such preeminent importance to the United States, the Church, and the world? Or is there, somewhere, a body of literature and a corps of experts coming from or encouraged by American Catholic universities which is somehow unknown to or lightly regarded by the Vatican? I would not undertake a judgment about either question here, but it would seem that such questions belong at the heart of the reevaluation of the goals, resources, and priorities of American Catholic higher education.

Thus we must ask, above all, what can American Catholic education do for the People of God in the United States and throughout the world? What can it do for all men who have a right to education, as well as a number of other rights, according to the Universal Declaration of Human Rights and the modern social teaching of the Church? If we take this perspective a number of current controversies about American Catholic universities diminish in importance. Suppose, for example, that American Catholic universities were imbued with a spirit of service on behalf of a universal Church, working from the base of the most affluent and powerful nation in the world. If this were the case, many of the issues currently debated would become secondary, if not trivial. The focus of the leaders of universities so highly motivated would be on issues and goals of such magnitude that mediocre, across-the-board imitation of other American universities, and the instilling of "Catholicism" through compulsory theology and philosophy courses would no longer seem important. Catholic theology and philosophy would live *in* and *through* the dedicated attention given to carefully selected areas of human concern which might range from America's problems in its cities and impoverished rural areas to its global responsibilities, including the obligation to assist in development. Surely the right to education is central to all of these responsibilities. If American Catholic universities cannot give major assistance to their nation and their Church with respect to these problems, then there would seem to be little reason to encourage their continued existence.

But if American Catholic higher education were to focus on individual attainment of the highest level of educational proficiency and on a world wherein education—and the other fundamental human rights—was available to "everyone," then it might more than justify its continued existence. With Christian commitment to all of God's creatures as the distinctive mark of Catholic colleges and universities, rather than the superficial "Catholicism" of compulsory theology and philosophy courses and emphasis on religious practice, Catholic higher education could enjoy a renaissance.[8]

American Catholic institutions so motivated could offer something distinctive to the American society and government, to the Church and to mankind. Such a revolutionary change could have a highly saluatory affect on the number, size, scope, and form of American Catholic institutions of higher education. For it could come to pass that, to borrow from the language of Mr. Robert McNamara, a kind of "moral cost effectiveness" test would increasingly be applied to the allocation of resources in American Catholic higher education. If each institution and its component parts were analyzed in terms of contribution to the moral responsibilities of the United States and the universal Church, presumably some institutions and some components would not pass the test—or would be dramatically altered.

There would obviously be profound repercussions for individual administrators, professors, and students. Each person would have to decide whether he really wanted to commit himself to the undertaking suggested here. There would be many discipline- or profession-oriented people in each category who would not choose to remain in such a new Catholic university. Given the unlimited expansion American education has been experiencing, it should not be difficult to find appropriate places for them.

On the other hand, movement of persons at all levels need not be one way. There must surely be administrators, professors, and students, non-Catholic as well as Catholic, who have avoided Catholic universities precisely because they shared the negative impressions summarized above. If being a "Catholic" university in the United States really meant what this paper suggests, talent that now goes elsewhere might very well be drawn to Catholic institutions. The well-known problems of financing and maintenance of standards would remain. But the *élan* would be there, and it is the present lack of *élan*, arising out of a lack of deep purpose and vision, that is the real root of the problem of contemporary American Catholic higher education.

Moreover, if American Catholic universities were reorganized along the lines indicated, perennial problems of separation of Church and State affecting government assistance might be alleviated. Suppose the emphasis was shifted from compulsory theology and philosophy courses and from claims in catalogues regarding the uniqueness in purely formal religious terms of "a Catholic education" (i.e. continuation of parochial education)? Suppose, instead, that courses of studies and programs, firmly grounded on Catholic thought and perspectives, took the form of service to the nation and to the world in fields where these perspectives are invaluable and possibly unique? Would it not then be more reasonable to justify public assistance to Catholic institutions as is already done, for example, in cases of conspicuous public service by medical schools and hospitals?

Reference has already been made to the possibility that non-Catholic as well as Catholic administrators, professors, and students might be attracted to the new Catholic universities envisaged here, whereas they are not interested in existing Catholic institutions. This is a most important aspect of the concept of a global educational mission for American Catholic higher education. One of the most positive developments in modern American history has been the fact that study, discussion, and action with respect to protection of fundamental human rights has led to unprecedented ecumenical understanding and cooperation. Whether the subject be race, poverty, development, or peace, ecumenism is a fixed feature of contemporary American life. On most great issues, for example, one finds attempts at coordinated or parallel efforts by, for example, the U.S. Catholic Conference, the National Council of Churches, The Synagogue Council of America, and the Union of American Hebrew Congregations.

This concept is beginning to take hold in American colleges. Unfortunately for the Catholic schools, the first wave of ecumenical exchange has apparently taken the form of a "brain drain" of some of the best Catholic scholars to the most prestigious universities, none of which is Catholic. Perhaps some of these *emigrés* could be lured back if they were really convinced that a "business as usual" sterility no longer characterized Catholic universities. But there are also signs that indication of a serious blending of technically competent empirical and moral analysis will draw highly reputable non-Catholic scholars to Catholic campuses. Thus Georgetown Medical Center has been able to attract Professor Paul Ramsey from Princeton to deal with the ethical problems of such subjects as birth control and heart transplants, a development which must surely be startling to many alumni of both institutions and which is most heartening to those who, through common concern over certain problem areas, have come to know persons of the erudition, wisdom, and personal integrity of Professsor Ramsey.

SOME AREAS OF CONCENTRATION FOR AMERICAN CATHOLIC UNIVERSITIES

This section will suggest some areas of concentration appropriate for American Catholic universities. Such concentration might well contribute to accomplishment of the global missions of the United States and the Church in defense of fundamental human rights. The writer will limit his suggestions and their scope to fields with which he is reasonably familiar. The following possible areas of concentration will be discussed:

1) Philosophy and theology;

2) Political and legal theory with respect to the international as well as to national communities;

3) The empirical social sciences:

    a) in terms of their present state of development and degree of reliability;

b) in terms of their normative assumptions and implications.

In addition, some concluding observations will be offered
concerning the organizational and methodological aspects of
a renewal of American Catholic higher education.

The basis for Catholic social thought relevant to the right
to education and to all other fundamental human rights is the
concept of natural law. This concept has its roots in Greek and
Roman philosophy, jurisprudence and positive law, and in the
adaptation of the Greco-Roman tradition of natural law by the
Scholastics, notably St. Thomas Aquinas, to a scholastic natural
law linked to Roman Catholic theology. The exact relationship
between Catholic theology and the scholastic natural law tradition in philosophy and ethics has been controverted. But it is
certainly clear that the natural law foundations of the Catholic
Church's social teaching rest on the assumption that the God
whom Christians worship has implanted in all men a share of
his divine reason. To the extent that men understand their God-
given nature, they understand how they should behave as individuals and as members of societies ranging from the local to
the national to the global level. Both the presumed reason-
ableness of natural law prescriptions and their morally binding
character ultimately are traceable to Christian theology and
philosophy.[9] If Catholics did not believe this, they would look
upon the social teaching of the Church, most of which is not
directly deduced from divine revelation, as purely optional
advice to be taken or not, depending on one's opinion of the
competence of the source of the advice with respect to the
subject matter.

Thus, if the Church says that there is a fundamental right
to education, it is not simply offering an opinion to the effect
that it would be a good idea to offer all men adequate, appropriate education. It is laying down a prescription to the effect
that, objectively, in Catholic theology and philosophy, certain
human rights are recognized, one of which is the right to edu-

cation. Therefore, the assertion of this right is not an opinion to be treated like any intelligent proposition, regardless of its source. It is an assertion to be considered seriously because it supposedly is derived from perennial first principles of the natural law.

Pacem in Terris, the most widely acclaimed modern Church document on human rights, is clearly in this natural law tradition. The same is true of the Pastoral Constitution on the Church in the Modern World, *Gaudium et Spes.* Thus, as it prepares to address itself to war-peace questions, *Gaudium et Spes* asserts:

> Contemplating this melancholy state of humanity, the Council wishes to recall first of all the permanent binding force of universal natural law and its all-embracing principles. Man's conscience itself gives ever more emphatic voice to these principles. Therefore, actions which deliberately conflict with these same principles, as well as orders commanding such actions, are criminal. . . .[10]

Such formulations of the nature of the "universal natural law" would appear to be indistinguishable from those of the scholastic tradition and those advanced during the neo-scholastic renewals of modern time. They carry the note of certainty and definiteness which characterizes the works of such authorities as Maritain, Messner, and Rommen. But one need not be either a theologian or philosopher to be aware, even from a casual reading of the Catholic press and journals of opinion, that we are witnessing revolutions within the Catholic Church in the fields of theology and philosophy. It is increasingly difficult to find a professor of theology or philosophy on the faculty of a Catholic university who would defend the traditional natural law concepts in the ways in which they have been historically presented, even very recently by modern natural law thinkers.[11]

As will be mentioned presently, there is a real problem for persons who want to take seriously the social teaching of the

Church, as regards the technical competence of this teaching in terms of the relevant empirical sciences. But, if there are also doubts as to the nature, scope, and binding character of the normative authority underlying such teaching, the utility of initiative, such as that of the Church in support of The Universal Declaration of Human Rights, is placed in jeopardy.

One area of obvious priority in shaping American Catholic higher education for the future is that of reviewing the theological and philosophical bases for the social teaching of the Church. Is there, in the opinion of contemporary Catholic theologians and philosophers, a "universal natural law?" What is its form and character? What is its content? Who may authoritatively decide these questions? What is the present state of all these questions? To those not professionally expert in theology and philosophy but who work in fields dependent on or greatly affected by those disciplines (e.g. law, politics), it appears that there is presently a lack of expert consensus concerning the answers to these questions. While we are advocating the right of education for "everyone," we must be reviewing the norms and processes by virtue of which the Church concluded that this and other human rights ought to be secured, not as a "good thing" but as a goal required by normative imperatives derived from principles of theology, philosophy, or both. To the best of my knowledge, such a review is not in progress in American Catholic universities, and it is at least questionable whether many of them would be able to conduct it. Surely, if American Catholic institutions of higher learning are unable to adequately deal with this fundamental problem area they have little basis for claiming uniqueness. Positive action in this area would contribute directly to the implementation of the right to education.

Directly related to the need for intensive review of the natural law bases for Catholic social thought is the need for practical and imaginative studies in political theory and jurisprudence. This applies equally to studies of the nature of the national and international political societies and legal orders.

Influenced by the need to reiterate the validity and viability of "the universal natural law," most Catholic political theorists and jurisprudential scholars in the United States have concentrated on the history of political thought and jurisprudence and on the refutation of "erroneous" theories. A single but critical example will be offered, namely, the lack of Catholic normative theory concerning revolution.

The phenomenon of violent revolution, a terrible commonplace in contemporary life in the United States, in the Third World, and throughout the international community, has hardly been touched by systematic Catholic theorists, whether they be theologians, ethicians, or scholars in the fields of political thought and jurisprudence. What are the presumptions for or against law and order, on the one hand, and justice achieved by violence, on the other? The scholastic natural law tradition tells us that a law that is contrary to the natural law is a nullity. One could, from this proposition, readily justify revolutionary disregard for purportedly unjust laws and systems. Yet most scholarly works in the natural law tradition are chary of any semblance of advocacy of violent revolution.[12] Pope Paul VI raises the question in the encyclical *Populorum Progressio*, but quickly drops it.[13]

Surely American Catholic institutions of higher learning should be producing scholars who can formulate the issues and propose preferred solutions with respect to such rampant phenomena as violent revolution and civil disobedience. Yet there is little evidence of recognition of the desperate need to develop such scholars and such analyses, much less that steps are being taken to meet it. In an age wherein moral arguments are raised in rapid crescendo from every conceivable ideological point of view with respect to revolution and civil disobedience, there is no American Suarez on the horizon. The need to motivate and train young American Catholic scholars to give informed and creative attention to the practical contemporary problems of political thought and jurisprudence must be recognized by American Catholic universities in a revolutionary age that confounds the American society, the Catholic Church and, indeed, the universities themselves as the revolutionary students storm the offices of their authorities and flout their laws and standards of conduct. Needless to say, the subject is now almost universally relevant to the right to education which is widely obstructed by student and other revolutionary behavior.

In addition to developing practical political and legal norms of a prescriptive and evaluative nature, American Catholic universities must be integrating normative theory with the findings and techniques of the empirical sciences. The record of Catholic thought in this respect is mixed. One must evaluate the empirical sciences from at least two perspectives: 1) the degree of reliability of each discipline; 2) the normative assumptions and implications of each discipline.

Gladly leaving such problem areas as population to others with more knowledge and greater courage, I would like to mention two areas vital to the Church, the world, and to the United States, wherein the problem of assessing the reliability of the empirical sciences is vital. They are: 1) international development; 2) arms control and disarmament.

In *Populorum Progressio*, Paul VI, having noted that earlier popes "did not fail in the duty of their office of shedding the light of the Gospel on the social questions of the times," asserted that, "today, the principal fact that we must all recognize is that the social question has become world-wide."[14] This opening statement has been widely construed by ardent supports and by critics of this and similar encyclicals (e.g., *Mater et Magistra*) to mean:

1) The political-economic-social programs, which can fairly be called "socialist" in a very broad sense, adopted within the nations primarily in the Western, advanced world in response to the Church's teaching on "the social question" and to many other appeals and pressures, have been proved technically sound and are, in effect, ripe for export to the underdeveloped Third World.

2) The technical experts (such as Barbara Ward) in the fields of development and foreign aid now have the expertise to "solve" the world-wide "social question," if only the wills and resources of the rich nations can be mobilized in this enterprise. Obviously, an extremely important part of this process of development would be the improvement of the state of education in the under-developed countries.

All of this strikes a note that is appealing to those in the affluent Western nations who are concerned about remaining items of business with respect to their domestic "social question" and who have developed a strong conscience with regard to the duties of the rich nations to assist in the development of the poor. But how far can we trust the judgment of the experts in the natural, social, and policy sciences in these matters? Most major American Catholic universities are in or near large cities. They are aware of the enormous difficulties, even where the will to do right is present, in solving the local "social question" and in producing "development" in the disadvantaged sectors of the society. They are painfully aware that well-intentioned but technically or socially impractical initiatives can do more harm than good. They are familiar with the phenomenon of "rising expectations," ever-mounting demands, the sense of frustration, and a revolutionary spirit which often results from the intervention of outside forces into an unjust but apathetic stable society. Such revolutionary spirit often results when the well-intentioned outside forces fail to live up to their promises or to meet the expectations (perhaps quite unrealistic) of those they are trying to "develop."

In addition, then, to theorists to set goals and standards for individual and collective behavior towards the disadvantaged, at home and abroad, we need experts to judge the technical feasibility of development measures. This calls for cooperation between the normative theorists and the technical experts. But it also calls for careful scrutiny by the normative theorists and all responsible participants in the processes of local, national, and international development of the state of the various empirical disciplines. Do the social psychologists, economists, area experts (whether the area be the urban United States or Black Africa) and the planners *really* have the answers? Is development exclusively a question of human and material resources and the will to make it work? Do we know enough about "social engineering" at home to export slightly modified programs of social engineering to other and very different countries?

The Church has made development the most central subject in its recent efforts in pursuit of international justice and peace. American Catholic universities, operating in the nation that has the greatest potential for contributing to the achievement of the goals set by the Church, must have the resources to assess these goals and the means advocated to accomplish them. This should clearly be an area for immediate, intense concentration in American Catholic universities.

Turning to another subject to which recent Catholic teaching has devoted great attention, there is a need for American scholars to assist the development of technically informed prescriptions and judgments in the fields of arms control and disarmament. American scholars have necessarily taken the lead in studies in this field. It is a field that affects everyone, but particularly Americans and Russians. The Soviets trail the United States in systematic studies of arms control; and, in any event, their internal debates are not available, and their public statements and studies must be read with considerable caution, in the light of their notorious and very effective propaganda components.[15]

Faced with an age of conflict, American scholars have given a great deal of thought and study to the phenomenon of international conflict and to conflict management. These studies range from internal conflict through a combination of such conflict and foreign intervention to the whole terrible gambit of conventional and nuclear war. American scholars have also necessarily given great attention to deterence, to the relation of deterence to conflict on the one hand, and to progress in arms control and disarmament, on the other.

Living with the constant contingency of making the nuclear decision, the United States has produced, to the best of its ability, experts and decision-makers who have sought to distinguish between what they hope for, what might come about, and what appears to be either likely or unlikely. This effort has engaged scholars and intellectuals from a variety of disciplines, and it is fair to say that ultimately normative concepts, restrictions, and rules of the game in the continued conflicts of our era have come overwhelmingly from the imaginative suggestions of American natural and social scientists rather than moral or legal scholars.[16]

It is clearly the duty of American Catholic universities to pass on whatever seems reliable from this body of knowledge, techniques of analysis, and individual insights to those who formulate official pronouncements on this subject, whether at the diocesan, national, or Vatican level. Happily, the final documents of Vatican Council II reflect the beginnings of such a collaboration.[17]

Again, however, it is necessary to raise the question of the degree of reliability of the knowledge and methods of the very new and precarious disciplines of international relations, peace research, problem-oriented arms control and disarmament studies, and the like.

It is now time to reflect briefly on the normative assumptions and implications of the empirical sciences. Although many practitioners of both the natural and social sciences tend toward the position that they are normatively neuter or "value free," these experts are human beings, not computers. As such, they have values, assumptions about human nature and about their disciplines, and goals which have a value content. Moreover, they usually have an interest in pursuing their respective disciplines so as to expand the limits of those disciplines. They have a natural tendency to look upon the challenges of problem areas, such as development and arms control and disarmament, as challenges to the capabilities of their disciplines. They often respond with a combination of enthusiasm and confidence which has to be carefully weighed.

Whether the subject be the possibilities of political sociali-

zation of some primitive tribes in an underdeveloped country
or detection of nuclear tests, there will usually be a technical
expert who looks upon the subject as a kind of experiment
which is technically "interesting." But all the time these technical experts are, in a very real sense, "playing God" with
human beings and sometimes with the future of mankind. The
moral implications of such experimentation ought to be constantly considered. American Catholic universities, in the center of the most advanced attempts to improve and control the
world by applied technical expertise, must shoulder the heavy
responsibility of monitoring these initiatives. Thus the questions to be asked of the empirical scientists are two-fold: 1)
What can you really accomplish? 2) What will be the human
effects—on individuals, on societies, on the international society, on the earth itself—if you can do what you say you can
do?

It should be evident that although the number of examples
given here of areas of concentration for American Catholic
universities is small, the magnitude of the tasks suggested are
sufficient to render absurd the contention that such universities
are no longer needed. This, of course, assumes that it is unlikely that these tasks could be adequately performed by institutions either controlled by the government or by the empirical
experts whose efforts are as much in necessity of normative
scrutiny as they are essential to achievement of the goals set by
the social teaching of the Church.

This brings us back to the central contention of this paper,
namely, that the future of American Catholic institutions of
higher learning should be defined in terms of the unique services which such institutions could or should be able to render
to their nation and their Church. I have sought to outline a few
of these services in terms of areas of concentration. The question remains: Are American Catholic universities presently organized to accomplish missions of the kind and magnitude
discussed, not to say of many other missions which persons
with other backgrounds could suggest.

The answer is probably negative. American Catholic uni-

versities tend presently to attempt to duplicate secular and
other private universities more or less across the board. They
cannot continue to do so, and there is no sufficient reason for
them to try. On the contrary their structure, programs,
emphases, personnel, and *élan* should stem from their dedication to tasks which they are uniquely qualified to undertake. If
a problem area requires a more or less orthodox school or
department, it would presumably be sufficient to reorganize
such a school or department so as to contribute to the study
and research appropriate to its contributions to U.S. and Catholic global goals. Thus, at Georgetown, to which I will limit
my examples because of long familiarity with that university, it
would seem quite feasible to continue the School of Foreign
Service as both an undergraduate school and a center for
thought and research of the kinds suggested. Likewise, the
departments of economics, government, history, and sociology
would continue their teaching functions while collaborating on
projects concerning such subjects as development with special
research centers such as the Population Research Center.

A law school might still justify its existence if, in addition
to providing regular legal education, it expanded programs
such as the Institute of Law and Human Rights and Social
Values, the Institute of Criminal Law and the Legal Interns
Program, all of which deal in both theoretical and practical
ways with the protection of human rights.

Almost any existing school, department, or research center
could justify its existence and perhaps its expansion if it mani-
festly contributed to the extension of the right to education.
Thus, to take another example from Georgetown's experience,
one would encourage the collaboration of the Summer School
with the departments of English, history, mathematics, chemistry, and biology in special programs to help disadvantaged
Washington primary and secondary students achieve their true
potentials. Likewise, the work of the university's Institute of
Languages and Linguistics in preparing Americans to teach
abroad and foreign students to teach languages in their own

countries is in the spirit of service to the nation, the Church, and those millions who have the human right of education.

But, at least on the basis of my experience at Georgetown University, I would have to conclude that the *proportion* between special programs of the kind I have mentioned and the volume of work involved in duplicating the educational efforts of other institutions of higher learning is heavily on the side of the latter. If this continues, those who proclaim the imminent demise of American Catholic education will probably be borne out. Financial and administrative problems will very likely drive these institutions out of existence completely or into some sort of merger with others that substantially removes their unique identities. But, as previously stated, the loss of *raison d'être,* the absence of a genuine spirit of renewal and unique service, will prove a psychological handicap which will be almost impossible to overcome. This, in the end, is the greatest problem of all. If, on the other hand, American Catholic universities and colleges seek out their appropriate roles in helping their country and their Church to expand efforts to ensure the right to education—and all fundamental human rights—to "everyone," it can be hoped that they will survive and make the contributions of which they are capable to the protection and extension of all the fundamental human rights.

THOMAS PATRICK MELADY

8: *The Right to be Educated in the New Africa*

When one speaks of human rights and Africa most persons will immediately think of the grave violations of the human rights of the black people of Southern Africa. This essay, however, will not be devoted to these grave problems in Southern Africa, but to the status of the right to an education in the new Africa.

In order to place the human right to be educated in focus it will be helpful to discuss the two following subjects: 1. Past and present ways of thinking about human rights in Africa's newly independent nations, and, 2. The role of church-related schools and the status of the human right to an education in the new Africa.

HUMAN RIGHTS IN THE NEW AFRICAN STATES

Perhaps the most serious problems in Africa arise from the danger inherent in the socio-political atmosphere in many independent African states of giving over-riding importance to the executive branch of the government. This is being done, it is said, so that all power can be focused on eliminating the triple curse of poverty, illiteracy, and disease. All of us who have seen the poverty in Africa can appreciate the desire for immediate change in the near subhuman standard of living.

There is, however, a danger to this. New states with a prolonged absence of strong constitutional safeguards to protect basic human rights can produce a climate dangerous to these rights. The author, a frequent visitor to Africa, raises his concern—as now is the time to stimulate discussion on this matter. Perhaps the concern is without foundation. But raising this concern is a proper activity of the academic community, and especially of the universities in Africa; those universities have a special educational responsibility to stimulate constructive review and to suggest safeguards which should, of course, reflect the basic cultural traditions.

The nationalist in Africa struggles for independence from colonial rulers in order to act in accordance with the democratic principles that exist in the metropolitan country—be it Britain or France. Among these principles are majority rule and the concept of the rights of the governed as the bedrock of government. In the law courts, this struggle manifested itself in clashes over public liberties or human rights. The nationalist argued for freedom of assembly, of the press, of information, of association, and freedom from arbitrary arrest and detention without a fair trial. The adage most frequently quoted by their lawyers was, "Justice must not only be done, but must also be seen to be done."

The focus on human rights was but one aspect of the general nationalist upsurge. For our purposes here, it must be stressed that, by and large, the nationalist's struggle for universal human rights won him moral and material support in parts of Europe and America—because of the belief and hope that independent Africa would uphold these rights for which she had strenuously fought. However, the new states of Africa are not acting too differently from the colonial authorities.

Basically, the crux of the human rights issue is the relation between the individual and the states, or rights versus duties. This is a major problem in jurisprudence and political philosophy—one that requires constant re-thinking in terms of changing social conditions. Generally, in established Western democracies human rights have been accepted and are observed. At any rate, there are set procedures whereby they can be safeguarded or curtailed in emergency cases such as war.

But in the new African states, there are peculiar conditions —hence the need for re-thinking the problem. Immediately after independence in 1957, Kwame Nkrumah wrote in his autobiography: "Ghana would need, for some time, measures of a totalitarian nature in order to protect and develop herself."

Nkrumah's words have been echoed and acted upon by many new African states. Their justification is that nation-building demands that human rights be curtailed until the consolidation of the nation-state has been achieved. It is argued that the State must be consolidated against internal and external forces of disruption. Among these forces are tribalism, parochialism, racialism; the latter may include subversion and oppression or threats thereof. If unchecked, both of these forces may endanger not merely the general welfare of the citizens, but the very existence of the state itself—hence the need for curbing rights and tipping the scales in favor of responsibility to the State. The arguments can be put with varying depths of persuasiveness, depending on expediency. However, free Africa did not start with expedient measures. On the contrary, she began the new era with human rights guaranteed by the protection of the law. On independence day, a good many of the African states had constitutional or other legal provisions designed to protect human rights. In most cases, these provisions were introduced to allay the fears of the minority groups.

In this respect, Nigeria offers a good example. In the constitutional conference held in London in September and October 1958, delegates from the minority ethnic groups urged the inclusion of definite constitutional provisions to protect their positions after independence. To show Nigeria's concern for human rights, these provisions were agreed on before the rest of the Constitution. A leading Nigerian jurist, later Federal Attorney-General T. O. Elias, showed in 1960 that in form and content these provisions were conducive to the establishment of the rule of law in Nigeria.[1] In the light of Nigeria's recent history, it must be pointed out that Elias was then aware that "fundamental rights in a constitution do not, in themselves, guarantee that they will necessarily be enforced after independence." Still, in his view such provisions were valuable: "They constitute a warning and a challenge to those who might later want to set the law at nought." He could have made his point more forcefully by saying that the safeguarding of human rights, ultimately, depends on human will.

John Stuart Mill said, in his *Representative Government:* "Political institutions are the works of men. They owe their existence to human will. Men did not wake up one morning and find them sprung up; nor do they resemble trees which keep on growing while men are sleeping." Human will—this is the foundation of political institutions, for their continual existence depends on the will of the majority to maintain them. This will has been lacking in Nigeria, in Ghana, and in some of the other states in Africa. For example, a study of the staff of the International Commission of Jurists, based in Geneva, examined Ghana's 1958 Preventive Detention Act, extensively used by Nkrumah to silence his opponents. The ICT study showed that the law courts refrained from investigating the grounds of Nkrumah's action in ordering detention. Furthermore, it scored such detention in peacetime as inimical to freedom. Conceding the need of such measures for security reasons, the study nonetheless added that preventive detention "must be hedged with reasonable safeguards to secure its proper, and not indiscriminate, use by the Executive."[2] Such safeguards include an independent judiciary, judicial review, and the submission of regular reports to the legislature. Not all of these safeguards to protect detainees can be found in Africa, or, for that matter, other subjects against whom executive action is being contemplated. Cases of deportation, expulsion, and censorship have been recorded.

In this regard, an illuminating article on censorship of literary material in Africa has been written by James S. Reed, Reader in African Law at the London School of Oriental and African Studies at the University of London. He showed that the governments of the English-speaking African states in transition have retained censorship regulations from the colonial era. These are now and then put into effect. A case in point is the banning by Kenya, in May 1967, of William Attwood's book, *The Reds and the Blacks.* "African literature has been long delayed by cultural colonialism. . . . it would be a tragedy indeed if African writers were now denied, by African governments, the conditions of free expression."[3] We must, however, add that Reed stresses that the wide powers legally given to the executive to whittle away human rights in the literary sphere, and in others, have not been used extensively. But the fact is that such powers do exist. The danger is that some governments may use these powers to expunge human rights and to victimize a regime's opponents, real and imaginary. Here lies the great danger and threat to human rights. What guarantee is there that these powers will be used judiciously?

It is not unreasonable to think that under certain conditions an African regime can be as ruthless as the minority and racist governments of southern Africa whose activities have been universally condemned. In 1960 the International Commission of Jurists made a study of human rights in South Africa which is still one of the best.[4] Other publications of the ICT have dealt with the violation of human rights in South West Africa and Rhodesia.

Southern Africa is the scene of the most glaring and the most systematic violation of human rights. Cultural and social genocide exists in the apartheid system of the Republic of South Africa. Southern Rhodesia, since its unilateral declaration of independence in 1965, is daily depriving the black African majority of their rights. These violations of human rights in Southern Africa are well documented and well publicized.

The independent African states, where the black Africans constitute the majority, have, so far in most instances, avoided anything like the violation of human rights occurring in Southern Africa. But we must recognize the dangers inherent in a situation where the executive has such broad powers. At present, these powers have been exercised rather sparingly. But their existence is a threat to human rights, and many of us hope that the new African states that brought the human right of independence to so many millions will recognize the dangers and institute legal safeguards and institutions that will safeguard internally the rights of minorities and opposition groups.

The potential dangers inherent in an excessively broad reservoir of power in the executive branch of government pose a particularly serious threat to education—a threat which, to date, has fortunately not been realized.

RIGHT TO AN EDUCATION IN THE NEW AFRICA

There is in Africa today an almost mystical faith in education. In a relatively short period of years, young educated Africans rose to the top positions in their country. Those who attended the universities returned to find their governments eager to employ them as diplomats, ministers, and the like. The danger, of course, is that this had led some to misconstrue the right to education as the right to a high position or a plush job after the completion of education. Nevertheless, education has proved to be a powerful tool for change in Africa, and the thirst for education still continues among the people.

Actually, the first forms of education were introduced in Africa by the Protestant and Catholic missionaries who began establishing schools long before colonial governments were functioning on the continent. The missionary efforts have continued to be a vital force in educating Africans. In 1965 it was estimated that half of the African children between the ages of six and eleven spent an average of six years in school. At least 60 per cent of these children studied in church-related or mission schools.

The main purpose of mission schools during the first missionary efforts in Africa was to teach Christianity. The colonial governments allowed them to remain, as most recognized the right of the people to learn and study about their respective religions. Gradually, however, these schools became increasingly secular in their curricula. The British colonial governments generally accepted the necessity of providing enough Africans with sufficient education to fulfill the manpower needs for the expanding administrative and commercial establishments. The French were more positive in their approach in that they provided some state schools (all of which, including missionary establishments, were rigidly supervised) and modeled them closely on the schools in metropolitan France. Their objective was to permeate the area with French culture and to provide a political and professional elite of a high intellectual quality in the French image. The Belgians were quite intent on building a strong technical corps of Africans, but did not provide for the training of a university-educated elite. In the Portuguese colonies the emphasis was, and still is, on Portuguese language and culture—with a strong sense of Portuguese nationalism. The Portuguese Government, in its educational policy, still attempts to insulate the African from the "heretical" doctrines of African nationalism.

The merits of the first educational efforts of the churches were great. Their continued insistence on the right to educate their members led eventually to the birth of the modern African states. The teaching of European concepts of democracy and freedom planted the seeds of African nationalism in many a young African student's mind. Furthermore, the churches were energetic and quite successful in arranging for university education of Africans, which was thought to be a dangerous enterprise by many colonial administrators. In the Catholic system of education seminaries with university status arose as a means to develop a native clergy. For many young Africans these seminaries were the only avenue to higher education.

These earlier educational patterns were European, but today there is a strong trend toward Africanization. With the growth of African nationalism not only does the African clamor for an education, but he insists on the right to know and be educated in an African sense, taking into account the wealth of African history and culture, its value and its application to the world today.

Although virtually every African government subscribes to the right to education and the statement of this right made in the *Universal Declaration of Human Rights*, there are some very important deficiencies in this commitment. In essence, Article 26 of the *Declaration on Human Rights* calls for free universal elementary education. Most African leaders are striving toward this goal, not only because they believe in the right itself, but also because they see the merits of eventual universal education for the betterment of their countries. Universal education would indeed be a way toward making the necessary changes in their societies and would help to meld the sometimes fragmented tribal societies into one nation.

The question remains, however, of how to implement this right. Financial resources and qualified personnel are needed. Certain basic decisions must be made in educational policy to reach the ultimate goal of universal education. Given the present limited resources, is it more profitable in the long run for a country to concentrate its financial energies on establishing universal free primary education or to strengthen and increase the capacity of the secondary schools? Is technical education more important at this point in their history than the prestige of university education? Is the basic general education for all more important than the intensive training of a select few for special professional and technical skills needed at this stage in their development? If expansion of primary education is attempted, are there enough teachers or would there necessarily be a dilution of teaching qualifications? All these questions are raised by leaders of government and educational policy in Africa, for they point out the practical problems in promoting education for the use of society as a whole, while at the same time providing for the exercise of the basic right to education for the individual. Where it is difficult to realize this ideal, sacrifices must be made.

Taking into account the wide existence of church-related schools in Africa, the driving thirst for education, and the governments' anxiety to promote (but control) the direction of education, there is bound to be some friction in working out the relationship between church-related schools and the state. This relationship has already taken several forms in the independent states of Africa. For example, in Ghana, through the Education Act of 1961, only two types of schools are recognized—state schools and unaided private schools. All Catholic schools which existed prior to 1952 were then absorbed into the public-school system, while remaining under direct Catholic management. In Tanzania, all denominational schools were absorbed into a national system and are regarded in exactly the same way as any other schools, in relation to recognition, building, staffing, and similar matters.

Another way is the grant-in-aid system which has provided very satisfactory results for the Catholic schools, in that they submit to government regulations and supervision in return for total or partial financial assistance, without losing ownership or management of the schools.

No matter what the relationship, certain problems arise. One of the greatest problems is in the area of the teaching of religion. Some countries have excluded religion from the curriculum; others have standardized texts which may be objectionable to some on religious grounds. Presently, these are the conflicts between the Church and her perceived right to educate, and the nationalistic African governments and their perception of their right to control education; in the future, similar tensions will undoubtedly arise from time to time. In practical everyday terms the Church, in adjusting to the situation, and the governments, in realizing the value of the Church's contribution to this area, seem to be able to cooperate at this time without too much sacrifice on either side. But the future of the right to an education in the new African states will almost inevitably be challenged and compromised by the actions of governments which are excessively heavy on the executive side, and by all the other complex forces of nationalism and racism which are sweeping the new Africa.

Amid all of these clashing forces and philosophies, the clear and challenging assertion of the inherent right to an education by every single person set forth twenty years ago in the *Universal Declaration of Human Rights* provides a focus and a Magna Carta for the new nations of Africa. One can only hope that the principles and prescriptions behind mankind's first universal proclamation of the human right to be educated will be heard and followed by the new nations of Africa.

JOHN B. SHEERIN

9: Ecumenical Implications of the Right to be Educated

Education is absolutely indispensable to civilization. Like religion itself, it exerts a powerful social influence in reconciling hostile factions and in building bridges of understanding across chasms of ignorance. Article 26 of the *U. N. Declaration of Human Rights* begins with the simple and unmistakable affirmation: "Everyone has the right to education." Then Section 2 of the Article elaborates:

> Education shall be directed to the full development of human personality and to the strengthening of respect for human rights and fundamental freedoms. It shall promote understanding, tolerance and friendship among all nations and racial or religious groups, and shall further the activities of the United Nations for the maintenance of peace.

The socializing role of education is evident also in the Second Vatican Council's *Declaration on Christian Education* which asserts that every man of whatever race, condition, and age is endowed with the dignity of a person and has "an inalienable right to an education." Then it states: "At the same time this education should pave the way to brotherly association with other peoples so that genuine unity and peace on earth may be promoted" (Article 1).

In its reconciling function and in its promotion of fraternal association, education plays a distinctively ecumenical role. Here I use the world "ecumenical" in its broad sense, meaning the unification of the whole human family. This ecumenizing role is specially laudable at this time in history when the men of our age have a new understanding of the world. Formerly, at least in the Christian West, men tended to think of divinity as a sort of brooding presence in the skies. Today, we see God at work among the emerging revolutions and kaleidoscopic events of our time, not as a far-off transcendent divinity, but as a God at home in the world he created, working among the children of God. To a certain extent the next world has lost its glow, but this world in which God is with us has taken on a stronger brilliance for us because we realize his presence more closely. Men talk of building a new world, and they enter into the task with an enthusiasm that is admirable, for they are intent on building a world where men can live a truly human existence and bring up their children in the decency that befits the children of God. So the present age is definitely oriented toward the neighbor, and the best minds of our time are profoundly concerned about problems such as war, racial injustice, and poverty—all the factors that divide man from man. Caught up in this movement for cooperative world order, governments are now enacting legislation that guarantees to every citizen the civil right to education. They aim to enshrine the moral right of every man to education in a civil law that will protect this right from violation—whether by the government itself or by powerful forces in the nation.

Through education men of all nations can come to know and appreciate the world religions and the religious aspirations of their members. There was a time when Western Europe thought of the non-Christian religions as being agents of darkness, their members beyond the saving power of Christ. Today the global revolutions in transportation and communication have brought us into close contact with these other religions, and we find that God has irradiated them with flashes of truth, a message of hope and love of neighbor. Education brings us new insights into these religions and in many cases helps us to rediscover features of our own Christian religion we had neglected. In short, God is at work reconciling men through these

other religions, as well as through Christianity, even though
they may not possess the revelation and means of grace given
by Christ. This universal ecumenism is not a species of religious indifference based on the notion that all religions are
equally valid. It is entirely consistent with orthodox Christianity to speak of uncovenanted graces and to say that God
moves in a mysterious way his wonders to perform. Through
education in the world religions, we can acquire a fuller appreciation of God's work outside the visible Church. It is the
Spirit within us seeking to discover the manifestation of the
Spirit in others. Ecumenical education in relation to the world
religions therefore means dialogue, patient listening to discern
the working of the Spirit outside the boundaries of Christianity
and to assist in the great enterprise of human reconciliation for
which God became man.

As there can be no universal ecumenism unless there is
recognition of the right to educate, so too there can be no
effective Christian ecumenism without recognition of this
right. Christian ecumenism is embodied in the ecumenical
movement. The proximate aim of that movement, as we find it
described in Roman Catholic, Protestant, or Orthodox periodi-
cals, is to promote the unity of Christians; and the ultimate
goal is the more effective preaching of the Gospel. Even here
education is imperative, else we will find ourselves thinking of
Christian unity as a pan-Christian ghetto that isolates us from
Jews and other believers, as well as from non-believers. Since
the ultimate aim of the ecumenical movement is the more
effective preaching of the Gospel, we wish not to offend Jewish
sensibilities by asking the Jews to participate in the promotion
of Christian unity. Yet we need them, and they need us. We
revere them not only for their ancient prophets and sacred
books, but also for the abiding vitality to be found in Judaism
today. They seek to share in the ecumenical spirit, if not in the
ecumenical movement, and we look to Christian-Jewish dialogue as a means of combating anti-Semitism and enriching
our knowledge of the Jewish tradition.

Just as there are special ecumenical problems in regard to the Jews, so too there are particular problems in Christian ecumenism as between Catholics and Protestants. I have in mind the problems that arise in the social and civic area which cause friction among Christians. These problems vary according to country, but in the United States one of the most formidable of these problems has centered around the question of religious liberty, with a particular focus on the right to educate in religion. The controversy over religious liberty has long embittered Catholic-Protestant relations in America and has spawned deep interfaith antagonisms. During the Second Vatican Council, Dr. John C. Bennett of Union Theological Seminary, New York, delivered an address in New York City in which he spoke about the fears of Protestants in regard to the Roman Catholic teaching on religious liberty:

> I believe that the American hierarchy has been right in giving so much attention to religious liberty because this has been the deepest source of misunderstanding between Catholics and Protestants in this country. I have found that it is a very common view of Roman Catholicism that, if the Roman Catholic Church were to be what it really intends to be, it would take as its model the Spanish Church.[1]

What the American Protestants feared about the Roman Catholic Church was that it might restrict the religious liberties of Protestants. They were acquainted with the "thesis, hypothesis theory" held by some Catholic theologians which asserted that when Roman Catholics are a minority in a country, they can demand the religious liberty they must suppress as soon as they come to power. The rapidly increasing Roman Catholic population conjured up before Protestant eyes the spectre of the unhappy day when Catholics would constitute a majority of the population, elect a Catholic President, and proceed to revoke the religious freedom guarantees of the First Amendment to the Constitution.

Vatican Council II, however, dispelled this fear to a large

extent when it approved the *Declaration on Religious Freedom*. The ecumenical overtones of this *Declaration* can be easily inferred from the fact that the *Declaration* was originally a part of the Council decree on ecumenism. For practical reasons, it was made a separate document before presentation to the Council for discussion. In this *Declaration* the Council states: "This Vatican Council declares that the human person has a right to religious freedom" (Ch. I, No. 2). The text goes on to affirm that this right of the human person must be recognized in constitutional law as a genuine civil right. This is not simply a private right, but is a social right as well. The Council declared that every man has a legal right not only to seek the truth privately, but to embrace it publicly and as a member of a religious association, according to the dictates of his conscience, and to teach it, communicate it, and enter into dialogue about it.

> Provided the just demands of public order are met, these religious groups have a right to immunity in order that they may govern themselves according to their own norms, honor the Supreme Being in public worship, assist their members in the practice of the religious life, strengthen them by instruction and promote institutions in which they may join together for the purpose of ordering their lives according to their religious principles (Ch. II, No. 4).

The U. N. Declaration of Human Rights has a somewhat similar section in which it speaks of a man's right to freedom of thought, conscience, and religion, and then states that this freedom includes, "the freedom either alone, or in community with others, and in public or in private, to manifest his religion or beliefs in teaching, practices, worship, and observance" (Article 18).

Proselytism is obviously an abuse of the right to educate in religion, but it is not a clear violation of the legal right. This, however, does not lessen the harm that it does to the ecumenical movement. Greek Orthodox clergy, for instance, frequently protest "sheep stealing" by Protestants and Roman Catholics.

The term "proselytism" includes all those practices that corrupt religious witness, practices such as bribery, undue influence, intimidation, falsification of beliefs of others, and all those spurious teaching devices designed to lure converts, such as comparison of the strong points of one's own religion with the weak points of another religion. These abuses are reprehensible, but it is dubious that they should be legally proscribed. For a government might use the charge of proselytism as a convenient excuse for repressing a minority religious group it considers politically undesirable. The *Declaration on Religious Freedom* says:

> However, in spreading religious faith and in introducing religious practices, everyone should always refrain from any manner of action which might seem to carry a hint of coercion or any other form of dishonest or unworthy persuasion, especially when dealing with poor or uneducated people. Such a manner of action would have to be considered an abuse of one's own right and a violation of the right of others (Ch. II, No. 4).

Rev. Thomas F. Stransky, C.S.P., in his commentary on the *Declaration,* questions whether any civil authority can legally repress any form of proselytism. Would this not lead to abusive interference in religious matters by a government judging that some religious group is acting in an "unworthy way?"[2]

In recognizing the right to religious liberty, and therewith the right to educate in religion, the Council did not go so far as to erect this civil right into an absolute right. The *Declaration* states that the right is subject to a certain amount of control by the civil authority. The American philosopher, Sidney Hook, some time ago chided U.S. Supreme Court Justice Hugo Black for claiming that religious liberty is an absolute under the First Amendment. Hook pointed out that no modern government would sanction the cultic practice of human sacrifice. American law does not regard religious liberty as an absolute. The American courts, for instance, have banned the Mormon practice of polygamy and have intruded on the religious liberties of the Amish in regard to compulsory education. An early version of the *Declaration on Religious Freedom* was worded to say that the right to manifest externally the rights of conscience can be and must be tempered for the sake of "the common good." Another version had it that religious liberty could be restricted in line with "the end of society." The final version, however, says that religious liberty can be controlled only if the just demands of "public order" so require. The "common good" or "common welfare" is the sum total of those conditions of social life which enable man to achieve a fuller measure of perfection with some relative ease and is a broader term therefore than "public order" (Ch. II, No. 6).

In permitting restriction of religious liberty (and of the correlative right to teach) only in cases in which the public order is threatened, the *Declaration* is safeguarding liberty with a broad and sweeping guarantee. Rare indeed is the instance in which religion might disturb "the public order." Totalitarian governments, however, have restricted religious liberty for the sake of the "common good," and this has given them wide scope for suppressing religious liberty.

Now that the Bishops in Council have approved the *Declaration,* the Catholic world looks anxiously to those Roman Catholic countries where the right of religious minorities to teach and evangelize has been suppressed in the past. This very anxiety has had a salutary effect here in the United States, in that it has made Catholics more sensitive to the religious liberties of Protestants and more reluctant to use any high-pressure methods that might possibly constrict the freedom of the Protestant conscience. In Roman Catholic countries apparently there still are some loyal supporters of the status quo who argue that the State has the right to defend the fabric of society against religious subverters from outside the country. Many Protestant missionaries who attempted to evangelize in Spain have come from foreign countries; and certain Spanish theologians hold that the Catholic religion is so intertwined with Spanish culture, history, and tradition that they constitute one social fabric and that foreign evangelists are, therefore, aggressors against whom the State can defend itself. This might seem plausible, but is not quite as convincing as the argument that a man's duty to follow his conscience takes precedence over the State's duty to preserve its culture.

The right to impart a religious education attaches especially to the family. The *Declaration* says that the family enjoys the right to live its own religious life under the guidance of parents and that the parents have the "right to determine, according to their own religious beliefs, the kind of religious education that their children are to receive" (Ch. II, No. 5). The *Declaration* goes on to say that civil authority must acknowledge the parents' right to make genuinely free choice of schools and of other means of education, and the use of this freedom of choice is not to be made a reason for imposing unjust burdens on parents, whether directly or indirectly. The rights of parents, moreover, are violated if their children are forced to attend lessons or instruction which go against religious beliefs (Ch. II, No. 5).

This question of choice of schools is a thorny question, from the ecumenical viewpoint, in many European countries, but especially in the United States. Perhaps the American experience may prove to be a lesson to Catholics in other countries, since the United States was one of the first nations to have a pluralistic society; and pluralism in religion seems to be the wave of the future.

The basic difficulty that has created so much ecumenical unpleasantness in America is that the First Amendment has been interpreted by the Courts to forbid the use of tax funds for any form of sectarian education. This use is alleged to fall squarely under the ban of the amendment by jurists who are fond of quoting Jefferson to the effect that the First Amendment erected a "wall of separation" between Church and State. Many Catholics, however, assert that this is a wrong interpretation of the amendment, which simply says "Congress shall make no law respecting an establishment of religion or prohibiting the free exercise thereof." These Catholics hold that there has been a venerable tradition of cooperation between Church and State in America and that justice demands that a fair share of the tax funds be allocated to Catholic schools. What complicates the problem and poisons the atmosphere is that from year to year rumors spring up to the effect that the Catholic hierarchy is exerting undue pressure on Catholic voters to secure the passage of laws permitting some form of aid to Catholic Schools, be it only free bus transportation to the Catholic School. Moreover, there are constant rumors that the hierarchy exert pressure on Catholic members of legislatures, state or federal.

Recently Catholics in New York State took part in a campaign to repeal the Blaine Amendment to the New York State Constitution which forbids any form of aid to religious schools. They were opposed by many Protestants, as well as by certain Jews. The attempt to repeal the controverted amendment was defeated, and when the smoke of battle had died down the ecumenical movement had been disastrously injured. The ecumenical euphoria that had hovered over the civic atmosphere in New York due to the passage of the Council's *Declaration on Religious Freedom* was replaced by an acid bitterness toward the New York bishops. One Protestant magazine,[3] usually well-disposed to Catholics, editorialized on "a Catholic power play" and "unsavory gambits" that had caused the editors to be "dismayed and chagrined." The hard work of ecumenists for years had been undone by a few months of civic warfare. From this hard lesson it is hoped that American Catholics will learn to infuse an ecumenical spirit into all discussions of the right of Catholic children or Catholic schools to share in tax funds. If Catholics discuss the question from a purely legal viewpoint, they will find the non-Catholic public becoming belligerent in controversy, for citizens are always disturbed by any issue that affects their bankbook. If Catholics, however, will enter into dialogue rather than debate, discussing these questions not in legal polemics but in an ecumenical spirit and in ironic fashion, other Christians will have no doubts about their ecumenical sincerity.

The "school question" has long been a source of community friction in European countries, and the probability is that it will continue to be a problem for many years to come in the United States. No solution is in sight. The American Government has always respected the right of Catholic parents to give their children a Catholic education, but at the present time there is no indication that it will change its stand on financial aid.

However, one would be rash to make any predictions about the future in view of the startling changes in the American educational system in the past. Originally the established churches in America controlled education. Many great American universities for instance were once religious schools. As the states disestablished their churches, the individual free churches found it difficult to support a whole system of education so the State took over the work of public education. The State continued to teach religious doctrine and practice, but it was a basic core of religious teachings acceptable to all the churches. Traditionally it had been felt that religion and morality was the warp and woof of American society, and that conviction seemed to be shared by the early Americans. However, this basic Christianity that was accepted as essential to American democracy, this civic religion, was not acceptable to Roman Catholics. They saw it as a form of evangelical Protestantism, and it was. As Sidney E. Mead says in *The Lively Experiment:*[4] "In this sense, the public-school system of the United States is its established church."

Down the years, however, the Christian element in this civic religion has been progressively corroded; and we have today a secularistic religion of democracy, and it has not been successful in directing lives for the good order and welfare of the community. On the other hand, the churches, according to

Mead, have also been unsuccessful in educating the public in moral and spiritual values. Dr. J. Paul Williams argues, therefore, that what is needed is that this democratic religion be taught with all the fervor that once accompanied the teaching of religion; for a culture is above all a faith, and the health of American culture depends on the maintenance of the faith in the hearts and minds of the American people. He feels, therefore, that the State should have coercive power to "bring the majority of our people to a religious devotion to our democratic way of life."[5]

It would be a grave error for a Christian parent or teacher to think of the right to educate merely as a legal right. True, it can be vindicated in a court of law, but a lawsuit happens rarely in the ordinary human life; and when it does happen, it seems to some litigants almost like a catastrophe. The parent or teacher, however, exercises the right almost daily, and should exercise it with prudence, sympathetic understanding of the child's mind, and with the aim of giving an ecumenical orientation to the child's mental processes.

"Catholics, who already have a proper grounding," says the *Decree on Ecumenism*, "need to acquire a more adequate understanding of the respective doctrines of our separated brethren, their history, their spiritual and liturgical life, their religious psychology and cultural background" (Ch. II, No. 9). This ecumenical attitude, however, does not spring up spontaneously in adulthood. It must be developed early in life. Ecumenism is an inescapable dimension of all Christian teaching today—whether of adults or children. The teacher and parent should foster an attitude of openness to all human values. In a recent article,[6] Carl J. Pfeifer, S.J., says: "Ecumenism on the elementary school level is an all pervasive dimension of the child's education fostering an attitude of openness to all that is of true value." He lists three basic attitudes that are radically Christian and ecumenical: objectivity, respect or reverence, and compassion. The child's mind must be opened to objective reality so that he can see beyond prejudices and inherited stereotypes. Our ecumenical age prizes intellectual honesty. Secondly, he must become accustomed to respecting other people, especially their conscience, else he will never find dialogue fruitful in the future. Thirdly, he must have compassion for the needs and troubles of all men. To achieve this in children, of course, the teacher or parent must first develop this ecumenical attitude in himself if he hopes to communicate it to the children.

Father Pfeifer crystallizes his main themes in these words:[7] "Elementary school ecumenism must be an all pervasive dimension of the child's education, fostering a genuine appreciation of all that is of value, a love of life characterized by honest objectivity, respect and compassion, and an integration of this love of life into love of Christ, the Word of Life, within the living tradition of the Church community."

In its concluding paragraphs, the *Declaration on Religious Freedom* calls attention to the ever-increasing unification of the human family today and the close bonds drawing men of different cultures and religions into a solidarity. It contends, however, that two further factors are imperative for strengthening peaceful relationships and global harmony—the constitutional guarantee of religious freedom and respect for that highest of man's duties and rights—to conduct a religious life freely in society (Ch. III, No. 15).

The Universal Declaration of Human Rights

WHEREAS recognition of the inherent dignity and of the equal and inalienable rights of all members of the human family is the foundation of freedom, justice and peace in the world,

WHEREAS disregard and contempt for human rights have resulted in barbarous acts which have outraged the conscience of mankind, and the advent of a world in which human beings shall enjoy freedom of speech and belief and freedom from fear and want has been proclaimed as the highest aspiration of the common people,

WHEREAS it is essential, if man is not to be compelled to have recourse, as a last resort, to rebellion against tyranny and oppression, that human rights should be protected by the rule of law,

WHEREAS it is essential to promote the development of friendly relations between nations,

WHEREAS the peoples of the United Nations have in their Charter reaffirmed their faith in fundamental human rights, in the dignity and worth of the human person and in the equal rights of men and women and have determined to promote social progress and better standards of life in larger freedom,

WHEREAS Member States have pledged themselves to achieve, in co-operation with the United Nations, the promotion of universal respect for and observance of human rights and fundamental freedoms,

WHEREAS a common understanding of these rights and freedoms is of the greatest importance for the full realization of this pledge,

NOW, THEREFORE, THE GENERAL ASSEMBLY PROCLAIMS this Universal Declaration of Human Rights as a common standard of achievement for all peoples and all nations, to the end that every individual and every organ of society, keeping this Declaration constantly in mind, shall strive by teaching and education to promote respect for these rights and freedoms and by progressive measures, national and international, to secure their universal and effective recognition and observance, both among the peoples of Member States themselves and among the peoples of territories under their jurisdiction.

Article 1. All human beings are born free and equal in dignity and rights. They are endowed with reason and conscience and should act towards one another in a spirit of brotherhood.

Article 2. Everyone is entitled to all the rights and freedoms set forth in this Declaration, without distinction of any kind, such as race, colour, sex, language, religion, political or other opinion, national or social origin, property, birth or other status.

Furthermore, no distinction shall be made on the basis of the political, jurisdictional or international status of the country or territory to which a person belongs, whether it be independent, trust, non-self-governing or under any other limitation of sovereignty.

Article 3. Everyone has the right to life, liberty and security of person.

Article 4. No one shall be held in slavery or servitude; slavery and the slave trade shall be prohibited in all their forms.

Article 5. No one shall be subjected to torture or to cruel, inhuman or degrading treatment or punishment.

Article 6. Everyone has the right to recognition everywhere as a person before the law.

Article 7. All are equal before the law and are entitled without any discrimination to equal protection of the law. All are entitled to equal protection against any discrimination in violation of this Declaration and against any incitement to such discrimination.

Article 8. Everyone has the right to an effective remedy by the competent national tribunals for acts violating the fundamental rights granted him by the constitution or by law.

Article 9. No one shall be subjected to arbitrary arrest, detention or exile.

Article 10. Everyone is entitled in full equality to a fair and public hearing by an independent and impartial tribunal, in the determination of his rights and obligations and of any criminal charge against him.

Article 11. (1) Everyone charged with a penal offence has the right to be presumed innocent until proved guilty according to law in a public trial at which he has had all the guarantees necessary for his defence.

(2) No one shall be held guilty of any penal offence on account of any act or ommission which did not constitute a penal offence, under national or international law, at the time when it was committed. Nor shall a heavier penalty be imposed than the one that was applicable at the time the penal offence was committed.

Article 12. No one shall be subjected to arbitrary interference with his privacy, family, home or correspondence, nor to attacks upon his honour and reputation. Everyone has the right to the protection of the law against such interference or attacks.

Article 13. (1) Everyone has the right to freedom of movement and residence within the borders of each state.

(2) Everyone has the right to leave any country, including his own, and to return to his country.

Article 14. (1) Everyone has the right to seek and to enjoy in other countries asylum from persecution.

(2) This right may not be invoked in the case of prosecutions genuinely arising from non-political crimes or from acts contrary to the purposes and principles of the United Nations.

Article 15. (1) Everyone has the right to a nationality.

(2) No one shall be arbitrarily deprived of his nationality nor denied the right to change his nationality.

Article 16. (1) Men and women of full age, without any limitation due to race, nationality or religion, have the right to marry and to found a family. They are entitled to equal rights as to marriage, during marriage and at its dissolution.

(2) Marriage shall be entered into only with the free and full consent of the intending spouses.

(3) The family is the natural and fundamental group unit of society and is entitled to protection by society and the State.

Article 17. (1) Everyone has the right to own property alone as well as in association with others.

(2) No one shall be arbitrarily deprived of his property.

Article 18. Everyone has the right to freedom of thought, conscience and religion; this right includes freedom to change his religion or belief, and freedom, either alone or in community with others and in public or private, to manifest his religion or belief in teaching, practice, worship and observance.

Article 19. Everyone has the right to freedom of opinion and expression; this right includes freedom to hold opinions without interference and to seek, receive and impart information and ideas through any media and regardless of frontiers.

Article 20. (1) Everyone has the right to freedom of peaceful assembly and association.

(2) No one may be compelled to belong to an association.

Article 21. (1) Everyone has the right to take part in the government of his country, directly or through freely chosen representatives.

(2) Everyone has the right of equal access to public service in his country.

(3) The will of the people shall be the basis of the authority of government; this will shall be expressed in periodic and genuine elections which shall be by universal and equal suffrage and shall be held by secret vote or by equivalent free voting procedures.

Article 22. Everyone, as a member of society, has the right to social security and is entitled to realization, through national effort and international cooperation and in accordance with the organization and resources of each State, of the economic, social and cultural rights indispensable for his dignity and the free development of his personality.

Article 23. (1) Everyone has the right to work, to free choice of employment, to just and favourable conditions of work and to protection against unemployment.

(2) Everyone, without any discrimination, has the right to equal pay for equal work.

(3) Everyone who works has the right to just and favorable remuneration ensuring for himself and his family an existence worthy of human dignity, and supplemented, if necessary, by other means of social protection.

(4) Everyone has the right to form and to join trade unions for the protection of his interests.

Article 24. Everyone has the right to rest and leisure, including reasonable limitation of working hours and periodic holidays with pay.

Article 25. (1) Everyone has the right to a standard of living adequate for the health and well-being of himself and of his family, including food, clothing, housing and medical care and necessary social services, and the right to security in the event of unemployment, sickness, disability, widowhood, old age or other lack of livelihood in circumstances beyond his control.

(2) Motherhood and childhood are entitled to special care and assistance. All children, whether born in or out of wedlock, shall enjoy the same social protection.

Article 26. (1) Everyone has the right to education. Education shall be free, at least in the elementary and fundamental stages. Elementary education shall be compulsory. Technical and professional education shall be made generally available and higher education shall be equally accessible to all on the basis of merit.

(2) Education shall be directed to the full development of the human personality and to the strengthening of respect for human rights and fundamental freedoms. It shall promote understanding, tolerance and friendship among all nations, racial or religious groups, and shall further the activities of the United Nations for the maintenance of peace.

(3) Parents have a prior right to choose the kind of education that shall be given to their children.

Article 27. (1) Everyone has the right freely to participate in the cultural life of the community, to enjoy the arts and to share in scientific advancement and its benefits.

(2) Everyone has the right to the protection of the moral and material interests resulting from any scientific, literary or artistic production of which he is the author.

Article 28. Everyone is entitled to a social and international order in which the rights and freedoms set forth in this Declaration can be fully realized.

Article 29. (1) Everyone has duties to the community in which alone the free and full development of his personality is possible.

(2) In the exercise of his rights and freedoms, everyone shall be subject only to such limitations as are determined by law solely for the purpose of securing due recognition and respect for the rights and freedoms of others and of meeting the just requirements

of morality, public order and the general welfare in a democratic society.

(3) These rights and freedoms may in no case be exercised contrary to the purposes and principles of the United Nations.

Article 30. Nothing in this Declaration may be interpreted as implying for any State, group or person any right to engage in any activity or to perform any act aimed at the destruction of any of the rights and freedoms set forth herein.

Adopted by the United Nations General Assembly
at its 183rd meeting,
held in Paris on 10 December 1948

APPENDIX B

Statement of the U.S. Catholic Hierarchy
on Human Rights

Following is the text of a statement issued Jan. 17 by Auxiliary Bishop John J. Dougherty of Newark, chairman of the U.S. Bishops' Committee for World Justice and Peace, and Bishop John J. Wright of Pittsburgh, episcopal chairman of the Social Action Department of the U.S. Catholic Conference, on the 20th anniversary of the adoption of the United Nations Universal Declaration of Human Rights. In the name of the U.S. Bishops, the spokesmen call on all Catholics actively to support the International Year for Human Rights.

During this Epiphany season we celebrate the event, which, in consummately revealing God's love for men, illumines their dignity and the bond which unites them with one another.

It was through love that God created man in His own image, giving him freedom and intelligence to rule over His creation. Through love He made of all mankind one family that they should seek Him and build up the earth in His design. Through love God sent His only begotten Son to be born like men, to share their life, seeking out the poor, the weak, the despised—and by love's gift of self, even to death—to show the way to the Father which is lost through pride and lack of love. Acceptance of these great truths and the desire to follow the example of Christ do not set His followers apart from the efforts and the society of other men. In fact, they are thereby impelled to greater responsibility for helping shape this society so that all men may develop themselves and attain their true destiny.

In the words of Vatican II's Pastoral Constitution on the Church in the Modern World: "Man has in his heart a law written by God: to obey it is the very dignity of man. . . . In a wonderful manner conscience reveals that law which is fulfilled by love of God and neighbor. In fidelity to conscience, Christians are joined with the rest of men in the search for truth, and for the genuine solution to the numerous problems which arise in the life of individuals and from social relationships."

Today, as in the past, these problems stem largely from refusal or failure to see God's image in every man and to love him as a brother. With the victims of such contempt and indifference —with their needs and anxieties—the People of God must identify in a special way. They are indeed the majority of the world's people, suffering every form of want and oppression both of body and spirit. Their condition cannot be substantially altered except through the universal cooperation of all men, which is proper to man's nature as it is organizationally and technically possible in the circumstances of modern global society.

A practical basis for organizing such cooperation for the benefit of men—because it had been agreed upon by peoples of all races, beliefs and degrees of development—exists in the Universal Declaration of Human Rights. Pope John called its adoption by the United Nations 20 years ago—as a common standard of achievement—an act of highest importance for the juridical-political organization of all the peoples of the world. For in it, he notes. . . . "The dignity of the human person is acknowledged to all human beings . . . there is proclaimed the right of every man freely to investigate the truth and to follow the norms of moral good and justice and . . . the rights to a life worthy of man's dignity, while other rights connected with those mentioned are likewise proclaimed."

This year marks the 20th anniversary of the Universal Declaration of Human Rights. In December, 1948, the General Assembly of the United Nations gave its approval to this noble and historic document. The 30 articles of the declaration are brief, but they paint a striking picture of man's dignity and his rights as a person, as a member of society, and as a citizen of his nation and of the world.

As Catholic Christians, we welcome this solemn assertion of man's basic and inalienable rights. These rights, the declaration notes, are to be granted to all. No form of discrimination based on race, color, sex, language, religion, political or other opinion, national or social, origin, property, birth, or other status is to be tolerated. "Everyone has the right to life, liberty, and security of person" (Article 3).

As American citizens we rejoice that the rights, liberties, and freedom asserted in our Constitution and the Bill of Rights are substantially present in this declaration. It is significant that the right to privacy and the right to one's honor and reputation are upheld by the United Nations (Article 12). There is a vigorous defense of the right of every human being to freedom of thought, conscience, and religion, including "freedom, either alone or in community with others and in public or private, to manifest his religion or belief in teaching, practice, worship, and observance" (Article 18).

Political freedoms are also upheld by the Declaration of Human Rights. These are expressed in a form which clearly indicates that the democratic form of government alone harmonizes with an enlightened view of man's dignity and freedom. Likewise the call for complete fairness in the administration of justice sets standards which all mankind might well honor.

There are rights set forth in this declaration which as yet have been only imperfectly realized in our nation. We refer, first of all, to Article 22, which asserts the right to social security for every citizen and calls upon each state to use its resources to secure "the economic, social, and cultural rights indispensable for his dignity and the free development of his personality." It is hardly necessary to say that the United States is still struggling with the problem of poverty. Too often our welfare programs for the destitute offer little in the way of assistance or incentive to help these persons rise above the level of poverty.

Likewise our country has failed to meet the ideal expressed in Article 23, which asserts that "Everyone has the right to work, to free choice of employment, to just and favorable conditions of work, and to protection against unemployment." It is a shameful fact that there are several million Americans without work. Even worse is the fact that the burden of idleness is disproportionately borne by American Negroes and particularly Negro youth.

We are also particularly sensitive to difficulties around the right to education. Article 26 states that "Parents have a prior right to choose the kind of education that shall be given to their children." While no law in the United States interferes with this right, severe economic burdens make it difficult for many parents to secure an adequate religious education for their children.

Finally we regret that the efforts of President Kennedy and of President Johnson to secure United States participation in the proposed international agreement relating to forced labor, have received little interest and little understanding from United States citizens.

These flaws are imperfections which should challenge the social conscience of every citizen. Our ideals have always proclaimed full equality for all Americans. We should never tolerate any form of discrimination or neglect that leaves millions of Americans alienated from our society. Poverty can be endured when it is unavoidable, but persistent poverty in this affluent nation can only breed bitterness and despair.

We appeal to Catholics of the United States, therefore, to examine how they can better translate the law of love into effective action in the social order as well as in the personal contacts of daily life.

To that end, we urge study in all Catholic institutions and organizations during 1968 of the Universal Declaration of Human Rights in the light of the Church's teachings, particularly as these are expressed in the documents of the council and in recent encyclicals, and in view of the concrete situations in which men find themselves today.

We urge American Catholics to cooperate wholeheartedly with their fellow-citizens of all faiths and with civic bodies in working for changes in our laws and in our social and economic institutions which may be necessary to minister to the dignity of those who suffer discrimination because of color and to the needs of those who are poor and underprivileged.

We support such action in the spirit of President Johnson's proclamation of the International Year for Human Rights in which he asked for deepened commitment by United States citizens to the defense of human rights.

Despite the fact that the rights embodied in the declaration are familiar to Americans and are indeed guaranteed by our Constitution and the efforts of our government, equal exercise of their rights by all our citizens, as noted above, is far from a reality, and equal opportunity is for many only a cruel myth.

Without a fundamental change of attitude by the comfortable, by the favored ethnic majority, and especially by those who profess themselves Christians, we cannot build the social order which will lift the burdens and remove the indignities inflicted by racial discrimination and material privation on our brothers and on our country.

Man and society must advance together. The force of our example would greatly contribute to human progress in other areas of the world, to which, moreover, we have direct responsibilities in shaping a peaceful world community.

To see how, in accordance with the possibilities inherent in an organized world, Christians might best support and participate in the efforts toward such a community, Pope Paul VI set up the Pontifical Commission for the Study of World Justice and Peace. The American bishops are cooperating in this endeavor through their own Committee for Justice and Peace established to encourage a more effective response on the part of American Catholics in these efforts. As American citizens, they are members of the world community and depend greatly on all other members of this community for their own material, cultural and spiritual development, while they in turn have an abundance to give. To fulfill our responsibilities in this regard it is therefore essential to deepen our knowledge and understanding of the efforts being made by the United Nations and other agencies of economic and social cooperation, both public and private, which contribute effectively to the implementation of human rights.

Man does not live by bread alone, but also from every word that comes from the mouth of God. The freedom of millions of men to receive or to seek the truth is still being denied and repressed. During the International Year for Human Rights we can do no less than renew our sense of solidarity with them, as with all who suffer oppression, through constant prayer and by working through international contacts and institutions to change the ways and the hearts of those who oppress them. It becomes increasingly apparent that the respect due man's dignity and his inalienable rights should be reflected in the positive law of all nations, and eventually of the international community itself.

In the light of the above considerations, we firmly believe that sincere and steadfast participation by American Catholics in the aims of the UN International Human Rights Year will help to hasten the wish expressed for the United Nations by Pope John XXIII in the encyclical, Pacem in Terris: "May the time come as quickly as possible when every human being will find therein an effective safeguard for the rights which derive directly from his dignity as a person, and which are therefore universal, inviolable and inalienable rights. This is all the more to be hoped for since all human beings, as they take an ever more active part in the public life of their own country, are showing an increasing interest in the affairs of all peoples, and are becoming more consciously aware that they are living members of the whole human family."

APPENDIX C

Statement of the Position of
the U.S. YMCA on Human Rights

THE INTERNATIONAL YEAR FOR HUMAN RIGHTS (1968)
*The following resolution was adopted by the National Board
of Y.M.C.A.s at Atlanta, Georgia, on October 22, 1967:*

Whereas, 1968 has been designated by the United Nations as
the International Year for Human Rights, and

Whereas, human rights and fundamental freedoms are major
concerns of the YMCA Movement around the world, therefore be it

RESOLVED, that The International Year for Human Rights
have the support of the National Board of Y.M.C.A.s, and furthermore be it

RESOLVED, that the National Board urge local Associations,
Area, and State YMCA organizations and the National Board staff,
committees, and assemblies

1. To initiate and co-ordinate programs, events, and procedures which will help promote the Year and the Universal Declaration of Human Rights; and

2. Through study and discussion to bring into focus for
thoughtful attention and action, as they deem appropriate,
problems, issues and programs having to do with religious
freedom, rights for women and children, race relations,
help for refugees, the war against disease and poverty, and
other areas of concern involving human rights and fundamental freedoms; and

3. To co-operate in whatever ways they deem appropriate
with other organizations which are giving attention to
these concerns

RESOLVED, that this resolution be implemented as soon as
possible through all appropriate Y.M.C.A. channels, and in cooperation with other religious and civic organizations

RESOLVED, that the staff of the National Board should co-operate on behalf of the National Board with the United Nations Association of the U.S.A. in support of the Human Rights Year and should provide information and guidance to local Associations.

Reflections on the aspects of human rights to which the present volume addresses itself may be found in the booklet, sponsored by the Y.M.C.A. and the United Nations Association of the United States of America, *Human Rights and Fundamental Freedoms in Your Community,* by Stanley I. Stuber (Association Press, 1968), 51-61, "The Right to an Education."

Resolution of the General Assembly
of the National Council of Churches
# of Christ Concerning

INTERNATIONAL YEAR FOR HUMAN RIGHTS

Whereas—the General Assembly of the United Nations on December 12, 1963 designated the year 1968, the twentieth anniversary of the adoption and proclamation of the Universal Declaration of Human Rights, as International Year for Human Rights; and on December 20, 1965 reaffirmed its belief that 1968 should be devoted to intensive national and international efforts and undertakings in the field of human rights, and also to an international review of achievements in this field; and

Whereas—the Universal Declaration of Human Rights has proved to be a valuable and effective instrument and source of inspiration for new legislation and judicial decisions in many countries, as well as a milestone in the history of the United Nations activities in the field of human rights; and

Whereas—the United Nations has called upon the government of all countries and the peoples of the world to intensify the struggle to safeguard fundamental freedoms and human rights; and to assure the complete and immediate elimination of such violation of human rights as racial discrimination and the policy of *apartheid;* and

Whereas—the advancement of human rights leads toward the strengthening of peace throughout the world and to friendship between peoples: be it

RESOLVED—that the General Assembly of the National Council of Churches of Christ reaffirm the Pronouncement on Human Rights adopted by the General Assembly (December 6, 1963) urging "the renewed dedication of our citizens and our government to the manifold concerns for human rights within our own country and in the growing world community and thus to larger measures of justice and freedom making for more peace on earth," and be it further

RESOLVED—that the General Assembly call on the member churches to observe 1968 as International Year for Human Rights and, when appropriate and feasible, in cooperation with the United Nations Association of the USA; and be it further

RESOLVED—that the General Assembly call upon the Senate of the United States to approve for ratification by the President of the United States those Human Rights Conventions already submitted to the Senate Foreign Relations Committee and others which represent the freedoms guaranteed by the Bill of Rights of the United States Constitution.

Adopted by the General Assembly, December 9, 1966

APPENDIX E

The Synagogue Council of America
Declaration of 1968 as Human Rights Year

Man, the Bible asserts, was created in the image of God. In a world seething with turbulence and freighted with the burdens of a machine age, religion is summoned to array itself resolutely with all forces of humanity seeking to enhance the dignity and exalt the stance of man.

The United Nations designated the year 1968, the twentieth anniversary of the adoption of the Universal Declaration of Human Rights, as International Year for Human Rights, and urges that 1968 be devoted to intensive national and international activities in its observance.

The Universal Declaration of Human Rights has been a source of inspiration through the world as well as a milestone in the history of the United Nations. We join all freedom-loving forces in calling upon the government of all countries and the peoples of the world to intensify the struggle to safeguard fundamental freedoms and human rights; and to hasten the elimination of all violations of human dignity and worth. In the thrusts of human history, the Jew can never subtract his innate sensitivity for the welfare of all individuals in every time and clime. It is destiny of the Jewish people in the spirit of prophetic teaching, to epitomize with unequivocal clarity the historic lesson that the advancement of human rights everywhere ineluctably conduces toward the strengthening of peace throughout the world and to friendship between peoples.

The Synagogue Council of America, speaking on behalf of the Jewish Religious Community in the United States, urges renewed dedication of our citizens and our government to the manifold concerns for human rights within our own country and the growing world community and thus to larger measures of justice and freedom and furthering peace on earth.

The Synagogue Council of America therefore calls upon Rabbis and Synagogues throughout the land to observe 1968 as International Year for Human Rights and to carry on appropriate activities and programs throughout the year in furtherance of the observance.

THE CONTRIBUTORS

Quentin Quade is professor of political science at Marquette University. He did his undergraduate study at Creighton University and his graduate study at Notre Dame, and taught at St. Louis University (1959-61). Dr. Quade's writing and teaching center around political institutions, normative political theory, and the relationships between ethics and politics.

Carlos Sacheri is Professor of Philosophy at Laval University, Quebec, Canada. During 1966-67 he was visiting professor of philosophy in Argentina. Dr. Sacheri has written extensively on natural law and Thomistic philosophy.

Germain G. Grisez is professor of philosophy at Georgetown University and author of *Contraception and the Natural Law* (Bruce, 1964). Dr. Grisez is a graduate of John Carroll University, Cleveland, and received his doctorate from the University of Chicago. He has been a lecturer in philosophy at the University of Virginia and received a Lilly post-doctoral fellowship in religion in 1963-1964. Dr. Grisez is author of numerous articles in scholarly journals such as *Ethics, Journal of Religion, Natural Law Forum,* and *The Thomist.*

Catherine Schaefer graduated from Trinity College, Washington, D.C., and received her M.A. from the Catholic University of America. For many years she has been closely identified with the United Nations as the Assistant for United Nations Affairs to the General Secretary of the U.S. Catholic Conference. She is a member of the board of the United Nations Association of the United States and a member of the Catholic Committee for Intellectual and Cultural Affairs.

Cornelius J. Murphy, Jr., is a graduate of the College of the Holy Cross and the Boston College Law School. He holds his doctorate in law from the University of Virginia Law School. He is a professor of law at Duquesne University Law School in Pittsburgh. Prior to this he was a professor of law at the University of Maine Law School. Professor Murphy is the author of articles in the *Natural Law Forum, University of Maine Law Review, Syracuse Law Review,* and other learned journals.

Neil McCluskey, S.J., has his doctorate in education from Columbia University, was formerly Academic Vice President of the University of Seattle, and is currently a visiting professor of education at the University of Notre Dame. He is the author of *Public Schools and Moral Education* (Columbia U. Press, 1958), and of *Catholic Viewpoint on Education* (Doubleday and Co., 1959).

William V. O'Brien is President of the Catholic Association for International Peace and Director of the Institute on World Policy, Georgetown University. He has written and lectured extensively on all aspects of international politics.

Thomas Patrick Melady is author of *The Revolution of Color* (Hawthorn, 1966) and six other books on Africa, race relations, and the Third World. He is visiting professor at Seton Hall University and an adjunct professor at Fordham University. Dr. Melady has served as the Pax Romana representative to the United Nations since 1965.

John B. Sheerin, C.S.P., has been editor of *The Catholic World* for many years. He is a graduate of Fordham University Law School and a member of the bar. He was a Peritus at Vatican Council II and is a member of the Ecumenical Commission of the U.S. Council of Bishops. He was also an unofficial observer at the 1968 General Assembly of the World Council of Churches in Uppsala, Sweden.

NOTES TO CHAPTER 2

1. *In I Pol.*, 1.1, n.40
2. *Summa Th.*, II-II, q.58, a.7, 2m
3. For the distinction between "temporal common good" and "supernatural common good," see Ch.de Koninck, *De la Primauté du Bien Commun contre les Personalistes* (Quebec, 1943); Nimio de Anquin, *La jerarquia de los bienes,* Actas del Congreso Int. de Filosofia de Barcelona, III, 1948; Santiago Ramirez O.P., *Pueblo y Gobernantes al Servicio del Bien Comun* (Madrid, 1957), and Jean Madiran, *Le Principe de Totalite* (Paris, 1963).
4. Aristotle, *Ethics* X, c.7-10
5. *Summa c.Gentiles,* II, c.28
6. *Politics,* I. c.5
7. S. Thomas, *Com in V Metaphys.*, 1.2, n.766-69; De Malo, q.3, a.3; Com. in II Phys., 1.5, n.5.
8. See Marcel Clément, *Traite de Formation Sociale* (Québec, 1961), 331.
9. J. Meinvielle, *Concepcion Catolica de la Politica* (Buenos Aires, 1961), 96.
10. *Summa Th.*, I-II, q.95, a.1
11. *Ethics*, I, c.6, 1097b
12. *Ethics,* X
13. *Summa Th.*, II-II, q.180-82
14. *Politics*, VII, c.1-2
15. *Summa c.Gentiles,* III, c.37: "Ad hanc [contemplatio veritatis] omnes aliae humanae operationes ordinari videntur sicut ad finem."
16. *Summa Th.*, I, q.82, a.3; De Ver., q.22, a.12; q.21, a.3; *Summa c.Gentiles*, III, c.26, 35 and 37.
17. *In IV Sent.*, d.26, q.1, a.2, c: "Ad perfectionem humanae multitudinis sit necessarium aliquos contemplative vitae inservire."
18. *Summa Th.*, I, q.14, a.16
19. *Com. in I Eth.*, 1.2, n.27
20. Pius XI, *Quadragesimo Anno;* John XXIII, *Mater et Magistra.*
21. *Op. cit.*, II, c.110-12
22. *Lettre á la Semaine Sociales de Grenoble,* 1960
23. Pius XII, *Christmas Message,* 1952
24. *Summa Th.*, I-II, q.87, a.8,1m; II-II, q.57, a.4
25. *Summa Th.*, Suppl, q.41, a.1, c.

26. S.Thomas, *in I Sent.*, d.19, q.5, a.2, 1m; *Suppl.*, q.41, a.1, 1m.

27. *Com. in De Causis*, prop. I

28. *In III Sent.*, d.23, a.2, qa. 5, 1m; *Com. in Ep.ad Eph.*, II, 1.20, n.130.

29. *De Ver.*, q.22, a.5; *Summa Th.*, I-II, q9.4, a.6, 2m

NOTES TO CHAPTER 4

1. Address to Fifth Annual Congress of the Union of Italian Catholic Jurists; see *Pattern for Peace*, ed. H. Flannery (Westminster, Md. 1962).

2. Address to new Cardinals on "The Function of the Church"; see *Major Addresses of Pope Pius XII*, I, ed. V.A. Yzermans (St. Paul, 1968).

3. Text of NCWC News Service, Washington D.C.

4. U.S. Catholic Conference, Washington D.C.

5. Papal statements, unless otherwise indicated, may be found in *Principles for Peace*, ed. H. Koenig (Washington, 1943).

6. See *Pattern for Peace*.

7. For texts of statements of American Bishops referred to in this chapter, see *Our Bishops Speak 1919-1951* (Milwaukee, 1952).

8. Text in appendix of *Pattern for Peace*.

9. For full text see Appendix III of *Code of International Ethics*, ed. John Eppstein (Westminster, 1953).

10. The various UN texts referred to hereafter may be found in the pertinent volumes of the *International Yearbook of Human Rights*, United Nations. For discussion, see Summary Records of the indicated sessions of the Human Rights Commission, United Nations.

11. See Philippe de la Chapelle, *Catholicisme et la Declaration Universelle des Droits de l'Homme* (R. Pichon et R. Durand Ozias, Paris, 1967).

12. U.S. Catholic Conference, Washington D.C.

13. *Pacem in Terris*.

NOTES TO CHAPTER 5

1. Hans Kelsen, *The Law of the United Nations* (New York, 1964), 40.

2. Hersch Lauterpacht, *International Law and Human Rights* (New York, 1950), 152.

3. Benjamin Nathan Cardozo, *The Nature of Judicial Process* (New Haven, 1921), 131.

4. Rosalyn Higgins, *The Development of International Law Through the Political Organs of the United Nations* (London, New York, Oxford University Press, 1963); Oscar Schachter, "Law and the Process of Decisions in the Political Organs of the United Nations," *Recueil Des Cours*, II (1963), 171.

5. Edward M. Wise, "Steps toward the Advancement of Human Rights," *Western Res L Rev.*, xviii (1967), 1548, 1567.

6. A/RES/2200 (XX1) 1966. See: *American Journal of International Law*, LX1 (1967), 861.

7. RESTATEMENT OF THE FOREIGN RELATIONS LAW OF THE UNITED STATES Section 165.

8. Constitutional Law No. 18-60 of 28 November 1960. See *Yearbook on Human Rights* (New York, 1960), 56.

9. Constitution of the Somalia Republic of 1 July 1960, Art. 35. See *Yearbook on Human Rights* (New York, 1960), 304.

10. Article A12 of the Constitution of Gabon guarantees that in public educational establishments, religious instruction may be given children at the request of the parents. See *U.N. Yearbook* (New York, 1960), 137. Brazilian Law also makes provision for religious teaching in public education. See *U.N. Yearbook* (New York, 1961), 31.

Parental right of choice is protected in the European community by Art. 2 of the Protocol to the *Convention For the Protection of Human Rights and Freedoms.* 213 U.N.T.S. 262 (1955). See also Arthur H. Robertson, *Human Rights in Europe,* (Dobbs Ferry, N.Y., 1963), 196. In the English case of Watt v. Kesteven County Council 1955 1 K. B. 408 it was held that provisions of the Education Act of 1944 providing for parental choice do not mean that a parent, exercising that option, can demand that state officials pay his full expenses, although he may obtain a contribution towards fees based upon a means test.

In Canada the right of a parent with respect to his child's religious education in a public school entitled his child to attend the school without being required to take prescribed religion courses. Chabot v. Les Commissaires d'Ecoles de Lamorandiere (1957) Q.B. 707.

11. In the United States, the state court decisions with respect to parental choice are uneven, although there is a tendency to uphold assistance directly given to children and to deny aid where

the institution is the immediate beneficiary. Compare Board of Education v. Allen 20 NYS² 109, 281 NYS 2799 228 N.E. 791; affirmed 36 *Law Week* 4532 (1968) with Opinion of the Justices, 233 A² 832 (N.H. 1967).

At the federal level, litigation challenging aid to parochial education under the Education Act of 1964 is pending in the Courts. A district court decision holding that the petitioners did not possess standing to sue has been reversed by the Supreme Court. Flask v. Gardner, 271 F. Supp. 1. 36 *Law Week* 4601 (1968). Time factors prevent a full discussion of the decision.

It has been held that compulsory school attendance laws do not infringe upon the religious freedom of an Amish parent who did not wish children to attend public schools. State v. Garber 197 Kan 567, 419 P² 896 (1966).

12. The First Amendment provides that the Congress shall make no law respecting an establishment of religion or prohibiting the free exercise thereof.

13. 333 U.S. 203 (1948).

14. School District of Abington Township v. Schempp, 374 U.S. 203 (1963).

15. Perceptive observers such as Professor Hook have seen the increase in demands for parochial assistance as an inevitable result of the Court's decision with respect to religion in the public schools; a result which he does not welcome because of the alleged divisiveness of parochial education. See Sidney Hook, *Religion in a Free Society* (Lincoln, Univ. of Nebraska, 1967), ch. V. It may be conceded that extreme concentration of children in separate schools is socially undesirable; however, those who deplore this tendency should give more attention to the religious dimension of public education. It is arguable that the zeal with which American bishops and concerned parents have extended parochial schools—often where the movement was objectively unwise—would have been more moderate if the public school milieu was more hospitable to the interests of religion.

16. See *Declaration Art.* 21.3 "The will of the people shall be the basis of authority of government. . . ."

17. Mark D. Howe, *The Garden and the Wilderness*, (Chicago, 1965), 4.

18. Hook, *op. cit.*, 93-94, 100-101. Critics of the Court on this point were numerous. In addition to Professor Hook's essay see Griswold, *Absolute is in the Dark. A Discussion of the Approach of the Supreme Court to Constitutional Questions, Utah L Rev.*, VIII (1963), 167.; Brown, "Quis Custodiet Ipos Custodes?

The School Prayer Cases," *Supreme Court Review* (1963), 1. Rice, *The Supreme Court and Public Prayer; The Need for Restraint.* (1964).

19. See Philip Kurland, *Religion and the Law* (Chicago, 1962), where the legal expression of the formula is cogently stated. The difficulty with the theory lies in its extreme logical positivism. In his desire to achieve uniformity and predictability, Kurland universalizes a categorical imperative from the too few particulars where conscious injection of the religious dimension into the legal process has historically resulted in uneven and, in some cases, unjust results. While the Court has been significantly influenced by this formula, it is also becoming aware of its oversimplicity. See Sherbert v. Verner, 374 U.S. 398 (1963).

20. There are numerous expressions of this philosophy by members of the Court in Church-State decisions and elsewhere. For illustrations, see Murphy, "The Supreme Court and Democratic Theory," *Syracuse Law Review*, XVII (1966), 642-647.

21. Paul Ramsey, "How Shall We Sing the Lord's Song in a Pluralistic Land?" *Journal of Public Law*, XIII (1964), 353, 360-361.

22. William Douglas, *The Bible and the Schools*, (1966), 35.

23. For a further elaboration of these ideas see my "Supreme Court and Democratic Theory," *supra*, note 20.

24. These ideas are being developed at a high level of abstraction, yet they are not without some practical relevance. Preparation of the Federal Education Act, now being challenged in the Courts, demonstrated the possibility of achieving some accommodation on these issues in a spirit of good will; an accomplishment by elected representatives of the people. The enactment, it should be noted, was not "pure politics"; the Congress gave careful attention to the First Amendment issued. See Wilber G. Katz, *Religion and American Constitutions*, (Evanston, Ill., 1964), 72ff.

The recent experience in New York, where the difficult question of financial aid to non-public education was submitted to the people in a referendum, also contradicts the thesis propounded by Justice Douglas.

25. Justice Stewart's dissent in the *Bible Reading Cases* is of considerable importance:

It might also be argued that parents who want their children exposed to religious influences can adequately fulfill that wish off school property and outside school time. With all its surface persuasiveness, however, this argument seriously misconceives the basic constitutional justification for permitting the exercises at issue in these cases. For a compulsory state educational system so structures a child's life that if religious exercises are held to be an impermissible activity in schools, religion is placed at an artificial and state-created disadvantage. Viewed in this light, permission of such exercises for those who want them is necessary if the schools are truly to be neutral in the matter of religion. And a refusal to permit religious exercises thus is seen, not as the realization of state neutrality, but rather as the establishment of a religion of secularism, or at the least, as government support of the beliefs of those who think that religious exercises should be conducted only in private (374 U.S. at 313).

26. Jacques Maritain, *True Humanism,* trans. Margot Adamson (London, 1946).

27. *Populorum progressio,* "On the Development of Peoples," (Boston, Daughters of St. Paul, 1967), 26.

NOTES TO CHAPTER 6

1. *The Church and Modern Society* (New York, 1903), I, 117-18.

2. *Records of the Massachusetts Bay,* II, 203.

3. *Life and Works,* II, 289-90.

4. *Ibid.,* 290

5. *Twelfth Annual Report,* facsimile ed., 116-17. Quoted in Neil G. McCluskey, *Public Schools and Moral Education* (New York, 1958), 91. This book contains an extended discussion of the historic issue.

6. By 1820 the estimated Catholic population was 195,000; a decade later it was 318,000; in 1840 it was 663,000 and in 1850, 1,606,000. On the eve of the Civil War, it had doubled and doubled again in both the census of 1880 and 1900. Estimates of today's Catholic population vary between 45 and 50 million or 23-25 per cent of the total population. See John L. Thomas, *The American Catholic Family* (Englewood Cliffs, N.J., 1956), 108, for the earlier figures. *The Official Catholic Directory* for 1968 gives (47, 468, 333), a conservative figure.

7. "The Changing Image of Catholicism in America," *Yale Review,* 48: 575 (June 1959).

8. John Gilmary Shea, *History of the Catholic Church in the United States,* (New York, 1886), 260.

9. John Gilmary Shea, *A History of Georgetown College,* (New York, 1891), 9.

10. Peter Guilday, ed., *The National Pastorals of the American Hierarchy*, 1792-1919 (Washington, D.C., 1923), 4.

11. *Ibid.*, 26

12. The New England *Primer* was a children's version of the Calvinist catechism. No textbook was more widely used. Between 1700 and 1850 the *Primer* sold 3 million copies.

13. *The National Pastorals*, 28.

14. 6th Decree, Fourth Provincial Council, 1840. Burns estimates that in 1838 there were 200 Catholic parochial schools (J.A. Burns, *The Principles, Origin and Establishment of the Catholic School System in the United States* [New York, 1912], 386). Cross makes much of the fact that the first *Catholic Almanac*, appearing in 1833, failed to mention the few parochial schools in existence. It did, but they were lumped into the category of "charitable institutions."

15. *National Pastorals*, 134

16. *Ibid.*

17. *Ibid.* One student of the period traces to this council the real beginnings of the Catholic drive for separate schools. (James E. Diffley, "Catholic Reaction to American Public Education, 1792-1852." Unpublished doctoral dissertation, University of Notre Dame, 1959). This is extremely doubtful though it is true that by 1840 the clash between certain liberal assumptions underlying public education and certain traditional Catholic principles was underway.

18. *Ibid.*

19. *Donahue v. Richards* (38 Maine, 376, 1854). The court ruled that the school board had "the legal and constitutional right to expel a child from school for refusing to read the Bible used by the school even though the child or its parents had religious scruples against doing so."

20. The New York *Freeman's Journal*, July 11, 1840. Cited in Edward M. Connors, *Church-State Relationships in Education in the State of New York* (Washington, 1951), 56.

21. Quoted in a pamphlet *The Public School Question* (Boston, 1876), 9.

22. *Ibid.*

23. Joseph Bayma, "The Liberalistic View of the School Question" *The American Catholic Quarterly Review*, II, 17.

24. *The Public School Question*, 9.

25. Quoted in Daniel F. Reilly, *The School Controversy* (1891-1893) (Washington, 1943), 107.

26. The full text of the document, "Petition of the Catholics of New York for a Portion of the Common-School Fund" is to be found in *Catholic Education in America*, ed. Neil G. McCluskey, (New York: Teachers College Bureau of Publications, 1964), 65-77.

27. Mary Peabody Mann, *Life of Horace Mann*, Centennial edition in facsimile, (National Education Association: Washington, D.C., 1937), 262.

28. J.A. Burns and Bernard J. Kohlbrenner, *A History of Catholic Education in the United States*, (New York, 1937), 82.

29. Richard J. Sabel, *Public Funds for Church and Private Schools* (Washington, 1937), 305-06.

30. *Ibid.*, 493.

31. The most competent treatment of these troubled years is still Ray A. Billington. *The Protestant Crusade, 1800-1860* (New York, 1938).

32. *The National Pastorals*, 190.

33. *Ibid.*

34. *Ibid.*, 191.

35. *Ibid.*, 215.

36. *Ibid.*, 216.

37. *Ibid.*

38. *Ibid.*, 217.

39. See especially Thomas T. McAvoy, C.S.C., "Public Schools vs. Catholic Schools and James McMaster," *The Review of Politics*, 28, No. 1, (January 1966) 19-46.

40. No area was more bitterly fought over in the conservative-liberal struggle within the Catholic Church of the latter nineteenth century than the state school. Father McAvoy's distinguished work is vital background here. See: Thomas T. McAvoy, *"The Great Crisis in American Catholic History 1895-1900* (Chicago, 1957).

41. *N.Y. Freeman's Journal*, July 1, 1871.

42. *Ibid.*, July 8, 1871.

43. *Ibid.*, Feb. 15, 1872.

44. The influence Miss Edes exerted in Rome on American Church affairs throughout the final 30 years of the nineteenth century was uncanny. Like McMaster a convert, she worked in Rome for the prefect of the Propaganda as a secretary and for several newspapers as a correspondent. Her instincts were all conservative. Her knowledge of Rome and her sense of *"Romanità"* made her an invaluable pipeline.

45. The original letter and *Memorandum*, quoted by McAvoy,

op. cit., 28, is in the archives of the Sacred Congregation of Propaganda Fide.

46. Wanting today's more highly developed journalistic ethics and libel laws, the journals and newspapers of the time were much more free-swinging than we are accustomed to today. Moreover, there was little church control over these media which generally were in private hands.

47. Archives of the Sacred Congregation of Propaganda Fide, Rome, *Lettere della S. Congregazione Anno 1874,* Vol. 370, fol. 147, 148. Copy in the University of Notre Dame Archives.

48. Quoted in McAvoy, 33-35. Original in the Baltimore Cathedral Archives.

49. Quoted in McAvoy, 35-36. Original in Rochester Diocesan Archives, McQuaid Papers, Bayley to McQuaid, Baltimore, June 25, 1874.

50. "Instruction of the Congregation of Propaganda de Fide concerning Catholic Children Attending American Public Schools, November 24, 1875," printed in *Catholic Education in America,* 121-26. The English translation reprinted here was first published in *The Pastor,* IV (June, 1886), 232-37. The Latin text appeared *in Acta et decreta concilii plenarii Baltimorensis tertii* (Baltimore, 1886), 279-82.

51. *Ibid.*

52. Quoted in *The School Controversy (1891-1893),* 286.

53. *Instruction.*

54. *Capita praecipua quae Emi. Cardinales S.C. de Propaganda Fide censuerunt a Rmis Archiepiscopis et Episcopis Foederatorum Statuum A.S. Romae congregatis praeparanda esse pro futuro Concilio.* Copy in Boston Archdiocesan Archives. The author is indebted to Fr. McAvoy for this reference.

These were the American prelates: Gibbons of Baltimore, William of Boston, Feehan of Chicago, Heiss of Milwaukee, Fitzgerald of Little Rock, Ryan of St. Louis, Corrigan of New York, Seghers of Oregon City, O'Hara of Scranton, Salpointe of Arizona and Chatard of Vincennes.

55. See "Minutes of the Roman Meeting Preparatory to the III Plenary Council of Baltimore" translated in *The Jurist,* III (1951), 121-31: 302-12: 417-24: 538-47. The school question is discussed on pages 422-24.

56. Chicago's Archbishop Feehan was chairman; the others were: Bishops Cosgrove of Davenport, Flasch of LaCrosse, and Spalding of Peoria. The eminently diplomatic Gibbons balanced

this group against a special deputation of bishops which reported to the council on Title VI: Heiss of Milwaukee, Francis McNeirny of Albany, Gilmour of Cleveland, and O'Farrell of Trenton.

57. Printed in Francis P. Cassidy, "Catholic Education in the Third Plenary Council of Baltimore," *Catholic Historical Review*, XXXIV (1948), 257-305 and 414-36.

58. *Interdict* bars the faithful from certain sacred acts, e.g., the bishop could order that no further masses are to be offered in a parish church. *Excommunication* is a sentence cutting a member off from association with the rest of the faithful.

59. Cassidy, 416.

60. *Acta et decreta councilii plenarii tertii* (Baltimore, 1886): Latin text of the decrees is found on page 104. The translation is the author's.

61. *Ibid.* The English text of the pastoral letter may be read in *Acta et decreta*, pp. lxxviii-lxxix, lxxxii-lxxxvi.

62. The change in Protestant policy is carefully documented in Francis X. Curran, *The Churches and the Schools* (Chicago, 1954).

63. The sections of the pastoral dealing with education may be found in *Catholic Education in America*, 86-93.

64. *Ibid.*, 93.

65. Ireland's letter to Cardinal Ledochowski, prefect of Propaganda, cites some of them: "I would not have Your Eminence, however, believe that I was the first ever to introduce such an arrangement into the United States or that the two villages above named are the only places where it actually prevails; on the contrary, Cardinal McCloskey, Archbishop of New York, instituted it 18 years ago in his diocese in the town of Poughkeepsie where it has been maintained there ever since by his successor, Archbishop Corrigan. It is in operation in 8 localities of the diocese of Archbishop Katzer of Milwaukee who also established it in his former diocese of Green Bay. It obtains in a great number of the schools of Bishop Zardetti in the diocese of St. Cloud; in the diocese of Savannah Bishop Becker has it in operation in all the Catholic schools of his Episcopal city. The Fathers of the Society of Jesus have applied the same plan with great success in their parish of Connewago in the diocese of Harrisburg; it also obtains in the dioceses of Albany, Erie, Buffalo, Rochester, Peoria, etc. etc." (See Appendix E, The School Controversy, 1891-1893, 255.)

66.

YEAR	CHURCHES	SCHOOLS	PUPILS	CHURCHES WITH SCHOOLS
1884	6,626	2,464	490,531	(37%)*
1885	6,755	2,621	492,949	(39%)
1886	6,910	2,697	537,725	(39%)
1887	6,829	2,606	511,063	(38%)
1888	7,424	3,024	585,965	(41%)
1889	7,523	3,194	633,238	(42%)
1890	7,523	3,194	633,238	(42%)
1891	7,947	3,482	694,513	(44%)
1892	8,431	3,585	731,385	(42%)
1893	8,512	3,610	768,498	(42%)
1894	9,309	3,731	775,070	(40%)
1895	9,501	3,361	796,348	(35%)
1896	9,670	3,438	812,611	(35%)
1897	9,570	3,636	819,575	(38%)
1898	10,002	3,581	815,063	(36%)
1899	10,339	3,811	854,523	(37%)
1900	10,427	3,812	903,980	(36%)

* Figures for 1884 are found in the 1885 *Catholic Directory,* not the volume for the year itself, etc. How accurate some of these statistics are is open to doubt. At least the suspicion is directed equally toward each year's findings.

67. Some of the statistics of the early Catholic Directories are inconsistent and suggest error. Boston, for example, in 1884 has 30 per cent of its parishes with schools and in 1894 goes up to 54 percent, but then drops in 1899 to 30 per cent. Milwaukee reports 26 schools in 1884 and five years later lists 125!

68. "The decline in employment in railroad building from 1882 to 1883 came to 500,000 men of a total national labor force of only 18 million. Steel rails, worth $71 a ton in January 1880, were selling for half that in December 1883." (Ray Ginger, *Age of Excess,* New York, 1965), 43.

69. Statistical tables printed in Ellwood P. Cubberley, *Public Education in the United States* (Cambridge, 1947 ed.), 627. Three out of four Americans now *finish* high school. In 1967 nearly 2.7 million students graduated and about 40 per cent started college.

70. Allen Sinclair Will, *Life of James Cardinal Gibbons, Archbishop of Baltimore* (New York, 1922), II, 238.

71. Complete text can be found in *Catholic Education in America,* 128-40.

72. *Ibid.,* 129-30.

73. *Ibid.*, 131. Ireland's opponents repeatedly cited these words as proof that he was an enemy of the parochial school. This was "dirty pool." The archbishop of St. Paul had been surpassed by few in building schools. As he wrote to Cardinal Ledochowski, Prefect of the Propaganda, "My opponents say that I deplored the existence of the parochial school. It is untrue. I deplored the necessity of the Catholics being obliged after paying in tax for the support of state schools to maintain again by voluntary contributions schools of their own, and asked the State for means to maintain schools Catholic as well as Protestant, . . ." (Appendix E, *The School Controversy*, 1891-1893, 251.)

74. *Ibid.*, 133.

75. *Ibid.*, 134.

76. *Ibid.*, 137.

77. *Ibid.*, 139-40.

78. Complete text in *Catholic Education in America*, 141-50. This citation, 146.

79. Peter M. Abbelen (1843-1917), vicar general of the Milwaukee archdiocese.

80. In 1890 and also in 1891 the German emigration societies, meeting in Lucerne, deplored what they considered great losses to the Church among the immigrants. Under the presidency of Count Peter Cahensley (hence "Cahensleyism" as a name for the movement), they urged the Holy See to provide the equivalent of "National" bishops.

81. Letter quoted in John Tracy Ellis, *The Life of James Cardinal Gibbons* (Milwaukee, 1952), I, 664.

82. There is an extended study of this philosophy in the author's *Public Schools and Moral Education* (New York, 1958).

83. "The Scope of Public School Education," an address in the collection *Means and Ends in Education* (Chicago, 1895). Reprinted in *Catholic Education in America*.

84. Ellis, I, 664.

85. The document is to be found in *Catholic Education in America*, 151-60.

86. F. J. Zwierlein, *The Life and Letters of Bishop McQuaid* III (Rochester, 1927), 191-93.

87. Letter reprinted in *Catholic Education in America*, 162-63.

88. Robert D. Cross, *The Emergence of Liberal Catholicism in America* (Cambridge, 1958), 145.

89. In sum, these concepts involved man's cooperation with grace and the action of the Holy Spirit, the importance of the nat-

ural virtues and the relevance of religious vows, new and irenic approaches to other religions.

90. See enrollment figures in following chart.

CATHOLIC AND PUBLIC (ELEMENTARY-SECONDARY) SCHOOL
ENROLLMENT IN U.S., 1960-1967

YEAR	CATHOLIC SCHOOL ENROLLMENT	Per-cent-age of Total	PUBLIC SCHOOL ENROLLMENT	Per-cent-age of Total	TOTAL CATHOLIC* PUBLIC SCHOOL ENROLLMENT
1900	854,523	5.2	15,503,110	94.8	16,357,633
1910	1,236,946	6.4	17,813,852	93.6	19,050,798
1920	1,826,213	7.8	21,578,316	92.8	23,404,529
1930	2,469,032	8.8	25,678,315	91.2	28,147,047
1940	2,581,596	9.2	25,434,542	90.8	28,016,138
1950	3,080,166	10.9	25,111,427	89.1	28,191,593
1960	5,288,705	12.7	36,086,771	87.3	41,375,576
1961	5,397,678	12.5	37,504,190	87.4	42,901,868
1962	5,613,956	12.6	38,836,610	87.4	44,450,566
1963	5,625,040	12.2	40,217,215	87.8	45,842,255
1964	5,662,328	12.0	41,416,289	88.0	47,078,617
1965	5,582,354	11.4	* 43,055,000	88.6	48,637,354
1966	5,473,606	11.2	* 43,152,000	88.8	48,625,606
1967	5,254,766	10.7	* 43,900,000	89.3	49,154,766

Sources: *Official Catholic Directory* (New York: P. J. Kenedy and Sons); *Biennial Survey of Education and School Life,* U. S. Office of Education.

* Estimate by the U. S. Office of Education.

91. All the canons dealing with education may be found in the author's translation in *Catholic Education in America*, 175-77.

NOTES TO CHAPTER 7

1. Andrew M. Greeley, *The Hesitant Pilgrim* (New York, 1966), esp. Part III, 139-214; Manning M. Pattilo, Jr., and Donald M. Mackenzie, *Church-sponsored Higher Education in the United States,* Report of the Danforth Commission (Washington, D.C., 1966), 200-208; Joseph F. Mulligan, S.J., "The Catholic Campus Today," *Commonweal,* Jan. 28, 1966, 497-499; John Cogley, "Catholic Universities: The Future of an Illusion," *Commonweal,* June 2, 1967, 310-316.

For a brief, incisive summary of the evolution and present

state of American Catholic education generally and an excellent annotated bibliography see Jack F. Bernard and John J. Delaney, *A Guide to Catholic Reading* (Garden City, N.Y., 1966), 118-126.

2. Neil G. McCluskey, S.J., *Catholic Education in America* (New York, 1965).

3. E.g. Jacques Maritain, *Christianity and Democracy*, Doris C. Anson, trans. (New York, 1944).

4. Address of Dr. Robert M. Hutchins at 175th Anniversary Convocation, Georgetown University, March 19, 1964. Dr. Hutchins stated:

> If we want to make the Athenian effort, we should be able to turn to the Catholic universities for leadership. I have had the impression from time to time that they were not prepared to give it. They have seemed occasionally to feel that their prime obligation was to show that they were just as American as the secular institutions. This they have done—or so it has sometimes seemed—by imitating, or even exaggerating, the vices of those institutions. They have offered as wide a range of trivial courses. They have set up as many pseudo-professional schools. They are sunk as deep in the slough of vocationalism and specialism as all the rest. They have either gloried in big-time, industrial football, or, when they have abandoned it, have been careful to give a true-blue American reason for doing so: they have said they were losing money. The battle against the culture, which every good university must wage, cannot be won on these terms.
>
> A good university is a center of independent thought. Its function is the critical appraisal and renewal of the intellectual heritage of the race. A great part of that heritage—I think myself the greatest—is the special work and possession of the Catholic church. The elucidation of that possession and its adaptation to the modern world is therefore the special task of the Catholic universities.

5. See, for example, "State of the Question: Do We Have Catholic Colleges?," responses by Fr. Christopher J. O'Toole, C.S.C. and Fr. R.J. Henle, S.J., *America*, Sept. 21, 1963, 296-299; and Brian A. McGrath, S.J., "Principles and Traditions of Jesuit Education," *Georgetown Papers on Jesuit Education* (Washington, D.C., 1966), 12-20.

6. See Fr. Greeley's chapter, "The Future of Catholic Education," *op. cit.*, 202-214 for an informed, balanced, and ultimately optimistic and imaginative treatment of this subject.

7. Andrew M. Greeley and Peter H. Rossi, *The Education of Catholic Americans* (Chicago, 1966).

8. Fr. Greely's *The Hesitant Pilgrim* provides a useful analysis of the problems of improving the spiritual life of American

Catholics on campuses and throughout the whole American society. By citing his work I seek to emphasize that I do not underestimate the function of the American Catholic institutions of higher learning in furthering the spiritual life of its students and faculty. Rather I seek to emphasize that this task has to be approached in an entirely different way in the post-Vatican II Church, generally, and on American Catholic campuses.

9. See Heinrich Rommen's monumental work, *The State in Catholic Thought* (St. Louis and London, 1945); Johannes Messner's *Social Ethics*, J.J. Doherty, trans.; (rev. ed; St. Louis & London, 1965); A.P. d'Entrèves, *Natural Law* (London, 1951); Illtud Evans, O.P., *Light on the Natural Law* (Baltimore, 1965); John Courtney Murray, S.J., *We Hold These Truths* (New York, 1960) esp. Chapter 13, "The Doctrine Lives," 295-336.

10. Walter M. Abbott, S.J., ed., *The Documents of Vatican II* (New York, 1966), No. 79, 292.

11. See, for example, Fr. Robert O. Johann's column, "Philosopher's Notebook," *America*, April 10, 1965, and the responses in "State of the Question: Right Reason and Natural Law," *America*, May 22, 1965, 754-771, by Malcolm P. Mullen, S.J., Germain G. Grisez, and Thomas J. Higgins, S.J., to whom Fr. Johann responds.

12. e.g., Messner, *op. cit.*, 369-371, 596-601.

13. United States Catholic Conference, *On the Development of Peoples, Populorum Progressio* (Washington, D.C., 1967), N31 "Revolution," 22-23.

14. *Ibid.*, #2 and 3, pp. 3-4.

15. The writer has prepared a selective bibliography covering this subject in *Nuclear War, Deterrence and Morality* (Westminster/New York/Glen Rock/Amsterdam/Toronto, 1967), 115-120.

16. e.g., Jerome Wiesner, Thomas C. Schelling, Amron Katz, Albert Wohlstetter.

17. This duty relates to the assertion of Article 26 of the International Declaration of Human Rights, paragraph 2, which calls for education which promotes "understanding, tolerance, and friendship among all nations, racial, or religious groups and shall further the activities of the United Nations for the maintenance of peace." For the most authoritative and exhaustive analysis of the Convention's treatment of this subject see Albert Verdoodt, *Naissance et signification de la Declaration Universelle des Droits de l'Homme* (Louvain/Paris, 1963), esp. 248-252.

NOTES TO CHAPTER 8

1. T. O. Elias, "The New Constitution of Nigeria and the Protection of Human Rights and Fundamental Freedoms," *Journal of International Commission of Jurists*, Vol. 3, No. 2 (Winter 1961), 79.

2. *Ibid.*, 46.

3. *South Africa and the Rule of Law* (Geneva International Commission of Jurists, 1960).

4. See also Edgar H. Brooks and J. B. Macaulay, *Civil Liberty in South Africa* (Cape Town, 1958).

NOTES TO CHAPTER 9

1. John C. Bennett, "A Protestant Views Religious Liberty," *The Catholic World*, Vol. 201 (September 1965), 362.

2. Thomas F. Stransky, C.S.P., Commentary on the *Declaration on Religious Freedom* (Glen Rock, N.J., 1966), Footnote 12, p. 73.

3. Robert W. Lynn, editorial in *Christianity and Crisis*, (Oct. 30, 1967), 243.

4. Sidney E. Mead, *The Lively Experiment* (New York, 1963), 68.

5. J. Paul Williams, *What Americans Believe and How They Worship* (New York, 1952), 371.

6. Carl J. Pfeifer, S.J., in "The Elementary School and Ecumenism," *Religious Education* (November-December 1967), 468.

7. *Ibid.*, 472.

Index

— Anita O'Day ?

— Toxico.

— Cary Grant ?

— Homo.

— Sénateur William F. Knowland ?

— Ivrogne.

— Chef Parker ?

— Ivrogne.

— Bing Crosby ?

— Ivrogne et tabasseur d'épouse.

— Sergent John O'Grady ?

— Mec du LAPD connu pour planter de la came dans le dos des musiciens de jazz.

— Desi Arnaz ?

— Chasseur de putes.

— Scott Brady ?

— Amateur d'herbe.

— Grace Kelly ?

— Frigide. Je l'ai sautée à une occasion et j'ai failli me geler le poireau.

Pete éclata de rire.

— Moi ?

Lenny eut un rictus.

— Roi de l'extorsion. Mac. Tueur. Et au cas où vous vous poseriez la question, je suis bien trop malin pour jamais essayer de déconner avec vous.

— Tu as le boulot, dit Pete.

Ils se serrèrent la main.

Sal le Fou franchit la porte, agitant deux tasses débordant de nickels.

peux plus attendre de me mettre sur mon trente et un, en femme s'il vous plaît, et vous inviter tous autant que vous êtes à dormir à ma soirée roupillon de la Bande !

Lawford fonça vers la scène.

Pete lui fit un croche-pied.

Visez-moi le plongeon du larbin, le cul par terre — classique instantané de tous les âges.

Frank Sinatra se fraya un chemin dans le salon. Les excursionnistes se transformèrent en une vraie clique de putains de givrés.

Sam G. l'intercepta. Sam G. lui murmura à l'oreille, doux, gentil et *ferme*.

Pete pigea le topo.

Lenny est avec l'Organisation. Lenny c'est pas le mec à rudoyer pour le plaisir.

Sam souriait. Ça le bottait bien, le Sam, le numéro de Lenny.

Sinatra fit volte-face. Entouré par une meute de lèche-culs.

Lenny remonta son zézaiement de plusieurs crans ;

— Frankie, reviens ! Peter, relève-toi donc, espèce de superbe andouille !

Lenny Sands était un merdaillon mignon et plein d'esprit.

Il glissa au chef de table de blackjack un mot à faire passer à Sands. Lenny fit son apparition à la cafétéria, ponctuel, à la minute près.

— Merci d'être venu, dit Pete.

Lenny s'assit.

— Votre petit mot parlait d'argent. C'est quelque chose qui attire toujours mon attention.

Une serveuse apporta du café. Des gongs de jackpot sonnaient, des machines à sous miniatures étaient boulonnées à chaque table.

— Kemper Boyd vous a recommandé. Il a dit que vous seriez parfait pour le boulot.

— Est-ce que vous travaillez pour lui ?

— Non. C'est juste une relation. Quelqu'un que je connais.

Lenny se frotta la cicatrice qu'il avait au-dessus de la lèvre.

— En quoi consiste le boulot exactement ?

— Vous seriez le dénicheur de *L'Indiscret*, le remueur de scandales. A déterrer de bonnes histoires et de bons petits scandales que vous refileriez aux rédacteurs.

— Je serai donc une balance ?

— En quelque sorte. Vous gardez bien le nez au ras des pâquerettes à L.A., Chicago et au Nevada et vous revenez au rapport.

— Pour combien ?

— Un bâton par mois, en liquide.

— Des cancans bien sales sur les vedettes de ciné, c'est ça que vous voulez ? Vous voulez toute la crasse sur les gens du spectacle ?

— Exact. Et sur les hommes politiques genre libéral.

Lenny se servit de crème dans son café.

— J'ai rien contre ça, à vrai dire, excepté les Kennedy. Bobby, je peux bien m'en passer, mais Jack, je l'aime bien.

— Vous avez été plutôt dur avec Sinatra. Il est pote avec Jack, pas vrai ?

— Il maquereaute pour Jack et lèche le cul de toute la famille, à en avoir le blair tout marron. Peter Lawford a épousé une des sœurs de Jack et c'est le contact lèche-cul de Frank. Jack est d'avis que Frank est bien utile pour une bonne marrade, mais pas grand-chose d'autre, et ce que je viens de vous dire, vous ne l'avez jamais entendu sortir de ma bouche.

Pete but une gorgée de café.

— Dites-m'en plus.

— Non. A vous de demander.

— Okay. Je suis sur Sunset et je veux tirer un coup pour un billet de cent. Qu'est-ce que je fais ?

— Vous voyez Mel, le mec du parking au « Dino's Lodge ». Pour dix *cents*, il vous enverra à une crèche sur Havenhurst et Fountain.

— Supposez que je veuille de la Négrillonne ?

— Allez au drive-in sur Washington et La Brea et touchez-en un mot aux patineuses de couleur.

— Supposez que les garçons, ça me botte ?

Lenny tiqua.

— Je sais que vous détestez les pédés, dit Pete, mais répondez à la question.

— Merde, je ne... Attendez.. le portier du « Largo » dirige un réseau de prostit mâles.

— Bien. Et maintenant, qu'est-ce qu'on raconte sur la vie sexuelle de Mickey Cohen ?

Lenny sourit.

— Elle est purement symbolique. La chatte, ça ne le botte pas vraiment, mais il aime être vu en compagnie de belles femmes. Sa quasi petite amie du moment s'appelle Sandy Hashhagen. Parfois, il sort avec Candy Barr et Liz Renay.

— Qui a effacé Tony Trombino et Tony Brancato ?

— Soit Jimmy Frattiano, soit un flic du nom de Dave Klein.

— Qui a la plus grosse queue d'Hollywood ?

— Steve Cochran ou John Ireland.

— Qu'est-ce que fait Spade Cooley pour prendre son pied ?

— Il s'avale des bennies et tabasse son épouse.

— Avec qui Ava Gardner a-t-elle trompé Sinatra ?

— Avec tout le monde.

— Qui faut-il voir pour un avortement rapide ?

— J'irais voir Freddy Otash.

— Jayne Mansfield ?

— Nympho.

— Dick Contino ?

— Brouteur de chattes suprême.

— Gail Russell ?

— Elle se tue à picoler dans une piaule bon marché de L.A.-Ouest.

— Lex Barker ?

— Coureur de chattes, avec une tendance à préférer les mineures.

— Johnny Ray ?

— Homo.

— Art Pepper ?

— Camé.

— Lizabeth Scott ?

— Gouine.

— Billy Eckstine ?

— Amateur de chattes.

— Tom Neal ?

— Dans la dèche à Palm Springs.

20

Washington D.C., 20 janvier 1959.

United Parcel déposa trois grosses caisses. Kemper les transporta dans sa cuisine et les ouvrit.

Bondurant avait enveloppé les joujoux dans de la toile huilée. Bondurant comprenait le concept de « gâteries ».

Bondurant lui envoyait deux mitraillettes, deux grenades à main et neuf automatiques, calibre .45, équipés de silencieux.

Bondurant y joignait un petit mot, succinct, non signé.

« A vous de jouer, Stanton et toi. »

Les mitraillettes étaient livrées avec chargeurs-camemberts pleins et un manuel d'entretien. Le .45 tombait à la perfection dans son étui d'épaule.

Kemper en fixa un et partit pour l'aéroport. Il prit la navette de 13 heures pour New York avec du temps à perdre.

Le 681 de la 5ᵉ Avenue était une forteresse Tudor haut de gamme. Kemper se plia en deux pour esquiver le portier et pressa le vibreur de l'entrée marqué « L. Hughes ».

Une voix de femme retentit dans l'interphone :

— Prenez le second ascenseur à gauche, s'il vous plaît. Vous pouvez laisser les courses dans le vestibule.

Il prit l'ascenseur, monta au douzième. Les portes s'ouvraient directement dans le couloir d'entrée d'un appartement.

Le vestibule avait la taille de son salon. La femme au vison était appuyée contre une colonne grecque de taille réelle : elle était vêtue d'un peignoir écossais et de pantoufles.

197

Elle avait les cheveux noués en arrière. Elle commençait ju-u-u-ste à sourire.

— Je me souviens de vous à la soirée Kennedy. Jack a dit que vous étiez l'un des policiers de Bobby.

— Je m'appelle Kemper Boyd, mademoiselle Hughes.

— Originaire de Lexington, dans le Kentucky ?

— Vous n'êtes pas loin. Nashville, Tennessee.

Elle croisa les bras.

— Vous m'avez entendue donner mon adresse au chauffeur de taxi et vous m'avez décrite au portier au rez-de-chaussée. Il vous a donné mon nom, et vous avez sonné.

— Vous n'êtes pas loin.

— Vous m'avez vue donner cette broche en diamant vulgaire. N'importe quel homme vêtu avec autant d'élégance que vous l'êtes apprécierait un geste comme celui-là.

— Seule une femme sans soucis matériels ferait ce genre de geste.

Elle secoua la tête.

— Ce n'est pas là une preuve de bien grande finesse de votre part.

Kemper s'avança vers elle.

— Alors essayons ceci. Vous avez fait ce geste parce que vous saviez que vous aviez un public. C'était le genre de chose qu'on attendrait d'un Kennedy, et je ne vous en blâme pas.

Laura resserra son peignoir.

— Ne soyez pas impertinent avec les Kennedy. Ne parlez même pas d'eux en termes impertinents car lorsque vous vous y attendrez le moins, ils vous trancheront les jarrets.

— Vous l'avez vu faire ?

— Oui, je l'ai vu.

— Cela vous est-il arrivé ?

— Non.

— Parce que vous ne pouvez pas vous débarrasser de ce que vous n'avez pas reconnu ?

Laura sortit un étui à cigarettes.

— Je me suis mise à fumer parce que la plupart des sœurs fumaient. Elles avaient des étuis comme celui-ci, alors M. Kennedy m'en a offert un.

— M. Kennedy ?

— Ou Joe. Oncle Joe.

Kemper sourit.

— Mon père s'est ruiné et il s'est suicidé. Il m'a laissé par testament quatre-vingt-onze dollars et l'arme dont il s'est servi.

— Oncle Joe me laissera beaucoup plus que cela.

— A combien se montent les émoluments du moment ?

— Cent mille dollars par an, plus les frais.

— Avez-vous décoré cet appartement de manière à ce qu'il ressemble à la suite Kennedy au Carlyle ?

— Oui.

— C'est très beau. Il m'arrive parfois de me dire que je pourrais vivre dans les suites d'hôtel indéfiniment.

Elle s'éloigna de lui. Elle pivota sur les talons et disparut dans un couloir d'une largeur digne d'un musée.

Kemper laissa passer cinq minutes. L'appartement était immense et silencieux — il n'arrivait pas à y retrouver ses marques.

Il s'engagea sur la gauche et se perdit. Trois couloirs le ramenèrent dans le même office ; les quatre entrées vers le salon le faisaient tourner en cercles. Il arriva à des intersections de couloirs, une bibliothèque, des *ailes...*

Les bruits de la circulation lui remirent les idées en place. Il entendit des frôlements de pas sur la terrasse derrière le piano à queue.

Il s'avança. La terrasse aurait englouti sa cuisine au moins deux fois.

Laura était appuyée contre la rambarde. Une brise faisait frissonner son peignoir.

— Jack vous a dit ? demanda-t-elle.

— Non. J'ai compris tout seul.

— Vous mentez. Les Kennedy et un de mes amis de Chicago sont les seuls à savoir. Est-ce M. Hoover qui vous l'a appris ? Bobby dit qu'il ne sait pas, mais je ne l'ai jamais cru.

Kemper secoua la tête.

— M. Hoover ne sait pas. Lenny Sands l'a appris à un homme du FBI de Chicago, qui est un de mes amis.

Laura alluma une cigarette. Kemper mit ses mains en coupe autour de l'allumette.

— Jamais je n'aurais cru que Lenny le dirait à âme qui vive.

— Il n'a pas vraiment eu le choix. Si cela peut vous conso...

— *Non*, je ne veux pas savoir. Lenny connaît de mauvaises gens, et les mauvaises gens peuvent vous faire dire des choses que vous n'avez pas envie de dire.

Kemper lui toucha le bras.

— S'il vous plaît, ne dites pas à Lenny que vous m'avez rencontré.

— Pourquoi, monsieur Boyd ?

— Parce qu'il a tant de relations bien placées que c'en est gênant.

— Non, vous ne comprenez pas. Je vous demande ce que vous faites ici.

— Je vous ai vue à la soirée Kennedy. Je suis sûr que vous compléterez le reste par vous-même.

— Ce n'est pas une réponse.

— Je pouvais difficilement me renseigner sur vous auprès de Jack ou de Bobby.

— Pourquoi pas ?

— Parce que Oncle Joe n'apprécierait pas, et Bobby ne me fait pas entièrement confiance.

— Pourquoi ?

— Parce que j'ai tellement de relations que c'en est gênant.

Laura frissonna. Kemper lui enveloppa les épaules de sa propre veste.

Elle montra son étui d'aisselle.

— Bobby m'a dit que les hommes du McClellan ne portaient pas d'armes.

— Je ne suis pas en service.

— Pensiez-vous vraiment que je m'ennuierais à un tel point, que je serais tellement amorphe qu'il vous suffirait de sonner à ma porte et de me séduire ?

— Non. Je pensais que je vous offrirais à dîner d'abord.

Laura éclata de rire et toussa sa fumée.

— Est-ce que « Kemper » est le nom de jeune fille de votre mère ?

— Oui.

— Vit-elle encore ?

— Elle est morte dans une maison de retraite en 49.

200

— Qu'avez-vous fait de l'arme que votre père vous avait léguée ?

— Je l'ai vendue à un étudiant de ma classe à la fac de droit.

— Est-ce qu'il la porte sur lui ?

— Il est mort à Iwo Jima.

Laura laissa tomber sa cigarette dans une tasse à café.

— Je connais tellement d'orphelins.

— Moi aussi. En quelque sorte, vous en...

— *Non.* Ce n'est pas vrai. Vous dites cela uniquement pour ne pas être en reste.

— Je ne pense pas que ce soit tellement exagéré.

Elle se rengonça sous sa veste. Les manches battaient au vent.

— La repartie, c'est une chose, monsieur Boyd, la vérité en est une autre. La vérité est que mon baron-voleur de père a baisé ma vedette de mère et l'a mise enceinte. Ma vedette de mère avait déjà eu trois avortements et ne voulait pas courir le risque d'un quatrième. Ma maman-vedette m'a reniée, mais mon « père » apprécie au plus haut point de m'afficher délibérément à la figure de sa famille légitime une fois par an. Les garçons m'aiment bien pour mes côtés provocateurs, et ils me trouvent superbe parce qu'ils ne peuvent pas baiser avec moi, parce que je suis leur demi-sœur. Les filles me détestent parce que je suis un message codé de leur père qui dit que les hommes peuvent déconner, mais pas les femmes. Est-ce que vous saisissez, monsieur Boyd ? *J'ai une famille.* Mon « père » m'a offert la pension et plusieurs universités. Mon « père » m'entretient. Mon « père » a informé sa famille de mon existence lorsque Jack m'a ramenée à la maison à l'issue d'une fête pour les diplômés de Harvard. J'étais un pion involontaire dans un stratagème plutôt vicieux que j'avais mis en branle pour être reconnue au sein de la famille. Imaginez sa surprise lorsque « père » a dit, « Jack, tu ne peux pas la sauter, c'est ta demi-sœur ». Petit Bobby, vingt ans et calviniste, a surpris la conversation et répandu la nouvelle. Mon père s'est dit, et puis après tout, rien à faire, tout le monde est au courant, et il m'a invitée à rester à dîner. Mme Kennedy a essayé un peu plus tard ce soir-là de s'engouffrer un paquet de somnifères. Notre ami Lenny Sands, celui qui « a tellement de relations que c'en est gênant » donnait des leçons de diction à Jack pour sa première campagne électorale au Congrès, et il se trouvait à la maison pour dîner. Il a empêché Rose de se suicider, et depuis lors, nous n'avons plus de secrets l'un pour l'autre. *J'ai une famille*, monsieur Boyd. Mon père, c'est le Mal incarné, il est avare, impitoyable, et il est prêt à détruire quiconque oserait ne serait-ce que regarder de travers les enfants qu'il reconnaît publiquement. Et je hais tout de lui, hormis l'argent qu'il me donne et le fait qu'il détruirait probablement quiconque essaierait de me nuire à moi aussi.

Des avertisseurs de voiture bêlèrent, longs et perçants. Laura indiqua du doigt une rangée de taxis en contrebas.

« Ils sont perchés là comme des vautours. Et c'est lorsque je joue Rachmaninov qu'ils font le plus de bruit. »

Kemper dégaina son calibre. Il prit en ligne de mire un panneau marqué YELLOW CABS ONLY — réservé aux taxis.

Il mit le bras en appui sur la rambarde et fit feu. Deux balles sectionnèrent le panneau de son poteau. Le silencieux fit *thwack*. Pete était bon fournisseur côté intendance.

Laura poussa un cri de joie. Les chauffeurs faisaient de grands gestes, sidérés, mystifiés, la trouille au ventre.

— J'aime vos cheveux, dit Kemper.

Laura les dénoua. Le vent les fit danser.

Ils parlèrent.

Il lui apprit comment la fortune des Boyd s'était évaporée. Elle lui apprit comment elle avait été virée de la Julliard School et avait changé du tout au tout en devenant une mondaine en vue.

Elle se qualifiait de dilettante musicienne. Il se qualifiait de flic ambitieux. Elle avait enregistré Chopin à compte d'auteur. Lui adressait des cartes de Noël aux voleurs qu'il avait arrêtés.

Elle dit qu'elle aimait Jack, mais ne pouvait supporter Bobby. Elle traitait Bobby de Beethoven des profondeurs, et Jack, de Mozart à son plus désinvolte. Elle dit de Lenny Sands que c'était son seul véritable ami sans faire état de sa trahison. Il lui dit que sa fille Claire partageait tous ses secrets.

L'Avocat du Diable se mit en place automatiquement, d'un seul coup. Il savait exactement ce qu'il fallait dire et ce qu'il fallait mettre.

Il qualifia M. Hoover de vieille tante vindicative. Il fit de lui-même le portrait d'un libéral pragmatique qui s'était accroché à l'étoile Kennedy.

Elle reprit le thème de l'orpheline. Il décrivit l'association des trois filles.

Susan Littell était prompte à juger de façon catégorique et à s'emporter. Helen Agee était courageuse et impétueuse. Sa Claire lui était trop proche pour qu'il pût savoir.

Il lui parla de son amitié avec Ward. Il dit qu'il avait toujours voulu un plus jeune frère à ses côtés — et le Bureau lui en avait offert un. Il dit que Ward adorait Bobby. Elle dit que Bobby avait un sens intuitif de la malfaisance d'Oncle Joe et qu'il pourchassait les gangsters pour compenser son patrimoine.

Il fit allusion à son propre frère perdu. Il dit que la perte de son frère l'avait entraîné à pousser Ward d'étrange manière.

Ils parlèrent, jusqu'à en être épuisés. Laura composa le 21 et fit monter un dîner. Le chateaubriand et le vin la rendirent somnolente.

Ils laissèrent les choses en suspens, sans parler.

Pas ce soir — la prochaine fois.

Laura s'endormit. Kemper visita l'appartement.

Deux circuits lui donnèrent une idée de la disposition des lieux. Laura lui avait appris que la bonne avait besoin d'une carte. La salle à manger aurait pu contenir une petite armée.

Il appela le numéro du responsable de poste à l'Agence de Miami. John Stanton décrocha immédiatement.

— Oui ?

— C'est Kemper Boyd. Je vous appelle pour vous dire que j'acceptais votre offre.

— J'en suis très heureux. Je reprendrai contact, monsieur Boyd. Nous avons des tas de choses à discuter.

— Bonsoir, en ce cas.

— Bonsoir.

Kemper retourna au salon de réception. Il laissa les rideaux de terrasse ouverts — les gratte-ciel de l'autre côté projetaient leurs lumières sur Laura.

Il la regarda dormir.

21

Chicago, 22 janvier 1959.

Le double de la clé du baisoir que possédait Lenny ouvrit la porte. Littell entailla l'huisserie jusqu'au pène pour simuler une effraction qui tiendrait le coup aux yeux des mecs du labo.

Il brisa la lame de son canif. Les chocottes cambrio lui avaient fait donner des coups trop violents.

Son premier cambrio d'essai lui avait montré la disposition des lieux. Il savait où tout se trouvait.

Littell referma la porte et se dirigea droit vers le sac de golf. Les quatorze mille dollars étaient toujours là, bien engoncés dans la poche à balles.

Il enfila ses gants. Il s'accorda sept minutes pour un peu de vandalisme symbolique.

Il débrancha la hi-fi.

Il vida les tiroirs et mit à sac l'armoire à pharmacie.

Il posa au sol une télé, un grille-pain et le sac de golf près de la porte.

Ça ressemblait à une effraction classique d'appart modèle camé. Butch Montrose n'irait jamais soupçonner autre chose.

Kemper Boyd disait toujours : *protège tes informateurs.*

Il empocha l'argent. Il emporta le butin jusqu'à sa voiture, roula jusqu'au lac et largua le tout dans une mare jonchée d'ordures diverses.

Littell rentra tard. Helen dormait sur son côté à lui du lit.

La place d'Helen était froide. Le sommeil ne voulait pas venir

— il ne cessait de se repasser le film de son effraction, à rechercher ses erreurs.

Il somnola plus ou moins jusqu'à l'aube. Il rêva qu'il s'étouffait sur un godemiché.

Il se réveilla tard. Helen lui avait laissé un petit mot.

Le devoir m'appelle. A quelle heure es-tu rentré ? Pour un homme du FBI apôtre d'un tel libéralisme (que je trouve consternant), tu es sans l'ombre d'un doute un chasseur de communistes très zélé. Que font donc les communistes à minuit ?

Je t'aime, je t'aime, je t'aime,

H

Littell s'obligea à avaler café et toast. Il rédigea son mot sur papier libre.

Monsieur D'Onofrio,

Sam Giancana a lancé un contrat contre vous. Vous serez tué, à moins que vous ne régliez les douze mille dollars que vous lui devez. Je connais un moyen de vous éviter cela. Retrouvez-moi cet après-midi à 16 heures. Le Kollege Klub, 1281, 58e, Hyde Park.

Littell mit le mot dans une enveloppe et ajouta cinq cents dollars. Lenny avait dit que la tournée d'excursionnistes était terminée — Sal devait être rentré chez lui.

Kemper disait toujours : *séduis tes informateurs par l'argent.*

Littell appela le service de messagerie Speedy-King. Le standard lui répondit qu'il envoyait un coursier immédiatement.

Sal le Fou ne perdit pas de temps. Littell repoussa sa bière sur le côté.

Ils disposaient de la rangée de tables tout entière pour eux seuls. Les étudiants au comptoir ne pourraient pas les entendre.

Sal était assis en face de lui. Ses rouleaux de lard s'agitaient et lui remontaient la chemise au-dessus du nombril.

— Alors ? dit-il.

Littell dégaina son arme et la posa sur ses genoux. La table le masquait.

— Alors, qu'avez-vous fait de ces cinq cents dollars ?

Sal se cura le nez.

— Je les ai placés sur les Blackhawks contre les Canadiens. A 10 heures ce soir, les cinq cents se seront transformés en mille.

— Vous en devez encore onze mille à Giancana.

— Qui est-ce qui vous a dit ça, putain ?

— Une source digne de confiance.

— Vous voulez dire une enculée de balance des Fédés. Vous êtes Fédé, pas vrai ? Z'avez l'air bien trop trouillard pour pouvoir être autre chose. Et si z'étiez de la police de Chicago ou des services du shérif du comté de Cook, je vous aurais déjà acheté, à l'heure qu'il est, et ch'serais en train de baiser votre femme et de titiller le troufignon de votre morveux pendant que vous êtes au boulot.

— Vous devez à Giancana douze mille dollars que vous ne possédez pas. Il va vous tuer.

— Dites-moi donc quelque chose que je ne sais pas.

— Vous avez tué un garçon de couleur du nom de Maurice Theodore Wilkins.

— Cette accusation, c'est du rassis. C'est du putain de réchauffé que vous avez sorti d'un dossier quelconque.

— J'ai simplement mis la main sur un témoin oculaire.

Sal se fourrailla les oreilles d'un trombone.

— C'est de la merde en barre. Les Fédés, y z'enquêtent pas sur les homicides de Négros et mon petit doigt m'a dit que ce môme a été tué par un agresseur inconnu au sous-sol du presbytère de l'église où il était en train de voler. Le petit doigt a dit que l'agresseur a attendu que les prêtres partent à un match de base-ball, et ensuite, il a découpé le petit Négro à la tronçonneuse après l'avoir forcé à lui tailler une pipe. Le petit doigt a dit qu'il y avait du sang partout, et que l'agresseur s'est débarrassé de la puanteur à coups de vin de messe.

Kemper Boyd disait toujours : *ne montre jamais ta peur ou ton dégoût.*

Littell posa mille dollars sur la table.

206

— Je suis préparé à régler votre dette. En deux ou trois versements, de manière que Giancana n'ait pas de soupçons.

Sal s'empara de l'argent.

— D'un côté, je prends. D'un autre côté, je prends pas. Pour ce que j'en sais, Mo pourrait bien décider de me dessouder pas'qu'il est jaloux de ma belle gueule.

Littell arma son pistolet.

— Reposez l'argent.

Sal s'exécuta.

— Et alors ?

— Alors êtes-vous intéressé ?

— Qu'est-ce qui se passe si je le suis pas ?

— En ce cas, Giancana vous élimine. En ce cas, je fais passer le mot comme quoi vous avez tué Tony Iannone. Vous avez entendu les bruits qui courent — Tony s'est fait buter juste devant un rade à homos. Sal, on lit en vous à livre ouvert. Seigneur, *tailler une pipe, titiller le troufignon.* On dirait que vous avez pris quelques habitudes à Joliet.

Sal reluquait le pognon. Sal sentait la sueur au tabac et la lotion Aqua Velva.

— Vous êtes un requin, vous prêtez à des taux d'usurier, Sal. Ce que je vous demande ne vous changera pas tellement.

— Et a-a-alors ?

— Alors je veux avoir accès à la Caisse de Retraite des Camionneurs. Je veux que vous m'aidiez à faire gravir les échelons à quelqu'un que je trouverai. Un homme avec des références qui cherche un prêt. Vous m'aidez à lui arranger le coup auprès de Sam et de la Caisse. C'est aussi simple que ça. Et je ne vous demande pas de cafter quiconque.

Sal reluquait l'argent.

Sal piqua une suée.

Littell laissa tomber trois mille dollars sur la pile.

— Okay, dit Sal.

— Apportez ça à Giancana, dit Littell. Ne le jouez pas.

Sal fit signe d'aller se faire mettre.

— Gardez vos leçons pour vous. Et rappelez-vous, votre mère, je l'ai baisée, ce qui fait de moi votre père.

Littell se leva et balança son revolver en arc de cercle. Sal le Fou se ramassa le canon en plein dans les dents.

Kemper Boyd disait toujours : *intimide tes informateurs.*

Sal cracha du sang et des plombages en or. Quelques mômes au comptoir contemplaient la scène, les yeux comme des billes de loto.

Littell soutint leurs regards et leur fit baisser les yeux.

22

Miami, 4 février 1959.

Le bateau avait du retard.

Des agents des Douanes américaines occupaient le ponton d'accostage. Le Service de Santé américain avait fait monter une tente dans le parc de stationnement juste sur l'arrière.

Les réfugiés seraient passés aux rayons X avec analyse de sang. Les contagieux seraient expédiés jusqu'à un hôpital d'Etat aux abords de Pensacola.

Stanton consulta sa liste de passagers.

— L'un de nos contacts sur l'île nous a fait passer une liste. Tous les déportés sont de sexe masculin.

Des vagues frappaient les piles. Guy Banister leur balança un mégot de cigarette.

— Ce qui implique qu'il s'agit de criminels. Castro se débarrasse de tous ses bons vieux « indésirables » sous l'étiquette de « politiquement indésirables », qui n'est qu'une couverture.

Des cabanes d'interrogatoire flanquaient le ponton. Des tireurs d'élite de la Patrouille des Frontières américaine se tenaient accroupis à leur abri. Leurs ordres : tirer pour tuer au premier signe de problème.

Kemper était debout, au-dessus des piles en bout de ponton. Des vagues venaient s'y fracasser et les embruns mouillaient ses jambes de pantalon.

Il avait pour tâche spécifique d'interroger Teofilio Paez, l'ex-patron de la sécurité de la United Fruit Company. Un guide explicatif de la CIA définissait ainsi la UF : « La compagnie américaine la plus importante et la plus rentable établie depuis le plus longtemps à Cuba même et le plus grand employeur de l'île de travailleurs de nationalité cubaine non qualifiés ou semi-qualifiés. Bastion de longue date de l'anticommunisme cubain. Les aides de la sécurité, de nationalité cubaine, et travaillant pour la compagnie, sont depuis longtemps d'une redoutable efficacité dans le recrutement de jeunes anticommunistes impatients d'infiltrer les groupes d'ouvriers et les institutions éducatives cubaines à tendances gauchistes. »

Banister et Stanton contemplaient l'horizon. Kemper se mit sous la brise qu'il laissa lui ébouriffer les cheveux.

Il y avait dix jours qu'il était agent sous contrat — deux réunions à Langley, et puis ceci. Il y avait dix jours qu'il était avec Laura Hughes — la navette de La Guardia facilitait leurs rendez-vous.

Laura se sentait légitime. Laura devenait folle dès qu'il la touchait. Laura disait des choses brillantes et jouait Chopin *con brio*.

Laura était une Kennedy. Laura dévidait ses petits récits Kennedy avec une verve superbe.

Il cachait lesdits récits à M. Hoover.

Avec la sensation d'une presque loyauté. La sensation d'un douloureux presque poignant — et celle de s'être compromis auprès de Hoover.

Il avait besoin de M. Hoover. Il continuait à l'alimenter de rapports téléphoniques, qu'il limitait néanmoins aux renseignements McClellan.

Il avait loué une suite au St. Regis Hotel, à quelques blocs de l'appartement de Laura. Le loyer mensuel faisait mal.

Manhattan vous entrait dans la peau. Ses trois chèques de salaire se montaient au total à cinquante-neuf mille dollars par an — loin de ce qu'il lui fallait pour mener le train qu'il désirait.

Bobby le tenait toujours occupé par d'ennuyeuses paperasseries du Comité. Jack avait laissé entendre que la famille pourrait bien lui avoir un emploi post-comité. Le poste le plus probable serait celui de chef de la sécurité pour la campagne.

Jack aimait beaucoup l'avoir à ses côtés. Bobby continuait à vaguement se méfier de lui.

Bobby n'était pas du genre disponible pour le premier venu — et Ward Littell le savait.

Il s'entretenait avec Ward deux fois par semaine. Ward faisait du battage à propos de sa nouvelle balance, un book/requin de l'usure du nom de Sal D'Onofrio.

Ward le Prudent disait qu'il avait mis « Sal le Fou » au pied. Ward le Furieux disait que Lenny Sands travaillait maintenant pour Pete Bondurant.

Ward le Furieux savait que c'était *lui-même* qui avait tout fait pour qu'il en soit ainsi.

Ward lui adressait des rapports de renseignements. Lui en supprimait des détails illégaux et les faisait suivre à Bobby Kennedy. Bobby connaissait Littell uniquement sous le sobriquet de « Phantôme ». Bobby priait pour lui et s'émerveillait de son courage.

Avec un peu de chance, ce courage se parait également de circonspection. Avec un peu de chance, le gamin sur son chariot à la morgue avait appris quelques petites choses à Ward.

Ward savait s'adapter et il était toujours prêt à écouter. Ward était lui aussi orphelin — qui avait grandi dans des foyers d'accueil jésuites.

Ward avait de bons instincts. Ward était convaincu qu'il existait effectivement un « double » des livres comptables de la Caisse de Retraite.

Lenny Sands était d'avis que lesdits livres étaient administrés par un vieux cacique de la Mafia. Il avait entendu dire que les recommandations se payaient en bon argent pour des prêts qui rapportaient d'énormes bénéfices.

Littell pourrait bien être sur la piste de sommes *considérables*. C'était le genre de renseignement lourd de possibilités qu'il fallait cacher à Bobby.

Il le cachait effectivement. Il supprimait toute référence à la Caisse dans les rapports du Phantôme.

Littell était malléable, tout zélateur qu'il fût. La *grande question* était la suivante : Pourrait-il continuer à cacher son travail à la dérobée à M. Hoover ?

Une tache sombre dansait sur l'eau. Banister regarda à la jumelle.

— Ils n'ont pas l'air bien remplumés. Il y a une partie de craps en cours à l'arrière de la barge.

Les douaniers débarquèrent sur le ponton. Ils arboraient revolvers, matraques et chaînes d'entraves.

211

Stanton montra à Kemper une photographie.

— Voici Paez. On se le chope tout de suite pour que la Douane ne puisse pas le réquisitionner.

Paez ressemblait à une version rondelette de Xavier Cugat[1].

— Je le vois maintenant, dit Banister. Il est tout devant, au premier rang et il porte des marques de coups et d'entailles.

Stanton fit la grimace.

— Castro hait la United Fruit. Notre Service de Propagande est tombé sur un pamphlet qu'il a rédigé à ce sujet il y a neuf mois. C'était une première indication, déjà à l'époque, qu'il puisse virer coco.

Les crêtes d'écume rapprochaient la barge du débarcadère. Les hommes se battaient de griffes, d'ongles et de pieds pour être les premiers à terre.

Kemper dégagea le cran de sûreté de son calibre.

— Où va-t-on les interner ?

Banister indiqua le nord.

— L'Agence est propriétaire d'un motel à Boynton Beach. Ils ont concocté une histoire fumeuse de désinfection et ont fait partir tous les locataires. On va entasser ces bouffeurs de fayots à six par pièce et on verra ceux qui pourront nous être utiles.

Les réfugiés hurlaient en agitant de petits drapeaux montés sur baguettes. Teo Paez était accroupi, prêt à jaillir pour son sprint.

— Préparez-vous ! hurla le chef des douaniers.

La barge cogna contre le ponton. Paez bondit à terre. Kemper et Stanton l'attrapèrent et le serrèrent, bras autour de la poitrine.

Ils le décollèrent du sol et se mirent à courir avec lui. Banister couvrait les interférences possibles.

— CIA ! Il est sous notre garde !

Les tireurs firent feu, en guise d'avertissement. Les réfugiés se baissèrent pour se réfugier à couvert. Les douaniers accrochèrent la barge au grappin et l'amarrèrent aux piles.

Kemper pressait Paez au-travers de la foule. Stanton courait en flèche et déverrouilla une cabane d'interrogatoire.

— Il y a un corps sur le bateau ! hurla quelqu'un.

Ils firent entrer leur bonhomme. Banister verrouilla la porte. Paez tomba au sol qu'il étouffa de ses baisers.

---

1. Chef d'orchestre cubain. (N.d.T.)

Des cigares tombèrent de ses poches. Banister en ramassa un et renifla l'emballage.

Stanton reprit haleine.

— Bienvenue en Amérique, monsieur Paez. Nous avons entendu d'excellentes choses à votre sujet, et nous sommes heureux que vous soyez ici.

Kemper entrouvrit une fenêtre. Le mort passa sur un chariot, lardé de coups de lame de la tête aux pieds. Les agents des Douanes firent aligner les exilés, peut-être une cinquantaine d'hommes au total.

Banister installa son magnétophone sur une table.

— Vous avez eu un mort sur le bateau ? dit Stanton.

Paez s'affala dans un fauteuil.

— Non. C'était une exécution politique. Nous avons estimé que l'homme avait été déporté pour servir d'espion antiaméricain. Après interrogatoire, il nous a révélé que c'était vrai. Nous avons agi en conséquence.

Kemper s'assit.

— Vous parlez un anglais excellent, Teo.

— Je parle l'anglais lent et exagérément correct des autodidactes. Les Américains de naissance me disent qu'il m'arrive de faire des impropriétés totalement hilarantes et de mutiler leur langue.

Stanton prit une chaise.

— Voyez-vous un inconvénient à nous parler maintenant ? Nous avons un joli appartement tout prêt, qui vous attend, et M. Boyd vous y conduira dans un petit moment.

Paez fit une courbette.

— Je suis à votre disposition.

— Excellent. Je m'appelle John Stanton, à propos. Et voici mes collègues, Kemper Boyd et Guy Banister.

Paez serra les mains à la cantonade. Banister empocha le reste des cigares et enclencha le magnétophone.

— Pouvons-nous vous offrir quelque chose à manger avant de commencer ?

— Non. J'aimerais que mon premier repas américain soit un sandwich au « Wolfie's Delicatessen », à Miami Beach.

Kemper sourit. Banister éclata de rire sans retenue.

— Teo, dit Stanton, est-ce que Fidel Castro est communiste ?

Paez acquiesça.

— Indubitablement. Il est communiste à la fois par la pensée et la pratique, et mon vieux réseau d'informateurs étudiants m'a appris que des avions chargés de diplomates russes ont récemment atterri à La Havane tard dans la nuit à plusieurs reprises. Mon ami Wilfredo Olmos Delsol, qui était sur le bateau avec moi, a mémorisé les numéros des vols.

Banister alluma une cigarette.

— Che Guevara est rouge depuis bien longtemps.

— Oui. Et le frère de Fidel, Raul, est lui aussi un porc communiste. En plus, c'est un hypocrite. Mon ami Tomas Obregon raconte que Raul revend l'héroïne confisquée à de riches drogués en essaimant dans le même temps, en hypocrite qu'il est, sa rhétorique communiste.

Kemper consulta sa liste de passagers.

— Tomas Obregon était sur le bateau avec vous.

— Oui.

— Comment pourrait-il disposer de renseignements sur le trafic d'héroïne à Cuba ?

— Parce que, monsieur Boyd, il a été personnellement impliqué dans le trafic d'héroïne. Voyez-vous, mes compagnons de voyage sont pour l'essentiel des raclures de criminels. Fidel voulait se débarrasser d'eux et s'en est déchargé sur l'Amérique, avec l'espoir qu'ils iraient pratiquer leur commerce sur vos rivages. Ce qu'il n'est pas parvenu à percevoir, c'est que le communisme est un bien plus grand crime que la revente d'héroïne, le vol ou le meurtre, et que même les criminels sont susceptibles de posséder le désir patriotique de réclamer leur terre natale.

Stanton bascula son fauteuil en arrière.

— Nous avons entendu dire que Castro s'était emparé des hôtels et des casinos qui appartenaient à la Mafia.

— C'est vrai. Fidel appelle ça la « Nationalisation ». Il a volé les casinos et des millions de dollars à la Mafia. Tomas Obregon m'a dit que l'illustre gangster américain Santos Trafficante Jr. est actuellement en détention au Nacional Hotel.

Banister soupira.

— Cet enculé de Castro a un grand désir de mort. Il joue au con à la fois avec les Etats-Unis d'Amérique et la Mafia.

Ward Littell haïssait Banister. Ward le qualifiait de « fêlé de droite, raciste à tous crins ».

— Il n'existe pas de Mafia, Guy. Tout au moins, c'est ce que M. Hoover a toujours dit.

— Kemper, même Dieu peut faire des erreurs.

— Ça suffit, dit Kemper. Teo, quel est le statut des citoyens américains qui restent à Cuba ?

Paez se gratta et s'étira.

— Fidel veut apparaître plein d'humanité. Il dorlote les Américains influents toujours à Cuba et les autorise à voir uniquement les prétendues bonnes choses que la révolution a faites. Il va les relâcher lentement, afin qu'ils retournent en Amérique comme des outils de dupe, prêts à dispenser la propagande communiste. Et, entre-temps, Fidel a brûlé nombre des champs de canne à sucre de ma bien-aimée United Fruit, il a torturé et tué nombre de mes informateurs étudiants en les accusant d'être des espions pour la United *imperialisto y fascisto.*

Stanton consulta sa montre.

— Guy, emmène Teo pour sa visite médicale. Teo, accompagnez M. Banister. M. Boyd vous conduira à Miami dans un petit moment.

Banister fit sortir Paez. Kemper les suivit des yeux qui se dirigeaient vers la cabane à radiographie.

Stanton referma la porte.

— Larguez le mort quelque part, Kemper. Je ferai passer le message à tout le personnel qui l'aura vu de n'en toucher mot à personne. Et ne secouez pas trop la cage de Guy, il est du genre explosif.

— C'est ce que j'ai entendu dire. On raconte qu'il a été adjoint au divisionnaire des forces de police de La Nouvelle-Orléans pendant une dizaine de minutes, avant qu'il ne se saoule et ne décharge son arme dans un restaurant bondé.

Stanton sourit.

— Et on raconte que, de votre côté, vous avez fourgué quelques Corvettes piquées.

— Touché. Et entre parenthèses, que pensez-vous de la petite donation armée de Pete Bondurant ?

— J'ai été impressionné. Nous songeons à faire une offre à

Pete, et je la soumettrai la prochaine fois que je m'entretiendrai avec l'adjoint du directeur.

— Pete a du talent, dit Kemper. Il est très doué pour tenir en bonne ligne les petits durs.

— Effectivement. Jimmy Hoffa se sert de lui à bon escient pour ses Tiger Kabs. Continuez dans cette voie, Kemper. Je sens que vous avez enfilé votre bonnet de penseur sérieux.

Kemper coupa le magnétophone.

— John, vous allez découvrir qu'un pourcentage non négligeable de ces hommes là-bas dehors sont des psychopathes échappant à tout contrôle. Votre idée de les endoctriner et de les entraîner comme guérilleros anti-castristes potentiels peut très bien ne pas marcher. Si vous les faites loger au milieu de familles d'immigrés cubains stables et si vous leur trouvez du travail, aux termes de votre plan existant, vous vous apercevrez qu'ils retomberont dans leurs anciennes tendances et prédilections criminelles dès que se sera un peu atténuée la nouveauté de se trouver dans ce pays.

— Vous êtes en train de me dire que nous devrions les passer au crible de manière beaucoup plus poussée ?

— Non. Je suis en train de dire que ce serait à *moi* de le faire. Je dis que nous devrions étendre la période d'internement au motel de l'Agence, et que ce serait moi qui aurais l'autorité de décider au bout du compte de ceux que nous allons recruter.

Stanton éclata de rire.

— Puis-je vous demander à quel titre ? Au nom de quelles qualifications ?

Kemper décompta sur ses doigts.

— J'ai travaillé sous couverture pendant neuf ans. Je connais les criminels, et je les aime bien. J'ai infiltré des réseaux de voleurs de voitures, j'en ai arrêté les membres et j'ai travaillé avec le bureau du procureur, à bâtir les dossiers de l'accusation pour le ministère public. Je comprends la nécessité qu'éprouvent certains criminels à se soumettre de leur plein gré à l'autorité. John, je me suis tellement trouvé proche de certains parmi ces voleurs de voitures qu'ils ont insisté pour ne confier leurs aveux qu'à moi, et à moi seul, l'agent qui les avait trahis et arrêtés.

Stanton siffla — tout à fait hors de propos pour le personnage.

— Seriez-vous en train de suggérer d'étendre vos fonctions et de rester auprès des hommes que vous aurez sélectionnés comme responsable de terrain ? Cela me paraît peu réaliste, étant donné vos autres engagements, et ils ne sont pas simples.

Kemper claqua la table.

— *Non*. Je suggère avec force de confier à Pete Bondurant la responsabilité de ce boulot. Ce que je suis en train de vous dire revient à ceci. Un contingent de criminels endurcis, convenablement endoctrinés et placés sous une autorité forte, pourrait être d'une efficacité redoutable. Prenons l'hypothèse que le problème castriste s'étende. Je pense que dès à présent, et nous n'en sommes qu'au tout début, il est sage et sans danger de présumer que l'Agence aura à sa disposition un vaste contingent de futurs déportés et de Cubains, émigrés légalement, au sein duquel elle effectuera sa sélection. Faisons donc de ces premières troupes des troupes d'élite. Elles sont à *nous*, John. Faisons en sorte qu'elles soient les meilleures.

Stanton se tapota le menton.

— M. Dulles était prêt à demander des cartes vertes pour tous les hommes. Il sera heureux d'apprendre que nous nous montrons aussi sélectifs à un stade aussi précoce. Il déteste aller mendier des faveurs auprès des Services de Naturalisation et d'Immigration.

Kemper leva la main.

— Ne déportez pas les hommes que nous rejetterons. Banister connaît bien quelques Cubains à La Nouvelle-Orléans, je me trompe ?

— Non. Il y a une importante communauté pro-Batista là-bas.

— Alors laissez Guy prendre en charge les hommes que nous rejetterons. Qu'ils se trouvent un boulot ou pas, laissez-les donc faire la queue comme tout le monde pour obtenir leurs visas en Louisiane.

— Combien d'hommes, à votre avis, vont-ils satisfaire vos exigences ?

— Je n'en ai aucune idée.

Stanton avait l'air enthousiaste et pressé.

— M. Dulles a donné son approbation pour l'achat de terrains bon marché dans le sud de la Floride destinés initialement à être notre camp d'entraînement. Je pense pouvoir le convaincre de garder là-bas notre cadre permanent, en nombre limité, et confiné à un espace restreint, si vous estimez que les hommes que vous sélectionnerez seront également à même d'entraîner les futurs arrivants avant que nous les dispersions vers d'autres camps qui, j'en ai la certitude, vont se multiplier.

Kemper acquiesça.

— Je ferai des compétences d'instructeur-formateur un de mes critères. Où est situé ce terrain ?

— C'est sur la côte, à côté d'une petite ville du nom de Blessington.

— Y a-t-il un moyen d'accès sur Miami ?

— Oui. Pourquoi ?

— Je pensais à la société de taxis des Tiger Kabs comme centre de recrutement.

Stanton eut l'air à la fois ennuyé et presque impatient d'approuver.

— Toutes connotations de gangsters mises à part, je pense que l'on pourrait utiliser les Tiger Kabs. Chuck Rogers y travaille déjà, nous avons donc déjà un homme dans la place.

— John, dit Kemper — très doucement.

Stanton donnait l'impression d'être en pleine extase.

— La réponse à toutes vos suggestions est *oui,* sous réserve de l'approbation du directeur adjoint. Et bravo, Kemper. Vous faites bien plus que répondre à mes attentes.

Kemper se leva et fit la révérence.

— Merci. Et je pense que nous ferons amèrement regretter à Castro le jour où il a expédié ce bateau de son pays.

— Que Dieu vous entende, et sans intermédiaire. Et, à propos, que pensez-vous que dirait votre ami Jack de notre petite barge de la liberté ?

Kemper éclata de rire.

— Jack dirait : « Où sont les femmes ? »

Paez était un vrai moulin à paroles. Kemper baissa sa vitre pour avoir un peu de répit.

Ils arrivèrent à Miami à l'heure de pointe. Paez continuait toujours à jacasser. Kemper tambourinait sur le tableau et essayait de se repasser son entrevue avec Stanton :

— ... et M. Thomas Gordean était mon patron à la United. Il

adorait la chatte, jusqu'à ce que sa tendresse pour le bourbon I.W. Harper le rende inapproprié. La plupart des cadres à la United sont partis après la prise du pouvoir par Castro, mais M. Gordean est resté derrière. Aujourd'hui, il boit encore plus. Il a plusieurs milliers d'actions de la United Fruit, et il refuse de partir. Il a acheté des miliciens pour qu'ils soient ses gardes du corps personnels et il commence lui aussi à pousser la chansonnette communiste. Ma grande crainte est que M. Gordean devienne communiste comme le Fidel que j'aimais tant il y a bien longtemps. Je crains qu'il ne devienne un outil de propagande par excentricité et...

— Des actions...

— Thomas Gordean...

L'étincelle se fit soudain et faillit l'aveugler. Kemper en quitta presque la route.

DOCUMENT EN ENCART : 10/2/59 : *Rapport du dénicheur de* L'Indiscret — *de Lenny Sands à Pete Bondurant.*

Pete,

Voici quelques pistes que j'ai pu relever. 1. — Mickey Cohen en est réduit à chasser les miettes. Il y a deux nervis (George Piscatelli et Sam Lo Chigno) prêts à monter ce qui pourrait bien être un racket d'extorsions sexuelles. J'ai eu ça de Dick Contino, actuellement à Chicago pour une soirée d'accordéon. Mickey en a eu l'idée en lisant les lettres d'amour de Lana Turner à Johnny Stompanato après que la fille de Lana a suriné Johnny. Johnny baisait de riches veuves et se faisait filmer par un caméraman au chômage. Mickey a quelques bouts de films de choix. Dites à M. Hughes qu'il est vendeur pour trois bâtons.

Salut,

Lenny.

DOCUMENT EN ENCART : 24/2/59 : *Rapport du dénicheur de* L'Indiscret *: de Lenny Sands à Pete Bondurant.*

Pete,

J'ai fait la tournée de Sal D'Onofrio et de ses excursionnistes. Voici quelques menus morceaux à se mettre sous la dent. 1. — Toutes les serveuses de l'équipe de minuit du Dunes Hotel de Vegas sont des racoleuses. Elles ont offert leurs bons services aux membres du Service secret du président Eisenhower quand Ike s'est adressé à la législature de l'Etat du Nevada. 2. — Rock Hudson s'enfile le maître d'hôtel du restaurant du Cal-Neva. 3 — Lenny Bruce est accro au dilaudid. Toute une brigade des services du shérif du comté de L.A. est prête à le piéger la prochaine fois qu'il met les pieds sur le Strip. 4. — Freddy Otash a trouvé un avorteur pour Jayne Mansfield. Le papa était un plongeur schwartze avec une biroute de quarante centimètres. Peter Lawford a des photos du mec en train de se la caresser. J'en ai acheté une à Freddy O. Je vous l'enverrai pour que vous fassiez suivre à M. Hughes.

5. — Bing Crosby est en train de s'assécher dans un coin discret de l'Eglise catholique réservé aux prêtres et nonnes alcooliques tout près de 29 Palms. Le cardinal Spellman lui a rendu visite. Ils se sont offert une virée et sont partis pétés pour L.A. Spellman a touché le flanc d'une voiture pleine de dos mouillés et en a expédié trois à l'hôpital. Bing a acheté leur silence avec des photos autographiées et quelques centaines de dollars. Spellman a repris l'avion de New York en pleine crise de *delirium tremens*. Bing est resté assez longtemps à L.A. pour passer son épouse à tabac avant de retourner à sa ferme de remise au sec.

Salut,
Lenny.

DOCUMENT EN ENCART : 4/3/59. *Note personnelle de J. Edgar Hoover à Howard Hughes.*

Cher Howard,

Je me suis dit que j'allais vous adresser un petit mot pour vous dire combien *L'Indiscret* s'est amélioré à mon humble avis depuis que M. Bondurant a engagé votre nouveau dénicheur de scandales. Voilà un homme qui ferait un excellent agent du FBI ! Je suis impatient de recevoir les rapports mot à mot que vous m'envoyez ! Souhaiteriez-vous, le cas échéant, accélérer leur livraison, demandez à M. Bondurant de contacter l'agent spécial Rice au bureau de Los Angeles. Merci une fois encore pour le petit film personnel de Stompanato et la photo du Nègre aussi prodigieusement gâté par la nature. Un homme averti en vaut deux : il faut connaître son ennemi avant de pouvoir le combattre.

Bien à vous,
Edgar.

DOCUMENT EN ENCART : 19/3/59. *Lettre personnelle — de Kemper Boyd à J. Edgar Hoover — Marquée EXTREMEMENT CONFIDENTIEL.*

Monsieur,

Ainsi qu'il en a été convenu lors de notre précédente conversation, je vous transmets des renseignements marquants sur la famille Kennedy, glanés auprès de Laura (Swanson) Hughes.

Je suis parvenu à gagner une part de la confiance de Mlle Hughes en liant avec elle une amitié de bon aloi. Mes relations avec les Kennedy me donnent de la crédibilité, et Mlle Hughes a été impressionnée par le fait que je sois parvenu à déterminer le secret de sa parenté sans avoir en réalité soulevé le sujet auprès des membres de la famille Kennedy et de ses autres amis au courant de la situation.

Mlle Hughes adore parler de la famille, mais elle limite ses sujets de conversation en termes directs à John, Robert, Edward, Rose et les sœurs. Elle a en réserve une furie considérable à l'égard de Joseph P. Kennedy Sr., cite ses attaches avec le mafieux de Boston Raymond L.S. Patriarca, ainsi qu'avec un « financier-bootlegger » de Chicago à la retraite du nom de Jules Schiffrin, se délecte à raconter des histoires sur les rivalités en affaires qui ont opposé M. Kennedy et Howard Hughes. (Mlle Hughes a adopté le nom de « Hughes » à son dix-huitième anniversaire, remplaçant le « Johnson » que lui avaient offert les Kennedy-Swanson pour tenter d'une certaine manière de fâcher son père, l'un des plus acharnés ennemis de Howard Hughes).

Mlle Hughes prétend que les attaches de Joseph P. Kennedy avec le monde des gangsters courent beaucoup plus profond que le *il a été bootlegger,* l'étiquette que lui a collée la presse en faisant référence à son affaire d'importation de scotch whisky d'avant la prohibition qui fut une très grande réussite commerciale. Elle est incapable de citer les noms spécifiques de gangsters intimes du père ou de se remémorer des incidents dont elle aurait été le témoin ou qu'elle aurait entendu rapporter ; néanmoins, sa perception d'un Joseph P. Kennedy comme profondément lié au monde des gangsters reste d'une force extraordinaire qui ne s'est pas encore totalement exprimée.

Je vais poursuivre mes relations d'amitié avec Mlle Hughes et vous rapporterai tous les renseignements saillants que j'obtiendrai sur la famille Kennedy.

Respectueusement,

Kemper Boyd.

DOCUMENT EN ENCART : *21/4/59. Rapport résumé — de AS Ward J. Littell à Kemper Boyd — « A remettre en forme et transmettre à Robert F. Kennedy ».*

Cher Kemper,

Les affaires continuent à suivre leur rythme rapide ici à Chicago. Je continue à poursuivre les communistes de l'intérieur aux termes de mon affectation officielle du Bureau, bien qu'ils me fassent tous l'effet d'être plus pathétiques et moins dangereux jour après jour. Cela étant dit, j'en arrive à ce qui nous tient à cœur.

Sal D'Onofrio et Lenny Sands continuent, en ignorant tout l'un de l'autre, à me servir d'informateurs. Sal, naturellement, a remboursé les douze mille dollars qu'il devait à Sam Giancana ; il en a été quitte pour un passage à tabac par Giancana. Apparemment, nul n'a fait le rapprochement entre mon vol des quatorze mille dollars de Butch Montrose et les douze mille dollars de Sal tombés du ciel. J'ai commandé à Sal de régler Giancana en trois versements et il a obéi à mes ordres. La violence dont j'ai initialement fait montre à l'égard de Sal s'est avérée payante à long terme : il semblerait que je sois parvenu à totalement en imposer à cet homme. Au cours d'une banale conversation, je lui ai appris que j'avais été séminariste jésuite. D'Onofrio, qui se décrit lui-même comme catholique fervent, a été impressionné par ce détail et me considère dorénavant comme une sorte de père-confesseur. Il a avoué six meurtres-tortures et je dispose naturellement de ses aveux (horriblement détaillés) pour renforcer mon emprise sur lui. Mis à part les quelques cauchemars occasionnels que ces aveux ont pu faire naître, il me semble que Sal et moi continuons à aller de l'avant sans heurts. Je lui ai dit que j'apprécierais beaucoup qu'il s'abstienne de commettre des meurtres et de s'adonner à cette frénésie destructrice du jeu tant qu'il sera sous mon aile et, jusqu'à présent, c'est ce qu'il semble faire. Sal m'a fourni quelques bribes de renseignements anti-Mafia de moindre importance (qui ne valent pas la peine d'être transmises, ni à toi, ni à M. Kennedy), mais il ne m'a été d'aucune aide s'agissant de me diriger vers un éventuel emprunteur potentiel susceptible de franchir les différents échelons de la Caisse de Retraite des Camionneurs. C'était à l'origine ma seule raison pour le soudoyer et l'obliger à devenir mon informateur, et il a failli à mon attente sur ce point. Je soupçonne fort qu'établir la preuve de l'existence de livres comptables « doubles » ne soit un processus de longue haleine, pénible et aléatoire.

Lenny Sands continue à avoir presque autant de cordes à son arc que toi. Il est le dénicheur des scandales de *L'Indiscret* (Seigneur, quel horrible travail ce doit être !), il est associé à Sal pour ses tournées d'excursionnistes, et sur un plan plus général, il est le parasite de la Mafia à Chicago. Il dit qu'il s'est engagé de manière très active à essayer de trouver des informations sur le fonctionnement de la Caisse de Retraite et il ajoute être convaincu que la rumeur selon laquelle Sam Giancana offrirait des primes pour des clients emprunteurs des Fonds de la Caisse est vraie. Il est également convaincu que des livres comptables « doubles », voire codés, détaillant les fonds cachés, existent bel et bien. En conclusion, il faut encore que je parvienne à glaner des renseignements solides soit de Sands soit de D'Onofrio.

Sur un tout autre front, M. Hoover semble vouloir éviter toute occasion potentielle qui mettrait un frein aux activités des membres de la Mafia de Chicago. Court Meade a intercepté la mention (en termes elliptiques) d'un cambriolage grâce au mouchard placé chez le tailleur. Des soldats de la Mafia de Chicago, Rocco Malvaso et Dewey Di Pasquale ont apparemment piqué quatre-vingt mille dollars dans une salle de craps (non-Mafia) aux enjeux élevés à Kenilworth. Des agents du PGC ont retransmis l'information à M. Hoover, qui leur a dit de ne pas les faire suivre aux agences concernées par une éventuelle enquête sur les faits. Seigneur, que les priorités de cet homme sont tordues !

J'arrête là. En guise d'au revoir : Tu continueras toujours à me sidérer, Kemper ! Seigneur ! Toi comme homme de la CIA ! Et maintenant que le Comité McClellan s'est séparé, que vas-tu faire pour les Kennedy ?

Adieu,

WJL.

DOCUMENT EN ENCART : 26/4/59. *Note personnelle — de Kemper Boyd à J. Edgar Hoover — Marqué : EXTREMEMENT CONFIDENTIEL.*

Monsieur,

J'ai pensé qu'il serait bon, par ce petit mot, de vous tenir au courant des derniers événements sur le front Ward Littell. Littell et moi continuons à communiquer régulièrement par téléphone, et je reste convaincu qu'il n'a pas entrepris d'actions anti-Mafia, ouvertes ou cachées, de sa propre autorité.

Vous m'avez signalé qu'on avait repéré Littell près de la boutique de tailleur « Chez Celano » et du poste d'écoute du Programme Grands Criminels. Je me suis discrètement enquis auprès de Littell sur ce point et je suis satisfait de sa réponse : comme quoi il retrouvait l'AS Court Meade pour déjeuner.

La vie personnelle de Littell semble tourner autour de sa liaison avec Helen Agee. Cette liaison a rendu ses relations avec sa fille, Susan, très tendues, car celle-ci désapprouve cette liaison. En temps normal, Helen est en contact étroit avec ma fille Claire, mais maintenant qu'elles sont étudiantes dans des universités différentes, la fréquence de leurs contacts a beaucoup diminué. L'aventure Littell-Agee semble se réduire à trois ou quatre nuits par semaine de retrouvailles domestiques. L'un et l'autre ont conservé des résidences séparées, et je pense qu'il continuera à en être ainsi. Je continuerai de mon côté à garder Littell à l'œil.

Respectueusement,

Kemper Boyd.

DOCUMENT EN ENCART : 30/4/59. *Note personnelle — de Kemper Boyd à Ward J. Littell.*

Ward,

Je te presse instamment de te tenir à l'écart de chez Celano et de sa boutique de tailleur ainsi que de la zone du poste d'écoute, et d'éviter qu'on te voie en compagnie de Court Meade. Je crois avoir étouffé les quelques petits soupçons que M. Hoover aurait pu avoir, mais tu ne saurais te montrer trop prudent. Je te conseille fortement de mettre un terme à tes échanges d'affectation avec Meade. Détruis cette lettre immédiatement.

KB.

DOCUMENT EN ENCART : 4/5/59. *Rapport résumé — de Kemper Boyd à John Stanton — Marqué : CONFIDENTIEL / A DELIVRER EN MAINS PROPRES.*

John,

Voici la remise à jour que vous avez demandée dans votre dernière livraison. Veuillez excuser mon retard mais, comme vous l'avez remarqué, j'ai « des emplois multiples ».

1. — Oui, le mandat du Comité McClellan sur les rackets de main-d'œuvre est arrivé à son terme. Non, les Kennedy ne m'ont pas encore offert d'emploi permanent. Je pense que cela ne saurait tarder. Il existe de multiples possibilités, dans la mesure où je suis à la fois juriste et flic. Oui, j'ai discuté de Cuba avec Jack. Il n'a pas d'opinion pour l'instant sur la pertinence de Cuba comme thème de sa campagne de 1960. Il est fortement anticommuniste, en dépit de sa réputation de libéral. Je suis optimiste.

2. — J'en ai terminé de mes « auditions » au Boynton Beach Motel. Aujourd'hui marque la fin de la période de séquestration de quatre-vingt-dix jours prescrite par le

directeur adjoint Bissell. Demain, le plus gros de nos hommes sera expédié en Louisiane. Guy Banister dispose d'un réseau de Cubains immigrés légalement prêts à les recevoir. Ils leur fourniront logement, emplois et références dans le but final de leur procurer des visas. Guy canalisera ensuite ces hommes jusqu'à son propre programme d'entraînement et d'endoctrinement.

J'ai sélectionné quatre hommes qui constitueront le noyau de notre groupe de Blessington. Je les considère comme les meilleurs des cinquante-trois passagers du bateau-banane du 4 février 1959. Dans la mesure où j'ai des « emplois multiples », je n'ai guère été présent lors de la période de séquestration, mais des officiers spécialisés très capables ont suivi les lignes directrices que j'avais établies quant aux tests d'endoctrinement et de psychologie.

Ces lignes directrices étaient excessivement rigoureuses. J'ai personnellement supervisé les tests au détecteur de mensonge destinés à déterminer la présence d'informateurs castristes infiltrés. Les cinquante-trois hommes ont passé l'épreuve avec succès (je crois que l'homme qu'ils ont tué sur le bateau était le faux expulsé). Des tests de confirmation au penthotal de sodium ont été administrés. A nouveau, tous les hommes ont passé l'épreuve avec succès.

Ont suivi les interrogatoires. Ainsi que je le soupçonnais, les cinquante-trois hommes possédaient tous à Cuba des casiers judiciaires lourdement chargés. Les crimes répertoriés allaient du vol à main armée jusqu'à divers « crimes politiques », en passant par les cambriolages, l'incendie volontaire, le viol, la contrebande d'héroïne et le meurtre. Un homme s'est avéré déviant, il avait agressé sexuellement et décapité six jeunes enfants à La Havane. Un autre s'est révélé être un pourvoyeur homosexuel méprisé par les autres exilés. J'ai estimé que ces deux hommes étaient dangereusement instables et j'ai mis un terme à leur formation selon les règles d'endoctrinement établies par le directeur adjoint.

Tous les hommes ont été soumis à des interrogatoires poussés à la limite de la torture. La plupart ont résisté avec grand courage. Tous ont été physiquement mis au pas et verbalement agressés à la manière pratiquée dans les camps d'entraînement du Corps des Marines. La plupart ont réagi avec un parfait mélange de colère et de soumission. Les quatre

227

hommes que j'ai sélectionnés sont intelligents, violents sous des dehors maîtrisés, physiquement habiles et doués, volubiles (ils feront de bons recruteurs pour Miami), consentants à l'autorité, et farouchement proaméricains, anti-communistes et anti-castristes. Leurs noms sont les suivants :

a) Teofilio Paez en personne. DDN 6/8/21. Ancien chef de la sécurité pour la United Fruit. Versé dans le maniement des armes et les techniques d'interrogatoire. Ancien homme-grenouille de la Marine cubaine. Expert dans le recrutement politique.

b) Tomas Obregon. DDN 17/1/30. Ancien guérillero de Castro. Ancien passeur de came à La Havane et cambrioleur de banque. Expert en jiu-jitsu et en fabrication d'explosifs.

c) Wilfredo Olmus Delsol. DDN 9/4/27. Cousin d'Obregon. Ancien brandon gauchiste ayant viré au zélateur de droite quand ses comptes bancaires ont été « nationalisés ». Ancien instructeur de l'Armée de Terre cubaine. Expert en armes légères.

d) Ramon Guttierez. DDN 24/10/19. Pilote. Pamphlétaire propagandiste de talent. Ancien tortionnaire de la police secrète de Batista. Expert en techniques de contre-insurrection.

3. — J'ai inspecté les alentours du terrain que l'Agence a acheté pour y établir les camps de Blessington. L'endroit n'est guère reluisant, peuplé de pauvres raclures de Blancs, dont un grand nombre sont membres du Ku Klux Klan. Je pense que nous avons besoin d'un Blanc pour diriger le camp, un Blanc qui fera impression, capable d'instiller la peur chez tous les péquenots du cru qui se sentent perturbés à l'idée d'être envahis d'émigrés cubains venant s'établir sans y avoir été invités sur leur territoire. J'ai recommandé Pete Bondurant. J'ai vérifié son dossier du Corps des Marines pendant la Seconde Guerre mondiale et j'ai été impressionné : il a survécu à quatorze charges au corps à corps à Saïpan, il a gagné la Navy Cross et est passé de simple soldat au rang de capitaine *via* une commission de campagne. Je vous presse fortement d'engager Bondurant dans les rangs de l'Agence sur une base contractuelle.

C'est tout pour l'instant. Je serai au St. Regis de New York si vous avez besoin de moi.

Bien à vous,

KB.

P-S : Vous aviez raison à propos du voyage de Castro aux Etats-Unis. Il a refusé de loger dans un hôtel qui n'admettait pas les Nègres, ensuite il s'est rendu à Harlem, où il a commencé à faire des déclarations antiaméricaines. Son comportement devant les Nations unies a été déplorable. Je salue votre prescience : l'homme voulait *effectivement* être « rejeté de force ».

DOCUMENT EN ENCART : 12/5/59. *Mémo — de John Stanton à Kemper Boyd.*

Kemper,

Le directeur adjoint a approuvé le recrutement de Pete Bondurant. J'ai quelques réserves mineures, et je veux que vous le chargiez d'une mission, de quelque sorte à l'essai, avant que nous le contactions. L'épreuve-test est laissée à votre discrétion.

JS.

23

Chicago, 18 mai 1959.

Helen beurra une tranche de toast.

— Susan tire un nez de six pieds de long et ça me monte à la tête. Je ne pense pas que nous nous soyons adressé la parole plus de trois ou quatre fois depuis qu'elle sait pour nous deux.

Il attendait le coup de fil de Sal le Fou. Littell repoussa son petit déjeuner, il n'avait absolument aucun appétit.

— Je lui ai parlé exactement deux fois. Parfois, j'ai l'impression d'avoir fait un troc pur et simple. J'ai gagné une petite amie et perdu une fille.

— Le fait de l'avoir perdue ne semble pas trop te tracasser.

— Susan se nourrit de ressentiment. Pour ça, elle est comme sa mère.

— Claire m'a appris que Kemper avait une liaison avec une femme riche de New York, mais elle se refuse à divulguer plus de détails.

Laura Hughes était à moitié Kennedy. L'infiltration des Kennedy par Kemper se transformait en campagne sur deux fronts.

— Ward, tu me parais bien perdu dans tes pensées ce matin.

— C'est le travail. Il me préoccupe.

— Je n'en suis pas si sûre.

Il était presque 9 heures — 7 heures du matin, heure de Gardena. Sal était un joueur lève-tôt invétéré.

Helen agita sa serviette à son adresse.

— Yoo hoo, Ward ! Est-ce que tu écoutes...

— Qu'est-ce que tu dis ? Qu'est-ce que tu veux dire, « je n'en suis pas si sûre » ?

— Je veux dire que ton travail à la Brigade Rouge t'ennuie et te contrarie. Tu en parles sans cesse avec mépris, mais depuis des mois, il t'absorbe complètement.

— Et alors ?

— Alors ? Tu te mets à avoir des cauchemars et à marmonner en latin dans ton sommeil.

— Et alors ?

— Alors ? Tu commences à te cacher de moi lorsque nous sommes dans la même pièce. Tu te mets à te comporter comme si tu avais quarante-six ans et moi, vingt et un, et il y a des choses que tu ne peux pas me dire tout simplement parce que je ne comprendrais pas.

Littell lui prit les mains. Helen se dégagea et fit tomber un rond de serviette de la table.

— Kemper dit tout à Claire. Je pensais que tu allais essayer de te faire son émule dans ce domaine.

— Kemper est le père de Claire. Je ne suis pas le tien.

Helen se leva et empoigna son sac à main.

— Je réfléchirai à ça en rentrant à la maison.

— Et ton cours de 9 h 30 ?

— Nous sommes samedi, Ward. Tu es tellement « préoccupé » que tu ne sais plus quel jour nous sommes.

Sal appela à 9 h 35. A l'entendre, il paraissait agité.

Littell fit gentil-gentil pour le calmer. Sal adorait les mièvreries.

— Comment se passent les petites tournées-plaisir ?

— Une excursion, c'est une excursion. Gardena, c'est bien pas'que c'est tout près de L.A. Mais ce putain de Lenny le Juif n'arrête pas de se tailler pour aller dénicher des merdes pour *L'Indiscret* et il arrive toujours en retard pour son numéro. Je crois que je devrais le découper en rondelles comme j'ai fait au mec qui...

— Ne fais pas d'aveux au téléphone, Sal.

— Pardonnez-moi, mon Père, parce que j'ai péché.

— Arrête ton numéro. Tu sais ce qui m'intéresse, alors si tu as quelque chose, dis-le-moi.

231

— Okay, okay. J'étais à Vegas et j'ai entendu Heshie Ryskind qui bavardait. Hesh a dit que les gars se faisaient de la bile, côté front cubain. Il a dit que l'Organisation avait payé au Barbu une chiée de pognon en échange de sa parole que leurs putains de casinos pourraient continuer à fonctionner s'il prenait le pouvoir dans son putain de pays. Mais maintenant, il est passé coco et il les a nationalisés, ces putains de casinos. Hesh a dit que le Barbu avait collé Santos T. en prison à La Havane. Les gars n'aiment plus beaucoup le Barbu ces temps derniers. Hesh dit que le Barbu, c'est comme le mec du dessous dans une partouze de mongoliens. Tu comprends, tôt ou tard, il va se faire baiser *pour de bon.*

— Et alors ? dit Littell.

— Avant de quitter Chicago, j'ai eu Ruby au téléphone. Jack était à court, alors je lui ai prêté un paquet de pognon pour qu'il largue sa boîte de strip pour s'en acheter une autre, le « Carousel » ou quelque chose. Jack rembourse toujours rubis sur l'ongle, pas'qu'y prête de son côté à ses moments perdus à Dallas, et...

— Sal, tu veux en arriver à quoi ? Dis-moi de quoi il s'agit.

— Whoa whoa whoa — je pensais que les flics aimaient les détails qui corroborent les faits.

— Sal...

— Whoa, écoutez. Jack a corroboré ce que Heshie avait annoncé. Il a déclaré qu'il avait parlé à Carlos Marcello et Johnny Rosselli, et les deux mecs ont dit que le Barbu coûte à l'Organisation soixante-quinze mille par jour en agios, en plus de leur bénef casinos quotidien réduit à des putains de clopinettes. Pensez un peu à ça, *Padre.* Songez à ce que l'Eglise pourrait faire avec soixante-quinze bâtons par jour.

Littell soupira.

— Cuba ne m'intéresse pas. Est-ce que Ruby t'a donné quelque chose sur la Caisse de Retraite ?

— Eh bien-ien-ien... dit Sal.

— Sal, nom de Dieu !

— Vilain, vilain, *Padre.* Vous me réciterez dix *Je vous salue, Marie* et après, écoutez-moi ça. Jack m'a appris qu'il avait adressé un pétrolier du Texas à Sam G. pour un prêt sur la Caisse de Retraite, y a comme qui dirait un an de ça. C'est un tuyau de première catégorie, faut savoir, et je mérite une récompense, et j'ai besoin d'un peu de putain de pognon pour couvrir mes paris, parce que les books et les requins qui n'ont pas de blé de réserve en voient de dures et y ne peuvent pas aller moucharder à des enculés de Fédés tout propres sur eux comme vous.

Qualification de Ruby par le PGC : porteur de valoches/requin de l'usure au petit pied.

— *Padre Padre Padre !* Pardonnez-moi parce que j'ai parié. Pardonnez-moi parce que...

— Je vais essayer de t'avoir un peu d'argent, Sal. *Si* je peux trouver un emprunteur que tu présenteras à Giancana. Et je te parle de quelqu'un que tu recommanderas sans intermédiaire, de toi à Sam directement.

— *Padre...* Seigneur.

— Sal...

— *Padre,* vous me baisez si fort que ça me fait mal.

— Je t'ai sauvé la vie, Sal. Et c'est pour toi la seule manière d'avoir le moindre centime de moi dorénavant.

— Okay okay okay. Pardonnez-moi mon Père, parce que je me suis fait enfiler côté chemin de traverse par c'te Fédé ancien séminariste qui...

Littell raccrocha.

La salle de brigade avait sa tranquillité des week-ends. L'agent chargé du standard l'ignora.

Littell s'installa au télétype et interrogea le Bureau de Dallas.

La réponse prendrait au moins dix minutes. Il appela Midway, les Renseignements aériens — et eut un coup de veine.

Une correspondance de la Pan-Am partait pour Dallas à midi. Le vol de retour le verrait de retour chez lui peu après minuit.

Les tuyaux demandés arrivèrent à la machine : Jacob Rubinstein : alias Jack Ruby, DDN 25/3/11.

L'homme avait été arrêté trois fois pour extorsion, sans condamnation : en 47, 49 et 53.

L'homme était soupçonné d'être maquereau et informateur pour la police de Dallas.

L'homme avait été l'objet d'une enquête de l'ASPCA[1] en

---

1. La Société protectrice des animaux aux USA. *(N.d.T.)*

1956. Il était fortement soupçonné de se satisfaire sexuellement de chiens. Il était connu pour faire l'usurier à l'occasion, et prêter à des hommes d'affaires et des prospecteurs de pétrole au désespoir.

Littell arracha le télétype. Jack Ruby valait le détour.

Le bourdonnement de l'avion et trois scotchs le bercèrent et il s'endormit. Les aveux de Sal le Fou se fondirent comme une compilation de morceaux au hit-parade.

Sal oblige le jeune Nègre à supplier. Sal fait avaler du Drano au mauvais payeur. Sal décapite deux gamins qui sifflent le passage d'une nonne.

Il avait vérifié ces morts. Toutes les quatre restaient « non résolues ». Les quatre victimes avaient été violées par le rectum *post-mortem.*

Littell s'éveilla en sueur. L'hôtesse lui tendit un verre sans qu'il l'eût demandé.

Le « Carousel Club » était un rade à strip-tease, un parmi d'autres qui s'alignaient. L'enseigne en façade affichait des filles en bikini.

Une autre enseigne disait : OUVERTURE 18 HEURES.

Littell se gara derrière le bâtiment et attendit. Sa voiture de location puait, une odeur de sexe récent et de gomina.

Quelques flics passèrent, en vitesse de croisière. Un homme lui fit signe. Littell comprit vite : ils croient que t'es un frère flic qui touche du fric de Jack.

Ruby arriva à 5 heures et quart, seul.

Il baisait les chiens et faisait le mac. Il allait falloir que ça se passe salement.

Ruby sortit et déverrouilla la porte arrière. Littell courut jusqu'à lui et l'intercepta.

— FBI, dit-il. Montre-moi tes mains.

Il dit ça à la manière Kemper Boyd, très classique.

Ruby eut l'air sceptique. Il portait un chapeau-tourtière en feutre ridicule.

— Vide tes poches, dit Littell.

Ruby obéit. Un rouleau de billets, des biscuits à chiens, et un .38 à canon court tombèrent au sol.

Ruby cracha sur le tas.

— Je sais à quoi ressemblent les petits braquages par des mecs étrangers à la ville. Intimement, si je puis dire. Je sais comment traiter avec les flics en costard bleu marine bon marché qui puent l'alcool. Alors tu prends ce que tu veux et tu me fous la paix.

Littell ramassa un biscuit à chiens.

— Mange-le, Jack.

Ruby se mit sur la pointe des pieds — à la manière d'un boxeur poids léger, ou tout comme. Littell sortit son arme et ses menottes.

— Je veux que tu manges ce biscuit pour chien.

— Ecoute...

— Ecoutez, *monsieur*.

— Ecoutez, *monsieur,* putain, pour qui vous...

Littell lui fourra le biscuit dans le bec. Ruby se mit à mâcher pour ne pas s'étrangler.

— Je vais exiger certaines choses de toi, Jack. Si tu ne t'y prêtes pas, le Service fédéral des Impôts va t'offrir un audit, les agents fédéraux vont passer tes clients à la fouille à corps tous les soirs, et le *Dallas Morning News* révélera au grand jour ton penchant sexuel pour les chiens.

Ruby se mit à mâcher. Ruby se mit à faire gicler des miettes. Littell lui chassa les jambes de sous lui.

Ruby tomba à genoux. Littell ouvrit la porte d'un coup de pied et fit entrer Ruby à coups de latte.

Ruby essaya de se relever. Littell le fit retomber, toujours à coups de pied. La pièce faisait trois mètres sur trois, le sol était jonché de piles de peignoirs de stripteaseuses.

Du pied, Littell balança une pile à la figure de Jack. Littell lui jeta un nouveau biscuit au creux des cuisses.

Ruby le mit dans sa bouche. Ruby fit d'horribles bruits comme s'il s'étranglait.

— Réponds à cette question, dit Littell. *As-tu jamais recommandé des emprunteurs à d'autres requins que toi et mieux placés* ?

Ruby hocha la tête — oui oui oui oui oui.

— Sal D'Onofrio t'a prêté l'argent pour acheter cet endroit. Hoche la tête si c'est vrai.

Ruby hocha la tête. Il avait les pieds entortillés dans des soutiens-gorge souillés.

— Sal tue les gens par simple routine. Est-ce que tu savais ça ?

Ruby hocha la tête. Des chiens commencèrent à aboyer une pièce plus loin.

— Il torture les gens, Jack. Il aime faire souffrir.

Ruby secoua la tête en tous sens. Il avait les joues gonflées comme le gamin mort sur son plateau à la morgue.

— Sal a brûlé un homme à mort au chalumeau. La femme du gars est rentrée à la maison de manière inopinée. Sal lui a fourré un chiffon imbibé d'essence dans la bouche et y a mis le feu. Il a dit qu'elle était morte en crachant des flammes comme un dragon.

Ruby pissa dans son pantalon. Littell vit la tache s'étendre sur les cuisses.

— Sal veut que tu saches un certain nombre de choses. Un, ta dette à son égard est effacée. Deux, si tu ne coopères pas avec moi ou si tu me balances à l'Organisation ou à l'un de tes amis flics, il viendra à Dallas, il te violera et il te tuera. Est-ce que tu comprends ?

Ruby hocha la tête — oui oui oui. Des miettes de biscuit jaillirent de ses narines.

Kemper Boyd disait toujours : *ne faiblis pas.*

— Tu ne dois pas contacter Sal. Tu ne dois pas connaître mon nom. Tu ne dois parler à personne de tout ceci. Tu devras me contacter tous les mardis à 11 heures du matin à un téléphone public de Chicago. Je t'appellerai et je te donnerai le numéro. Est-ce que tu comprends ?

Ruby hocha la tête — oui oui oui oui oui oui. Les chiens se mirent à gémir et à gratter à grands coups de griffes une porte située à quelques mètres devant lui.

— Je veux que tu trouves un emprunteur à répondant élevé pour Sal. Quelqu'un que Sal peut adresser à Giancana et la Caisse de Retraite. Hoche la tête si tu es d'accord, et hoche la tête deux fois si tu comprends toute la situation.

Ruby hocha la tête trois fois.

Littell sortit.

Le bruit que faisaient les chiens se changea en cacophonie.

Son vol de retour atterrit à minuit. Il rentra à la maison en voiture, à cran et épuisé.

La voiture d'Helen était garée en façade. Elle allait être debout ; elle allait se montrer pressante ; elle devait vouloir à tout prix se réconcilier.

Littell se rendit dans un magasin de spiritueux et acheta une demi-pinte. Un poivrot lui demanda la pièce. Il lui donna un dollar — le pauvre connard avait un air de Jack Ruby.

Il était 1 heure du matin. C'était dimanche. Peut-être que Court Meade était de service au poste d'écoute.

Il appela. Personne ne répondit. Un mec du PGC était en train de sécher son poste.

Kemper l'avait pressé d'éviter le poste d'écoute. Peut-être que Kemper — qui sait ? — ne trouverait pas une dernière petite visite trop risquée.

Littell alla jusque-là et entra. L'émetteur du mouchard était débranché. La pièce avait été récemment nettoyée et rangée. Un mot collé à l'adhésif sur la console principale expliquait pourquoi :

Mémo

La boutique du tailleur de Celano doit passer à la désinfection du 17/5 au 20/5. Toutes opérations dans les lieux seront suspendues pendant cette période.

Littell fit sauter la capsule de sa bouteille. Quelques gorgées lui redonnèrent vie, et ses réflexions s'éparpillèrent en rafales dans des millions de directions.

Quelques circuits de neurones se mirent à grésiller et à se recouper.

Sal avait besoin d'argent. Court Meade parlait d'un braquage d'une partie de craps. M. Hoover avait dit de laisser filer.

Littell consulta les transcriptions de conversations du mouchard. Il tomba sur une discussion portant sur le braquage en question, classée là le mois précédent par l'AS Russ Davis.

18/4/59. 22 heures. Seuls à la boutique du tailleur : Rocco Malvaso et Dewey Di Pasquale, dit « le Canard ». Ce qui ressemblait à des toasts de célébration a été brouillé par des bruits de marteau-piqueur et de chantier au-dehors, sur Michigan Avenue. Deux minutes se sont écoulées : apparemment, les deux hommes se sont rendus aux toilettes. Ensuite s'est engagée la conversation qui suit.

Malvaso. — *Te salud*, Canard.

Di Pasquale. — Couin, couin. Ce qui est sympa, tu sais, c'est qu'ils ne peuvent pas le signaler.

Malvaso. — Les flics de Kenilworth en chieraient dans le froc. Cette ville, c'est la ville des caves entre toutes les villes de caves. La dernière fois que deux beaux queutards comme nous avec plein de couilles se sont farcis quatre-vingts bâtons pendant une partie de craps, ç'a été le dernier mois du grand jamais, putain de merde.

Di Pasquale. — Couin, couin. Je dis que ce sont des indépendants et que ça leur pendait au nez. Je dis que quand on est pas couvert par Momo, sous protection de la Mafia, on est que de la merde. De Canard. Hé, on portait des masques et on a déguisé nos voix. En plus de ça, ces empaffés d'Indy ne savent pas qu'on est du milieu. Je me sens comme Super Canard. Je suis en train de me dire que je devrais m'offrir un déguisement de Super Canard et de me le mettre sur le dos la prochaine fois que j'emmènerais mes mômes à Disneyland.

Malvaso. — Couin, couin putain, espèce d'enfoiré de palmipède. Y a quand même fallu que tu fasses cracher ton pétard, hein ? Comme si ça pouvait pas exister, une putain de cavale, une fois le coup fait, sans un empaffé de palmipède qui fait parler la poudre.

(Note : La police de Kenilworth signale des coups de feu non expliqués au bloc 2600 de Westmoreland Avenue — 23 h 40 — 16/4/59.)

Di Pasquale. — Hé, couin, couin. Ça a marché. On a planqué le paquet bien en sécurité et...

Malvaso. — ...là où c'est un peu trop public à mon goût, bordel.

Di Pasquale. — Couin, couin. Soixante jours, ça fait pas

238

long, à attendre pour le partage. Donald a bien attendu vingt putains d'années pour sauter Daisy, pas'que Walt Disney voulait pas le laisser faire. Hé, tu te souviens, l'année dernière, Lenny le Juif, quand il est venu me faire ma soirée d'anniversaire ? Il a fait son numéro, celui où Daisy taille une plume à Donald avec son bec, quelle putain de rigolade.

Malvaso. — Couin, couin, espèce d'enfoiré.

(Note : les bruits de chantier ont rendu le reste de la conversation inaudible. Bruit de porte qui claque à 23 h 10.)

Lenny consulta les fiches d'identification du PGC. Malvaso et Di Pasquale vivaient à Evanston.

Il repassa la bande du 16 avril 1959 et la compara à la transcription. Russ Davis avait oublié de noter les dernières répliques de départ.

Le Canard fredonnait, *Chattanooga choo-choo.*

Malvaso chantait, « *I got the key to your heart* » — « J'ai la clé qui ouvre ton cœur. »

« Trop public », « Clé » et « Choo-choo ». Deux voleurs *habitant la banlieue* qui attendent soixante jours pour le partage.

Il existait une quarantaine de gares de banlieue reliées à Chicago.

Avec une quarantaine de salles d'attente où s'alignaient des casiers-consignes.

Les casiers-consignes se louaient au mois. En liquide exclusivement, sans traces, sans registre, sans délivrance de reçus, sans noms.

Deux voleurs. Deux clés *séparées* par porte de casier.

Les serrures étaient changées tous les quatre-vingt-dix jours — aux termes de la loi T.A.[1] d'Illinois.

Des milliers de casiers. Des clés sans signe distinctif. Soixante jours jusqu'au partage — trente-deux s'étaient déjà écoulés.

Les casiers étaient d'acier blindé. Les salles d'attente, gardées vingt-quatre heures sur vingt-quatre.

1. Transit Authority. *(N.d.T.)*

Littell passa deux jours entiers à réfléchir à toutes les possibilités. Qui se résumaient au bout du compte à ceci :

Il pouvait filer les deux hommes. Mais lorsqu'ils iraient récupérer l'argent, il serait impuissant.

Il ne pouvait en filer qu'un seul à la fois. Et il en arrivait à ceci : les chances, déjà bien minces au départ, étaient divisées par deux. Contre lui.

Il décida d'essayer malgré tout. Il décida de gonfler de baratin ses rapports de la Brigade Rouge et de filer les deux hommes, un jour sur deux, pendant une semaine.

Jour 1 : il file Rocco Malvaso de 8 heures du matin à minuit. Rocco fait la tournée, ses repaires de loterie des nombres, ses antennes du Syndicat, et le domicile de sa petite amie à Glencoe.

Rocco ne s'approche ni de près ni de loin d'une gare de chemin de fer.

Jour 2 : il file Dewey le Canard de 8 heures du matin à minuit. Dewey fait la tournée : il relève ses nombreux compteurs de trottoir.

Dewey ne s'approche ni de près ni de loin d'une gare de chemin de fer.

Jour 3 : il file Rocco Malvaso de 8 heures du matin à minuit. Rocco se rend à Milwaukee et balafre au pistolet des macs rétifs.

Rocco ne s'approche ni de près ni de loin d'une gare de chemin de fer.

Jour 4 : il file Dewey le Canard de 8 heures du matin à minuit. Dewey, déguisé en Donald le Canard, amuse la compagnie au cours de la fête d'anniversaire en plein air de Dewey Jr.

Dewey ne s'approche ni de loin ni de près d'une gare de chemin de fer.

Jour 5 : il file Rocco Malvaso de 8 heures du matin à minuit. Rocco passe tout son temps avec une call-girl au Blackhawk Hotel de Chicago.

Rocco ne s'approche ni de près ni de loin d'une gare de chemin de fer.

Jour 6, 8 heures du matin : il prend sa filature de Dewey le Canard. 9 h 40 : la voiture de Dewey refuse de démarrer. Mme Canard conduit Dewey à la gare d'Evanston.

Dewey traîne dans la salle d'attente.

Dewey reluque les casiers-consignes.